Y0-BUO-496

GARLAND STUDIES IN

THE HISTORY OF AMERICAN LABOR

edited by

STUART BRUCHEY
UNIVERSITY OF MAINE

A GARLAND SERIES

ASIAN AND HISPANIC IMMIGRANT WOMEN IN THE WORK FORCE

Implications of the United States Immigration Policies since 1965

FUNG-YEA HUANG

GARLAND PUBLISHING, INC.
NEW YORK & LONDON / 1997

Library of Congress Cataloging-in-Publication Data

Huang, Fung-Yea, 1962–
Asian and Hispanic immigrant women in the work force : implications of the United States Immigration policies since 1965 / Fung-Yea Huang.
p. cm. — (Garland studies in the history of American labor)
Includes bibliographical references and index.
ISBN 0-8153-2615-7 (alk. paper)
1. Women alien labor—United States. 2. Women immigrants—United States. 3. Alien labor, Asian—United States. 4. Alien labor, Latin American—United States. 5. United States—Emigration and immigration—Government policy. I. Title. II. Series.
HD6095.H75 1997
331.4'08968073—dc20 96-42261

Printed on acid-free, 250-year-life paper
Manufactured in the United States of America

To my father, for his love and support along the way

Contents

List of Tables

Preface

In 1930, 52 percent of immigrants entering the U.S. were women. Since then, women continued to outnumber men at least until 1980. Most research on the labor market experience of immigrants, however, has continued to concentrate on men. The experience of women has received much less attention than their numbers and economic importance warrant. This book examines the work experience of women from two of the largest contemporary immigrant groups, Asians and Hispanics. It is known that immigrant women from these groups differ substantially by country of origin in labor market behavior and attainment. Of married immigrant women aged 18 to 44, about 49 percent of Mexican origin participated in the labor force as compared to 81 percent of Filipino origin in the late 1980s. Once in the labor force, Mexican women earned an average of $6.8 an hour while Filipino women earned $11.7 an hour. One possible explanation for the differences is "migration selectivity." Immigrants differ from people who remain at home in a number of ways. Depending on the level of risks and costs associated with migration, those who seek to settle in foreign land tend to be young, adventurous, energetic, and hard-working. The nature of migration selectivity is influenced by a number of factors, one of which may be the immigration policy of the receiving country. It is often argued that, family reunification policy, filtering potential immigrants based on family connection rather than skills, may in fact select people who do not have the best skills for fast adaptation to the labor market. This book seeks to answer the following questions: Does migration selection contribute to the observed ethnic difference in the labor market performance of Asian and Hispanic immigrant women? If so, what role do immigration policy play in the selection of women from Asia and Latin America?

The migration of women is highly conditioned by the status of women in the sending countries. As societies confine/encourage the mobility of women in various ways, the extent to which immigrant women differ from non-immigrant women also varies by country of origin. Single women from societies that discourage the migration of "unattached" women are likely to perform better in the receiving country than single women from other countries. An immigration policy that favors family reunification is likely to further polarize the selection of single women because the policy makes it difficult for them to migrate. Chapter 2 reviews literature on why women migrate, who they are, and how well they fare in the receiving country. Chapter 3 illustrates the changes of U.S. immigration policy in historical context. It reviews literature on how the volume and patterns of Asian and Hispanic immigration have responded to the family reunification emphasis since 1965 and its implications toward the selection of immigrants. Evidence has suggested that men migrating to join their families do not adapt as well in the labor market as those migrating on their own. The extent to which family reunification has affect the selection of women and their labor market outcomes remains unexploited.

It is well-documented in the labor economic literature that the context in which labor supply decisions are made differs substantially between single women and married women. While discussing the migration of women in general, this book limits its empirical analysis to the labor market performance of married women. Chapter 4 develops a conceptual framework that incorporates migration selectivity into the neoclassical married women's labor supply model.

This study proposes marital status at migration and migration pattern as empirical measures of female migration selectivity and evaluates how these selectivity measures interact with the labor market performance of immigrant women. National data containing both the migration and adaptation experiences of immigrant women have been extremely rare. Chapter 5 reviews potential sources of empirical data and evaluates their usefulness for this study. This book constructs marital status at migration, migration pattern, and labor force data for a nationally representative sample of Asian and Hispanic immigrant women through linking individuals across several supplements of the Current Population Survey (CPS).

The results show that migration selectivity significantly differentiates immigrant women in labor supply, but not in earnings. Among women who are married at the time of arrival in the United States, those who migrate before their husbands are most likely to participate in the labor force, while those who migrate after their husbands are least likely to do so. Since the implementation of family reunification policy in 1965, the number of female Asian and Hispanic immigrants in the U.S. have increased drastically. However, the selection with respect to marital status and migration pattern of women appears to vary substantially by country of origin. In addition, the selectivity effects on the immigrant women's labor supply and earnings also differ by country of origin. Overall, Asian women are more likely to be married at the time of their arrival in the U.S. than are Hispanic women. Asian women, from East Asia in particular, who migrate after their husbands, earn substantially lower wages in the U.S. labor market than their respective ethnic counterparts. Refugee women typically migrate in the same period as their husbands. Among refugee women, those with this migration pattern are most likely to participate in the labor force and gain the highest wage. A statistical test shows that, however, migration selectivity does not have a significant contribution toward explaining the ethnic differences in immigrant women' labor market outcomes. Chapter 6 details the findings. Chapter 7 discusses policy implications and provides future direction.

This book was formerly my doctoral dissertation submitted to the graduate school of Cornell University in January 1995. The faculty, staff, and my fellow graduate students at the Department of Consumer Economics and Housing had provided generous support for this study. Dr. Robert Avery encouraged my pursuit of the subject and provided numerous feedbacks in the development of the study. His empirical approach greatly influenced this book. Discussions with Dr. Peter Chi helped me think through the conceptual model of the book. Discussions with Dr. Douglas Gurak deepened my understanding in migration theory and practice. Dr. Steven Schwager read through the methodology chapters and contributed useful comments in the presentation of statistical concept. His interests in and support for the study meant a lot. Friends who enrich my Ithaca and Boston experiences, Nicky Morris, Barbara Johnson, Barbara Moeykens, Jieyu Li, and David Weakliem, have encouraged and helped in the publication of the book. As a freshman in book publishing, I am indebted to Dr. Stuart Bruchey at the University of Maine for critical review and to Mr. Robert McKenzie and Ms. Elizabeth Manus at Garland for editorial suggestions. A special thanks goes to every member of my family. In particular, my sister Fung-Yin and her husband Jason helped tremendously in the production of the tables of the book.

Boston, Massachusetts
July 1996

Asian and Hispanic Immigrant Women in the Work Force

1

Introduction

The volume and composition of U.S. immigration streams have undergone drastic changes since the implementation of the Immigration and Nationality Act Amendments of 1965. The amendments trigger a revival of mass immigration in the post-war era mostly through unlimited family reunification by U.S. citizens. In the 1950s, about 2.5 million legal immigrants were admitted to the U.S. Three decades later, the figure more than doubled to 5.8 million (INS 1990, p.1). The resulting foreign-born stock reached 19.8 million in 1990, the highest level of foreign-born counted in U.S. history (USDC 1993a, p.2).

Nationals of certain countries appear to be more willing and able to take advantage of the family reunification provisions than others. The administrative records of the Immigration and Naturalization Service show that from 1820 to 1960, 81 percent of the 42 million legal immigrants were European (USDC 1993a, p.2). Between 1960 to 1990, only 2.7 percent of the 15 million legal immigrants were European. In fact, over 80 percent of the legal immigrants entering the U.S. in the 1980s were from Asia, Mexico, Caribbean and Latin America (INS 1990). Accordingly, the country-of-origin composition of the foreign-born population in the U.S. has shifted from 3 percent Asians and Hispanics at the turn of the century to 68 percent in 1990 (USDC 1993a, p.2). As new immigrants settled down, they have contributed substantially to the rapid growth of the Asian and Hispanic populations in the U.S. in recent decades.

Given the volume and the diversity of the post-1965 immigration, public concerns have centered on its impacts on the U.S. economy. First, what are the contributions of the new immigrants to the U.S. labor force? Second, what is the skill composition of the new immigrants? Do they tend to be less skilled and thus more likely to replace unskilled native workers? Third, are immigrants likely to accept wage offers lower than those taken by comparable natives and thus suppress the wage, and deteriorate the work conditions? Fourth, can immigrants adapt to the U.S. economy, and achieve parity with their native-born counterparts in a timely fashion or will they become long-term burdens to the welfare system? Fifth, as new members of the U.S. minority groups, do immigrants differ in their adaptation experiences by country of origin, and thus contribute to the existing racial/ethnic stratification in the labor market?

These questions call for evaluations of the role of the U.S. immigration policy in selecting the levels and types of skills that immigrants bring with them and the economic adaptation experiences of the new immigrants as a result of the selection. It is generally maintained that the post-1965 immigrants are less skilled than previous waves of immigrants, and the deterioration of qualities over time is also apparent among the post-1965 immigrants. The decline of immigrant qualities is attributed to (1) the shift in the country-of-origin composition; (2) the extensive utilization of family reunification of the recent immigrants; and (3) the increasing phenomenon of aliens entering the U.S. and staying without proper documents. The underlying assumptions to these speculations are (1) immigrants from developing countries are either less skilled or possess skills that are less transferable to the U.S. economy; (2) immigrants admitted through family reunification are less skilled than those admitted through occupational preferences; and (3) immigrants entering the U.S. without legal status are less skilled than legal immigrants. Empirical research addressing these issues have been based exclusively on immigrant men, and uncovered a mixed picture due to a lack of data specifically designed to answer each question.

Research has shown that the emphasis of the U.S. immigration policy on family reunification since 1965 is not gender-indifferent (Houstoun et al. 1984; Boyd 1990; Jasso and Rosenzweig 1990), and in particular, female immigrants are much more likely to be admitted as spouses than male immigrants. Despite the fact that over half of the recent immigration streams are women, the evaluation of the economic impacts of immigrants have mostly ignored the female experiences due to the implications of a conventional image of immigrant wives accompanying husbands (Morokvasic 1984a). Immigrant wives, particularly those from developing countries with more traditional gender roles than others, are often portrayed as inactive and transitory in the U.S. labor market. However, recent research has suggested that Asian and Hispanic immigrant wives in the U.S. are highly responsive to their market potentials in making their labor force participation decisions (Stier 1991; Stier and Tienda 1992). Moreover, their economic contributions have been found to be critical for their families in achieving self-sufficiency (Perez 1986a; Reimers 1984b; Bach and Bach 1980). Very little is known regarding the skill level and composition of the post-1965 immigrant women, and how the family reunification policy exert an impact on the selection of immigrant women.

Existing research on the comparison of female labor force participation behavior among various immigrant groups has attributed observed ethnic differences to differential adaptation processes and/or cultural factors (Stier 1991; Ong 1987; Reimers 1984a; Ortiz and Cooney 1984; Wong and Hirschman 1983; Bean et al. 1982). Differential adaptation processes are viewed as the result of differences in structural factors in the host society, such as discrimination or economic opportunities which may vary over time. Cultural factors are viewed as generating ethnic differences either through differential stock of human capital, such as education, motivation for upward mobility and entrepreneurship, or through different values placed on kinship networks (Hirschman 1982). Within this conceptual framework, ethnic differences are taken as exogenous, and the role of the U.S. immigration policy in shaping ethnicity is obscured. Questions as to why some groups come into the U.S. with a more advantaged stock of human capital or are more likely than others to rely on ethnic enclaves remain unsolved.

In filling these gaps, this book examines the effects of the immigration selectivity of the Asian and Hispanic immigrant wives on their labor market performances. Previous studies along this line have suffered from a small number of observations and/or a lack of a combination of both immigration status and labor force data. By pooling information over rotated samples from Current Population Survey (CPS) supplements, this study was able to combine critical marital history, immigration history and labor market information for a sufficiently large number of immigrant wives. It provides a new and direct opportunity to empirically examine policy impacts on the economic adaptation of immigrant wives. The current study focuses on the experience of Asian and Hispanic women since these two groups constitute the bulk of recent immigrant women to the U.S. and there have been concerns raised over the role of third world women in the family migration process, how they fare and interact with the native-born and other minority women in the U.S. As married women face choices in whether to stay at home or participate in the labor force, while going to work is less of a choice for single immigrant women, this study restricts its analysis on the economic adaptation of immigrant wives.

The central questions addressed in this research are as follows. First, is there female migration selectivity, and how can we measure it? Second, does the migration selectivity matter in the immigrant wives' labor market performances? Third, does the selectivity vary by country-of-origin groups? Fourth, what are the labor market consequences of implementing the family reunification provisions since 1965? Do the changes in policies encourage more married women to accompany husbands than before? Can marital status at migration and migration patterns account for the differences in the labor market incorporation of immigrant wives entering the U.S. at various historical times?

Migration literature suggests that migration selectivity may occur due to differential cost and benefit calculation along both observed and unobserved dimensions (Gurak et al. 1987; Chiswick 1978; Borjas 1987). Specifically, this study argues that immigrant women differ in their selections of when to migrate and how to migrate. As rational actors, their choices of migration patterns reflect their unobserved labor market qualities. In particular, single women migrating on their own find it more difficult to obtain visas than married women. It is apparent that marital status and spousal migration patterns are important indicators of female immigrants' family responsibilities and migration motivation, as well as their future ability to adapt to the receiving countries. Since those migrating to join their husbands or family members are most likely to face lower costs of migration and have more prior information about the U.S. than those migrating on their own, they are likely to be less competitive in the U.S. labor market.

Immigration policy in the receiving country may result in differential selectivity across country-of-origin groups. Historically the U.S. immigration legislation has imposed differential costs on immigrants based on national origin through numerical limitation and a preference system. Lobo (1992) argued that because the preference system was applied to western countries one decade later than to eastern countries, the U.S. has drawn less selective Hispanic than Asian immigrants. Furthermore, the selectivity of the previous cohorts of a given country of origin may influence the selection of future immigrants through family reunification. Very little empirical investigation testing the policy effects on differential selection among countries of origin has been conducted.

Research also suggests the home country characteristics to be decisive factors explaining the differential selection. Borjas (1987; 1991a) assumed that men migrate in search for better economic rewards and argued that countries with higher income inequality than the U.S. tend to send those with skills below the national average to immigrate the U.S. His empirical studies found that a few political and economic factors of the home countries explained notable variations of the earnings differences among immigrant men. Similarly, the participation of women in the migration process depends largely on their attachments to their families as well as to their cultural heritages. To summarize, the structural and cultural differences across home countries interacting with the terms provided by the U.S. immigration legislation further intensify the differential selection among female immigrant groups, and consequently widen the gap of their economic achievements.

This book contributes to the literature by integrating the migration selectivity literature with married women's labor supply literature. It identifies the immigrant wives' marital status at migration and migration patterns as indicators of the immigrant wives' unobserved migration selectivity and examines the significance of these factors in the young Asian and Hispanic immigrant wives' labor market performances. Furthermore, it examines how much migration selectivity accounts for the well-documented disparity in the labor market achievement of women migrated from various countries in the world at different periods of time.

To examine the patterns of migration selectivity, descriptive statistics indicating the demographic and labor market characteristics of the immigrant wives are presented. To examine the consequence of migration selectivity in labor supply, this study estimates the significance and magnitude of the marital status and migration patterns in the Asian and Hispanic immigrant wives' labor supply and earnings equations. To examine how migration selectivity interacts with country of origin and timing of migration, this study compares the immigrant wives' labor supply and earnings before and after inclusion of their marital status and migration pattern variables in the models. The empirical data utilized for this study are the June 1986, 1988, and 1991 and the November 1989 CPS supplements. Only young Asian and Hispanic wives aged 18-44 with husbands present at the time of survey are included.

The remainder of the book is organized as follows. Chapter 2 reviews the theoretical and empirical literature on the selectivity of female immigration. The labor market consequences of female immigration are discussed. Chapter 3 portrays the historical evolution of the U.S. immigration policy applied to Asia and Latin America. Policy implications on gender composition and female immigrant characteristics across national-origin groups and over time are highlighted. Chapter 4 describes the conceptual model and empirical model. In addition, it specifies the variables constructed as well as the empirical questions and hypotheses. Chapter 5 describes the sources of data employed for this study, documents the imputation procedures undertaken, and reports the sample statistics. Chapter 6 presents the empirical results. Finally, Chapter 7 discusses the implications as well as limitations of the results, and proposes future directions.

2

Female Immigration, Selectivity, and Settlement

The migration process involves several stages and is dynamic in nature. Chang (1981, p.306) proposes that a general theory of migration must be able to answer the following series of questions: "who are the migrants?" (selectivity); "why do they move, stay or return?" (causes of migration); "how and where do they move?" (migration patterns); "when do they move?" (migration cohorts); and "what are the effects of such actions on the migrants and on others?" (consequences of migration). Each phase of migration is clearly interrelated. To evaluate the consequences of migration, the answers to the above questions need to be addressed.

This chapter reviews hypotheses and evidence on why women participate in the migration process, their characteristics as compared to non-migrants, and their subsequent labor market adaptation. Section 2.1 examines the causes of female migration, drawing conceptual and empirical references from conventional migration theory. A review of the literature of female migration, and in particular, internal female migration, reveals the gender-specific variations in the causes, patterns, and selectivity of migration process. Section 2.2 defines immigration selectivity and summarizes empirical evidence on selectivity. Section 2.3 addresses the economic adaptation of female immigrants. Factors contributing to group differences are discussed.

2.1 DETERMINANTS OF FEMALE IMMIGRATION

The conventional migration wisdom reflects an image of a young male seeking a better opportunity elsewhere. This "male bias" stems from the traditional male role as the major provider and decision-maker (Morokvasic 1984). From a broad perspective, the phenomenon of female immigration is induced by similar forces and subject to similar constraints as male immigration. However, females may react to these forces and constraints differently, and the impact of these factors on women may be substantially different from those of men. Morokvasic (1984b) argues forcefully that gender is an important factor in immigration studies since immigration often involves two countries of different stratification systems. Furthermore, immigration policies, which filter potential immigrants, usually have different implications for men and women.

This section is composed of two parts. First, the enormous conventional migration literature provides a common ground and language in immigration studies. Second, gender-related determinants in the migration context are addressed. Since the research on female migration originated and flourished in examination of internal migration, the discussion utilizes materials from both internal and international migration.

2.1.1 Conventional Migration Theory

The conventional migration theory originated from efforts devoted to specifying a universal principle that would explain aggregate human movements. Ravenstein (1885; 1889) points to the inverse relationship between the rate of migration and distance. Gravity model predicts that distance tends to discourage population movement between two places. The deterrent effects of distance are due to the fact that distance measures physical and psychic costs of moving, and the availability of information, conditional on technology and communication.

Push-Pull Framework. Analyzing migration data in England from the 1881 census, Ravenstein (1885; 1889) concluded that people were pushed out of the originating country due to factors such as famine or bad weather, whereas they were attracted to certain areas in response to better opportunities. Lee (1966) elaborated on this push-pull framework, and hypothesized four groups of factors affecting the migration decision: positive/negative factors associated with the sending area; positive/negative factors associated with the receiving area; intervening factors (e.g. geographical barriers; distance); and personal factors. The positive factors in the sending area, negative factors in the receiving area and intervening factors discourage migration whereas the negative factors at sending area, and positive factors at the receiving area encourage migration. Finally personal characteristics differentiate among migrants and non-migrants given the same sets of factors in both the sending area and the receiving area, as well as intervening factors. criticized Lee's framework on its attempt to generalize all migration processes and reliance on hypotheses.

Despite of criticisms on its generality (Todaro 1976; Gaude 1976), the push-pull model in fact provides a basic framework in the formulation of subsequent advanced and refined migration theories and hypotheses. The following describes the two most important theories in migration studies, and relates them back to the push-pull framework.

Neoclassical Theory. The neoclassical economic theory treats labor as a source of input, which is allocated within and among countries by the forces of supply and demand. High demand in the receiving area clearly raises the potential wages of workers and thus "pulls" migrants out of their low-paying areas of origin. These pull factors in the receiving areas are often created by labor scarcity, or by recruitment by multinational organizations. In contrast, high supply of labor in the sending areas will lower the offered wage for the workers, and hence "push" out the marginal workers who can't find a job or can't maintain a living in the sending areas. This "surplus labor" hypothesis is based on unlimited labor supply from the rural areas in the development and industrialization process (Lewis 1954).

At the micro level, the classical economic model postulates that the migration from region A to region B is mainly determined by the wage differential between the two regions and the human capital of the individuals at region A. However, the theory does not provide specific guidance on which wage differential the potential migrants actually respond to. Empirical studies have employed measures of wage differentials such as: absolute differential, relative differential and expected differentials (Todaro 1976). Since the theory is mainly developed and researched in the context of internal migration, it is to be detailed later.

To explain the aggregate level of migration flows, the neoclassical theory relies on the international trade theory. The theory portrays the flows of capital and labor between two nations as the result of specialization based on each nation's comparative advantages in resources and international trade (Lim 1989; Martin 1991). A nation which has substantial capital will specialize in capital-intensive production, and import cheap labor from labor surplus nations.

Economic Theory of Internal Migration. The economic maximization theory postulates that people choose residence wherever the discounted present value of the expected net benefits is greatest (Todaro

1969; 1976; De Jong and Fawcett 1981; DaVanzo 1981). The calculation of the present value is based on the decision maker's utility function, which includes subjective values and objective environmental variables. The costs of migration include (1) direct transportation costs (factors such as distance or technology are good measures of transportation costs); (2) information costs; (3) psychic costs; and (4) opportunity costs in foregone earnings if not migrate.

Derived to explain the increasing urbanization in the process of development, two major economic models are both based on a rural-urban comparison. Lewis-Fei-Ranis models (Lewis 1954; Todaro 1976) assume a perfectly responsive supply of rural labor pushed out by overpopulation and new technology in agriculture, while pulled into the cities by growing employment opportunities. In contrast, Todaro (1969; 1976) postulates that migration decisions are made by individuals who compare expected earnings between rural and urban areas. He suggests that the expected returns can be measured by (1) the differences in real income between rural and urban job opportunities; and (2) the probability that a new migrants will get a job in the urban areas. Furthermore, he assumes that the higher the probability of obtaining a job in urban areas, the lower the urban unemployment rate.

Subsequent modifications of the models have benefitted from the human capital theory and the neoclassical trade theory. The human capital model views migration decision as an investment in human capital (Becker 1964). Hence, people make decisions to migrate if they expect increases in productivity (e.g. earnings potential) as a result of the move (Sjaastad 1962). Criticisms of the neoclassical economic model are (1) the simplified assumption of rationality and maximization; (2) the ambiguity regarding unit of decision-making; (3) that they offer little insight on how the utility function is shaped (Goodman 1981) and (4) the assumption of perfect information (Stark and Bloom 1985; Stark 1984).

A variation of the microeconomic-type model considers the family as the unit of decision-making and that the main objective is to maximize total family income. If individual interests don't agree with the goal of maximizing family income as a result of family migration, he/she is often referred to as a tied-mover (DaVanzo 1981). Alternatively, the couple may decide to live apart temporarily or even permanently if the individual loss exceeds the gain of staying together. Migration may sometimes be used as a family strategy in which the family take out a loan to finance the migration of the family member most likely to benefit from moving and expects remittances in return.

Stark and Taylor (1986; 1989; 1991) found that rural households in Mexico migrate not only to maximize their household incomes but also to get ahead of other villagers. Poor households are likely to engage in U.S.-bound migration if their household incomes are ranked among the lower end of their village's household income distribution. Nonetheless, regardless of how their income compared to others', most households appear to be able to utilize their resources efficiently by allocating members across labor markets (Stark and Taylor 1991).

In most cases, prospective migrants know very little about the receiving areas prior to the actual move, the assumption of perfect information embedded in the neoclassical model that enables the comparison of expected gains/losses seems unrealistic. A second variation in the microeconomic model concerns imperfect information. Since established migrants often feed information back to those who are left behind in the sending areas, Ritchey (1976) suggests migrant stock to indicate the flow of information. Imperfect information tends to lead to (1) a lower incidence of mobility; and (2) concentration of the mover in certain locations (Goodman 1981).

To sum up, based on the push-pull framework, the neoclassical theory implicitly assumes that individuals are making rational choices based on the calculation of expected gains and losses associated with migration. The calculation of gains and losses is evaluated by the differences in offered wages in the originating area and offered wages in the destination. The causes in wage differentials between areas or countries may be a result of uneven resources endowment or uneven economic development.

Economic Development Hypothesis. As described previously, the neo-classical economic model of migration asserts that economic differentials determines migration, which implies a net migration flow from less-developed countries to develop countries. Given this prediction, the way for developed countries to virtually control immigration is to help promote economic development in less-developed countries. However, the actual phenomenon of migration did not seem to confirm this hypothesis. In light of the failure of prediction, major attention has been paid to the formation of a migration network in the process of economic development and its role in facilitating further migration.

Linking migration and development, Martin (1991) describes how the efforts of recruitment, return migration and remittances may often induce further migration in practice. The recruitment helps build the migration network, which greatly reduces the cost of migration, and encourages further migration. Likewise, the spending of remittance on mainly consumption commodities rather than investment pushes up inflation and augments income inequality among the villagers, and hence induces more emigration.

Massey (1988; 1990) challenges the misconception that economic development will reduce mass migration in the short run. Instead, he postulates that peasants are in fact separated from the land and traditional ties in the development process. In a sense, they are displaced by capital and new technologies. Migration to cities or other nations is an alternative. The first among them to migrate across national borders encounters high costs in the presence of unknown future. The costs and uncertainty decline as more and more people participate in the move and more information about the destination becomes readily available. Lowered costs induce further migration, and further migration enlarges the migration network. Gradually, immigration grows independent of the economic conditions that originally caused it.

Structural Theory. "Historical Structuralists," "dependency theorists," and the imperialist model of migration" argue that the international trade order was structured by international division of labor. Dependent of the supply of capital investment from developed countries (or "core countries,") less-developed countries (or periphery countries) were subject to inferior term of trade ((reubens 1981; Grasmuck and Pessar 1991). In less-developed countries, the collapse of agricultural economies has caused migration from rural to urban areas. Due to limited capacities to absorb these displaced labors in cities, export of labors to developed countries becomes a sensible alternative. This strategy is welcomed by developed countries through aggressively recruiting cheap labors from the less-developed countries to fill jobs undesirable to their native workers. In this view, the individual migrants, often the unskilled laborers, were said to be drawn by macro-forces, instead of income-maximizing actors (Burawoy 1976).

The world system hypothesis and the system approach renewed the structuralist arguments and paid special attention to account for the interdependence between countries. The world system hypothesis postulates that migration flow from region A to region B is caused by the capital penetration from region B to region A and a demand for cheap labor in region B (Portes 1987). It emphasizes the role of the network between region A and region B by linking populations residing across the system. As network matures, it help stabilizing migration flow through assisting newcomers and eventually migration flow grows independent of its original drive.

The systems approach postulates that migratory flows from region A to region B are triggered by (1) macro or formal associations between the two regions such as geographic proximity, colonial ties, and political relations; (2) micro networks, or informal factors such as recruitment, family or communities; and (3) structural differences between region A and region B such as economic, demographic, social and political forces (Kritz & Zlotnik 1992). The impacts of the first two sets of factors are accumulated in dynamic processes, whereas the impacts of the last set of factors are specific at points in time. This hypothesis states that migration does not start randomly; instead, it starts with institutional factors, such as migrant networks. System approaches emphasize the dynamic aspects of migration processes and the interdependence and feedback between migration flows (Boyd 1989). According to this approach, networks serve as linkages between migrants and non-migrants across space and time and are a critical element of migration processes.

Unit of Analysis. Migration research distinguishes between micro- and macro-level studies (De Jong and Gardner 1981). Micro-level analyses focus on individual or family decision-making while macro-level analyses describe the features, volume and direction of migration flows at an aggregate level. Each approach points to a different conceptualization of the empirical model to test its related theory and hypotheses. The micro-level analysis examines the probability of migration of individuals by their demographic characteristics. In contrast, the macro-level analysis examines the rate of migration of areas with given features (Todaro 1976).

Two kinds of macro-level variables may be further distinguished (Gardner 1981). Contextual variables refer to aggregations of individual characteristics. Setting variables are characteristics of the whole population or environment which can't be attributed to any single individual. Income inequality and education level are examples of contextual variables whereas historical connection with a foreign group, or government policy are examples of setting variables.

It is obvious that macro-level and micro-level factors may interplay. One such example is that macro-level factors may influence individual decisions through conceptualization and value formation (Gardner 1981; Hugo 1981). De Jong and Fawcett (1981) proposed a value-expectancy-based model where both individual and societal factors are taken into account. In this model, individual and household demographic characteristics, the societal and cultural norms, and the opportunity system for migration are hypothesized to shape individuals' values and expectancy of migration. Values and expectancy jointly determine migration decision.

In addition to the simplistic micro versus macro distinction, family or household decision may determine individual migration outcomes. Studies indicate migration of an individual may be a household strategy for survival or social advancement of the household (Pessar 1982).

A few studies have pointed to the necessity of combining the two levels of analysis (Parkin 1975; Taylor 1969; Tienda 1983; Perez 1986). In particular, Parkin suggests regarding the macro context as a "given" in a micro study of migrants, although very little research has adopted such an approach. The potential use of multilevel analysis in studying the determinant of female migration is stressed (Bilsborrow and Zlotnik 1992).

To summarize, conventional migration theories differ from one another in the types of migration forces they identify and the unit of analysis they are dealing with. Recent development in the theory has focused on (1) the need of integrating both micro- and macro- levels of analyses; (2) the cumulative process of migration; and (3) the interdependence between countries and regions. The discussion provides a conceptual framework in migration analysis, be it male or female immigrants. The next section reviews studies on the determinants of female migration.

2.1.2 Determinants of Female Migration

Research on female internal migration has emerged in the late 1960s due to rapid urbanization in developing countries. Morokvasic (1983) attributes the emerging literature on female migration from the mid-seventies onwards to the wider feminist movement and increasing women's participation in economic activities. Although cultural and societal differences as well as legal control over population movement are involved across national boundaries, similar arguments or findings from internal migration may be extended to international migration.

Associational versus Autonomous Migrants. From an individualistic perspective, a common typology used to describe female migration is to characterize female migrants as either associational or autonomous migrants. The former is defined in relation to their family connections, whereas the latter assumes the predominance of economic motivations. Family, as an economic maximization unit and a socialization unit, clearly has close impact on the motivations of females as family members (Lim

1990). Female migration is also said to be conditioned by the broad macro-factors. Bogue (1961) describes the migration of women as a by-product of a mature migration stream to joining their pioneer male relatives. The economic factors motivating female migrants to cities and towns in developing countries are seen as the consequence of economics development and social change undergone in these areas.

At the individual level, women migrants do seem to react to income differential between areas just like their male counterparts. Nonetheless, Todaro and Thadani (1979) observed two gender-specific factors, the desire for social mobility and marriage mobility in predict female migration. Furthermore, the process of modernization and changes in reproductive technology may have played an important role in encouraging women migration. Delayed marriage and child birth and the promotion of few children through family planning tend to free women from child-bearing and child-rearing activities and thus increase the likelihood of their engaging in autonomous migration (Bilsborrow and Zlotnik 1992).

Structural Determinants of Female Migration. In the process of economic development and modernization, the change in institutional factors, mode of production and distribution, and societal values and norms may served as structural constraints and pressures on female emigration. Arizpe (1984) contends that it is the conditions and the dynamics of social structure in the sending areas that ultimately determines who will be most likely to migrate. In particular, the commercialization in the peasant society has, to a certain degree, freed women from the social organization and norms of the rural communities and hence are suitable candidates for migration. Despradel (1984) observed that the introduction of cash crops to the Caribbean has limited the participation of women in local production and hence encouraged emigration.

The preponderance of female migration in Latin America and Southeast Asia, particularly the Philippines since the 1960s and more recently in East Asia is well-documented (Boserup 1970; Youssef et al. 1979). This phenomenon has been attributed to both women's residual function in local production (Boserup 1970) and the growing opportunities in domestic service, trade and light industry that mostly appeal to women in cities around the world (Boserup 1970; Connell et al. 1976). Boyd (1990) summarized the situations under which female migration rather than male migration is more likely to occur: (1) where the majority of land is owned and farmed by men; (2) where the peasants' land ownership is highly uneven as a result of economic restructuring; and (3) where domestic non-agricultural production is completely substituted by import goods.

The nature of the structural factors driving female migration seem to differ from that of male migration (Morokvasic 1984b). First, immigrant women are particularly seen by the recruitment agents in the receiving country as a source of cheap and flexible labor force that are easy to control. Second, the discriminatory attitudes and practice towards women rather than men in the sending societies push women to immigrate to developed countries. Morokvasic (1984b) identifies the disadvantaged position of women in paid work in southeast Europe as the main cause of female emigration. Abadan-Unat (1984) attributed the phenomenon of female emigration in Turkey to the discriminatory clauses of property ownership system. In their study of Dominican Republican households, Grasmuck and Pessar (1991) suggest that the emigration of sons and wives is often an escape from patriarchal dominance and generational conflicts over disputes on land inheritance. Once settled and in the United States, Dominican wives often refused to either quit jobs or return to their home towns with their husbands. This observation appears to coincide with the reported high incidence of female-headed households among Dominican women in New York city (Grasmuck and Pessar 1991; Gurak and Kritz 1984).

In addition to being a cause of female migration, structural factors may also determine the patterns of migration. In Latin America, it is reported that women sometimes migrating ahead of their husbands if their skills are more needed in the destinations than their husbands' (Whiteford 1978).

Status of Women and Female Immigration. The increasing phenomenon of female migration in the less-developed world is seen as closely related to the changing roles and status of women (Bilsborrow and Zlotnik 1992). Lim (1990) defines women's status as follows:

> The status of women refers to women's position vis-a-vis men and vis-a-vis each other over the life course within a particular socio-economic, cultural and politico-legal context. (p.6)

Based on this definition, she describes a society with low women's status as: (1) where women have little control over resources; (2) where women are unable to make decisions for themselves and to influence other people; and (3) where women are deprived of prestige and respect. Empirically,

Donato and Tyree (1986) suggest indicators such as the ratio of secondary school enrollments for boys and girls or the ratio of earnings of adult men and women of the origin population as measures of the status of women.

Lim (1990) elaborates on the interplay of status of women and female immigration. She hypothesizes that a woman, particularly if single, who is well-respected in her family and society and has control over her life is least likely to migrate. She contends that the migration patterns of married women, whether following husbands or staying behind, reflects how well the culture accepts the separation of husband and wife. She identifies marital status, educational attainment, and stage in the life cycle as key factors determining migration for women. Other research has also noted the significant distinctions between married and single women in studying the motivations and consequences of female migration (Fawcett, Khoo and Smith 1984; Hong 1984). At working and marriageable ages, single women tend to have strong motives to migrate. When society emphasizes the reproductive and domestic roles of married women, female migration at reproductive ages may be least common. Thus, age and duration of marriage may be used as proxies for life-cycle stage. While acknowledging the importance of marriage and life-cycle factors, Arizpe (1984) cautions that these factors are subject to the ideological control and social norms of individual society.

Internal Migration versus International Migration. International migrants and internal migrants differ in many ways. On average, international migrants tend to be better educated and are more willing to take risks. A few factors may account for these differences (Weeks 1986). First, since international migration usually means confronting a new culture and institutional system, international migration is more influenced by the political climate and the opportunity structure. Second, internal migration is seldom regulated by government, whereas international migration may involve forced or illegal migration. Third, international migration usually is sometimes not achievable by everyone due to immigration regulations and distances between nations.

Immigration policies regarding the admissions or adaptation of immigrants are often not gender-neutral. Houstoun (et al. 1984) underline the sex discrimination feature in the U.S. immigration policy which permitted wives to reunite with their husbands but not the other way around, until 1952. Boyd (1986) shows that immigrant women in Canada, taken as dependents by the admission practice,, were often denied the access to government-sponsored language or job training programs.

To summarize, this section describes four sets of factors that affect the migration of women: (1) individual motives, such as economic or marriage; (2) structural determinants in the home town, such as the local mode of production; (3) status of women in the sending areas; and (4) legislation in both sending and receiving areas that promote or constrain the migration of women. These factors clearly attract different pool of immigrant women. The next section presents evidence on female migration selectivity.

2.2 FEMALE MIGRATION SELECTIVITY

Migration is a selective process. As described in section 2.1, the relative economic structures, the social norms and the political systems between the originating society and the receiving society, and the individuals's characteristics circumscribe the likely pool of potential immigrants. Furthermore, the individuals' connections to the existing migration networks, as well as the family/household migration strategies under which migration was initiated play an important role in determining who will migrate. Due to the distinct gender role defined in the originating society and family, the female migration selectivity may be highly affected by the functions of migration networks and the actions of family/household. This section discusses hypotheses and empirical evidence on migration selectivity, emphasizing the gender aspect of it. Migration selectivity is further examined in relation to migration network and family/household.

2.2.1 Definition and Facts

Bogue (1961) provides a technical definition of "differentials in migration (or selectivity of movement)" as follows:

> Evidence of differential migration exists with respect to a given category whenever a disproportionately greater or smaller percentage of migrants falls into that category than is found in the base population with which they are compared. (Bogue 1961, p.405)

Based on this definition, he suggests a measure of differential migration as the difference between the percentage distribution of the migration population and the percentage distribution of the base population.

Apparently, the measures of differential selectivity vary depending on the base population employed. Therefore, the selection of base population is critical in drawing inferences from such a calculation.

Several facts regarding the nature of migration selectivity are summarized as follows (Bogue 1961; Lee 1966; Todaro 1976; Yap 1977). First, migration induced by economic growth, technological improvement, or an expansion in white-collar jobs tends to consist of better-educated people than the average of the origin population. This selectivity is particularly true for longer distance movement. As people with high education are better-informed of opportunities available and are more likely to migrate in response to high rewards. Second, the relative size of migration flow and its counterflow between two points indicates the degree and types of selectivity. If these two migration streams are comparable in size, those who move are usually not too different from those who remain at home. Third, migration flows caused mainly by pushed factors tend to consist of less selective migrants than migration flows induced by pull factors. The nature of the push and pull factors also intensify/reduce the degree of selectivity. Refugees who are pushed out by famine, war, or natural disaster tend to be least selective out of their population of origin. Fourth, migration is highly circumscribed by life cycle stage. High mobility is often observed among those reach maturity.

The selectivity of migrants may be most profound where barriers of migration exist. The deterrent effect of distance on migration is well-documented (Todaro 1976; Yap 1977). However, in the presence of expected sizeable economic differentials, highly educated people are not likely to be discouraged by distance (Schultz 1975). Level of education is therefore positively associated with distance (Todaro 1976; Yap 1977). The less educated immigrants are more reliant on friends and relatives providing information than the educated, who tend to be deterred by distance (Schwartz 1973).

Due to the political obstacles in international migration, migration selectivity may be related to the legal status in the receiving country. Studies have shown that illegal Mexican women in the United States tend to be younger, more unmarried, and less educated than their legal counterparts (Simon and DeLey 1986). However, the illegal Mexican women as a whole are not drawn from the bottom of the socioeconomic ladder in Mexico. The evidence further suggests that single women may have a more difficult time immigrating legally, which seems to coincide with the implications of the family reunification provisions.

This section defines migration selectivity as the deviation from the mean of the population that the immigrants are compared to. It is generally true that migration involving greater costs, as measured by distances or legislative constraints tend to induce more selective immigrants. The next section discusses female selectivity as contrasted with male selectivity.

2.2.2 Gender Selectivity

The selectivity of female migration is often compared to male selectivity of the same country of origin. A few facts concerning the demographic characteristics of migrants exist (Lee 1961; Youssef et al. 1979). First, regardless of sex, migrants tend to be relatively young since young people are less attached to the origin communities (Gallaway 1969; Hugo 1981; Connell et al. 1976). Young people can also expect higher returns through migration as compared with old people. The tendency of migration seems to peak between ages of the late teens and early twenties as well as in the over 50 ranges. Second, females tend to predominate in short-distance migration, whereas males tend to predominate in long-distance migration. Third, female migrants are more concentrated on certain ages and educational levels than male migrants (Youssef, Buvinic and Kudat 1979; Smith, Khoo and Go 1984; Abadan-Unat 1984; Eviota and Smith 1984). Internal female migrants in Latin America, Southeast Asia and East Asia are disproportionally young single females. Female migration in older ages is also prevalent in Latin America and international migration (Smith, Khoo and Go 1984). Fourth, divorced or widowed women are more likely than other women to leave their origin communities. Briody (1987) found a significant percentage of divorced women among Mexican immigrants in South Texas. Changes in or disruptions of life-cycle patterns are all stages that heighten the probability of migration (Findley 1987).

Immigrants are usually selective in terms of level of education. Todaro (1976) noted that coherent evidence has suggested a positive correlation between education and probability of migration, even after controlling for age. This positive relationship may be less evident under international migration where human capital can't be easily transferred. Nonetheless, Donato (1993) found that Mexican women who have little education, no previous U.S. experience, and/or own land in their home communities are not likely to immigrate to the U.S. As the educational attainments of the origin population improve over time, the educational composition of immigrant streams is likely to changed as well. Ducoff

(1961) provides evidence of improving education attainments of Salvadorean migrants for the post-1950 cohorts as compared to the earlier cohorts, and suggested the improvement in education facilities and the reduction in illiteracy in the late 1950s may contribute to the change in cohort composition, instead of change in selectivity itself.

Given the vast majority of the literature has focused on the comparison between males and females, comparisons with women in both origin and destination are needed to enhance the understanding regarding the determinants and consequences of female migration (Bilsborrow and Zlotnik 1992). The selectivity in female immigration clearly is highly related to the family/household migration strategy, and the utilization of migration networks. The following two sections review literature describing the functions of family/household and migration network in selecting immigrants with certain demographic characteristics.

2.2.3 Family/Household Migration Strategy

Families/households play an important role in sharing risks in time of crisis and in coordinating resources in pursuit of higher total income (Stark and Levhari 1982; Stark 1984a; 1984b;.Stark and Bloom 1985). By exercising various strategies, they determine the selection of immigrants. In areas where migration is mainly pushed by famine or heavy taxation at home, migration of household members may be a household strategy for survival. In areas where migration is mainly pulled by better opportunities elsewhere, migration of household members is often a strategy for mobility (Findley 1987; Bilsborrow and Zlotnik 1992). Emigration of young girls in Latin America and in the Philippines is an example of households exercising their survival strategy (Jelin 1978). Young girls and single women were selected for migration because they did not have any viable alternative in the village while they could get employment as domestic servants in the cities.

The cooperative nature of the household is usually sustained through intra-household resource allocation. Who among the household members first gets selected, and the patterns of migration, clearly depends on the type of strategy, the age and sex structure of the household, the resource levels of households, the stage of the family life cycle and the socioeconomic structure that conditions the local production (Pessar 1982; Harbison 1981; Schmink 1984). Migrants are generally found to be from large families, which may be a result of diversification of the family investment portfolio (Connell et al. 1976) and/or small inheritance

(Harbison 1981). Birth order may matters in deciding the best candidate to send to the cities or abroad (Connell et al. 1976). The youngest son may be forced to leave because of not inheriting any land (Wyon and Gordon 1971). Medina and Natividad (1985) found the eldest child of the family to be the most likely candidate as the pioneer migrant of the family, irrespective of gender.

Sending a young educated male, who is likely to be the member having the highest earnings potential, is usually a rational choice for the household. However, in Southeast Asia, the consideration that daughters are more likely to send remittances back, may alter the selection (Bilsborrow and Zlotnik 1992). Dinerman (1978) further observed that the sex and age distribution of the household is important in deciding who should migrate. When there is no eligible man to migrate, i.e. a household consisting of only old men or there is no free hand from the household production, woman may go. In general, social norms prevent migration of women, except for old women.

Not every household can afford to employ a migration as strategy. Immigration to the U.S. is most likely for Mexican rural households with sufficient economic resources to support the trip and with extra labor to cover household production (Dinerman 1978; Pessar 1982; Briody 1987). Accordingly, an extended household is more likely to send members to the U.S., provided its supply of income is secured. Household size appear to matter the most in the case of international migration where foregone opportunity costs are highest (Taylor 1986). The head of household is less likely to migrate due to stronger attachment with the origin community than other members of the household.

While Mexican migration is often described as a male-led phenomenon, females and children often follow the men later on as the men accumulate more U.S. experiences (Reichert and Massey 1980; Massey 1985). Briody (1987) surveys previous research and suggests a pattern of household migration among Mexicans to South Texas in the 1970s. The expanding employment opportunities in the agricultural sector in the same period appear to have facilitated the trend. In her own study, she observes that a substantial number of Mexican immigrants were separated from their families for a certain period. This pattern of partial household immigration is intended to take advantage of low living expenses in Mexico, avoiding the risk associated with illegal status, and difficulties in finding shelter and caring for all family members in the U.S. Consequently, those undocumented households and households at the early stage of life cycle are identified as more likely to have adopted this strategy (Briody 1987; Browning and Rodriguez 1985).

The types of potential jobs at the destination is likely to effect the immigrant women's migration patterns. British West Indians often migrate alone to the U.S. Gordon (1981) explains this phenomenon by noting the prevalence of West Indian female engaged in private household work, which discourages the presence of the other family members.

The definition of a household in the migration context has been expanded beyond co-residence. Evidence in the Philippines supports that existence of the "shadow household" containing individuals residing elsewhere who are committed and obliged to that household (Caces et al. 1985). They find that young unmarried women constitute the majority of "shadow households", which may be a result of their least attachment in their originating area. In general, the rest of the household members will join the shadow household, the shorter the distance, the faster.

This section describes, under various family/household strategies, individual member of the family/household of certain characteristics have higher chances of migrating than other members. The selection of the family/household member depend on (1) the demographic size and composition of the household; (2) the need of the local production; (3) the attachment of the individual member to the local community; and (4) the chances of the member successfully migrated and prospering at the destination.

2.2.4 Migration Network and Selectivity

Network is critical in migration process through its adaptive, selective, and channelling functions (Gurak and Caces 1992). The adaptive function of a migration network facilitates the integration of immigrants, or insulates immigrants in the destination society while at the same time maintains migrants' connections to the origin society. The selective function of the migration network influences the selection of migrants and households within originating areas, and the selection of the destination given chosen migrants. The channelling function of the migration networks feeds information and other resources among migrants and potential migrants, and shape the size and momentum of migration.

The existence of migration networks also reduce costs and risks involved with migration. Acknowledging that migration involves uncertainty and risk, Taylor (1986) argues that migration networks provide risk-reducing information, and furthermore, the higher migration risks are, the greater the impact of networks will be. Since international migration involves more risk, less information and higher penalties for making bad predictions than internal migration, networks are hypothesized to have greater impacts on the former than the latter.

Empirical findings based on Mexican data show that access to network connections greatly increases the probability of emigrating to the U.S. (Taylor 1986; Massey and Garcia-Espana 1987; Massey et al. 1987). Massey and Espana found that villagers having a relative in the U.S. were five times more likely to migrate to the U.S. than others. Those whose fellow villagers had prior U.S. experience were more likely to conduct a U.S. trip themselves than others. Using the Filipino data, DeJong and colleagues (1986) shows the importance of personal contacts in providing information, regardless of the type of relative present in the United States.

The existence of a kinship network may effect migration selectivity in various ways. Tilly and Brown (1967) hypothesize (1) a higher degree of reliance on kinship in migration process for persons of lower status and few abilities; and (2) a slower process of assimilation for persons migrating under the sponsorship of kinship. Utilizing village-to-city migration data, their empirical findings show that blue-collar workers, the oldest, and the youngest tend to migrate under the assistance of kin. It is conceivable that the selection effects of kin network is greatest among immigrants from less-developed countries where interaction among kin members remain strong (Goodman 1981). Long distance migrants face higher uncertainty, and therefore may be more reliant on friends and relatives than short distance migrants (Goodman 1981).

A critical component in sustaining migration networks is through return migration. Information is spread over the originating area through return migrants. One may expect heavier reliance on kin in places where there is little return migration. Those who migrate under the auspices of previous migrants are likely to reside in the ethnic community, form large households, and engaged in same occupations and industries.

As networks develop, migration tends to become less selective. Furthermore, despite the fact that migration networks encourage further migration, as length of stay increases, and more kin are present in the receiving country, the amount and frequency of remittances may diminish (Massey 1987; Massey and Garcia-Espana 1987; Massey et al. 1987; Portes and Bach 1985). These accumulative effects change the network resources the subsequent immigrants encounter, and thus the effects of migration networks may be reduced.

While the phenomenon of migration selectivity has been widely noted, few research efforts have explicitly attempted to specify actual selectivity mechanisms and magnitude (Gurak, et al. 1987). Empirically, it is not clear whether it is the migration network itself that contributes to the continuation of migration flow or that both migration network and migration flow are motivated and sustained by the same set of macro factors. Specifically, distance and contacts may be correlated since previous migrants may also be attracted by the same distance factor. Thus the significance of contacts may not necessarily be due to information (Yap 1977). Nelson (1959) points out that since the geographic location of migrants is closely related to the location of past migrants, it is also closely related to all the factors that influence past migration. Greenwood (1970; 1972) confirms this hypothesis through empirical data.

Network literature has predominantly focused on male experiences. Boyd (1989) calls for research on how females develop, maintain and utilize networks in the migration and adaptation processes. Recent research suggest that the presence of immediate relatives in the U.S. protects the women who migrate, and therefore encourages the migration of Mexican women (Lindstorm 1991). Similarly, Donato (1993) found that Mexican women are likely to immigrate to the U.S. if someone from their immediate family is a migrant during the same period.

To summarize, the existence of migration network tends to facilitates further migration. As the migration network developed, potential migrants gain more information about the destination and expect more assistance from the network, new immigrants become close to or below the average of the general population in the sending area. The selective function of the migration network is clearly dynamic and varies by the type of network and how closely the individual migrants involved in the network. Given that immigrants are selective in many dimensions, they tend to fare differently based on how they self-selected themselves to migrate in the first place. The next section describes the adaptation experiences of female immigrants in the U.S.

2.3 CONSEQUENCES OF FEMALE IMMIGRATION

Hirschman (1982) suggested three broad sets of factors influencing the socioeconomic progress of immigrants: (1) the human capital the immigrants possess upon migration; (2) the structure of economic opportunities; and (3) the institutional factors, such as discrimination against immigrants/minorities in the host country. These factors, however, can not fully describe the dynamics of the adaptation experiences of women. Clearly, the settlement of migrant women is conditioned by their cultural heritage, their position in the family and migrant community in the receiving society (Berg-Eldering 1984), their family and household situations, and the life-cycle stage at which migration occurs (Lim 1990). Accordingly, immigrant women's labor market performance in the receiving country will be impacted by their initial human capital characteristics, migration patterns, household structure, communities environment, and the structural factors in the receiving society.

The literature examining the economic adaptation experiences of immigrant wives in the U.S. has focused exclusively on their labor force participation and occupational mobility, very little has been done looking into their earnings or hours of work. This section addresses how these factors will impact on the immigrant women's labor force participation. It also reviews literature on the relationship between migration selectivity and migration adaptation. The discussions rely on mainly U.S. examples unless otherwise noted.

2.3.1 Immigrant Women's Labor Supply

This section examines the impact of migration-related factors on immigrant women's labor force participation. In particular, the discussion addresses the following factors: observed human capital characteristics, functions of households, utilization of ethnic networks, and the structural factors.

Cultural Backgrounds and Characteristics at Migration. Individual demographic characteristics at migration reflect the human capital stock that the immigrant women brought with them, their bound to their countries of origin and their exposure to the receiving society and are thus closely related to their subsequent labor market performance. Boyd (1982) finds that age at migration is closely related to Canadian immigrant women's subsequent labor market incorporation. In particular, women migrating as a child (under age 17) appear to perform as well as Canadian-born women in the labor market.

Level of education and English proficiency were found to be important variables in determining the economic adaptation of immigrant and minority women (Reimers 1984a; Wong and Hirschman 1983; Ortiz and Cooney 1984). The immigrant women may accumulate U.S.-specific experience as the length-of-stay increases. However, Long (1980) showed that as the duration-of-stay increases, immigrant wives' earnings deteriorate. The author speculated that immigrant wives may enter the labor force immediately upon arrival to supplement family income. As their family income improve over time, they may withdraw from the labor market and reallocate their time to housework.

As in the case of immigrant men, the labor market performances of immigrant women is also highly related to their motivation for migration. The high incorporation of Cuban immigrant women into the U.S. labor force has been related to their refugee status, with their striving to regain their status in the U.S. (Portes and Bach 1985; Prieto 1986). Due to their relative unfavorable demographic characteristics, the Southeast Asian refugees have lower labor force participation than the U.S. population on average in 1982 and 1983. However, the gap between refugee women and U.S. women is much narrower than that between refugee men and their U.S.-born counterparts (Bach and Carroll-Seguin 1986). North (1981) reports a similar gender differential, except a much better labor market performance of refugees than their U.S. counterparts, which may be attributed to the higher selectivity of the early refugee cohort.

Fertility is generally found to deter the labor force participation of immigrant wives in the U.S., although the degree varies depending on ethnic origin (Bean et al. 1985). Immigrant wives may reduce their fertility level or postpone child-bearing to remain in the labor force. In general, immigrant fertility is lower then that of the natives in the 1970s. The increase in the immigrant fertility in the 1980s can largely be explained by the shifting national-origin and demographic composition of the immigrant flow (Kahn 1991). Evidence is found to be supportive of a disrupted version of the immigrants' fertility, indicating an initial low level of fertility shortly upon arrival and a gradual catch-up (Kahn 1991). Asian immigrants in the U.S., except Southeast Asian refugees and Filipinos, have a lower fertility rates than the natives (Kahn 1991; Rumbaut and Weeks 1986; Massey 1981). Immigrants from the Western Hemisphere exhibit a mixed picture of fertility, with relatively high fertility for immigrants from Mexico, Guatemala, Peru and Ecuador, and low fertility for Cubans.

Migration patterns may effect the immigrant women's labor market behaviors by circumscribing the environment migrant women confront upon arrival. Gordon (1981) suggests that Caribbean women who migrate first to the U.S. tend to be under greater economic pressure to work. Bilsborrow and Zlotnik (1992) summarized that in general, married women, particularly those who migrated with their husbands, were less likely than single women to participate in the labor force in the receiving country.

In examining the labor force participation differences among Asian, among Hispanic, or among native-born and foreign-born women in the U.S., substantial racial/ethnic differences remain even after controlling for the observed demographic differences (Wong and Hirschman 1983; Ortiz and Cooney 1984; Reimers 1984; Cooney and Ortiz 1983; Stier 1991; Stier and Tienda 1992). Cultural factors may prohibit or encourage the labor force participation of immigrant women. Empirically, however, it is not clear what is the best way to pinpoint cultural factors. Ortiz and Cooney (1984) find that sex-role attitudes unimportant in explaining the labor force behavior of Hispanic females.

Immigrant women are found to respond to different factors in making labor force decision by where they came from. Stier (1991) compared similar Asian immigrant wives by their country of origin and found substantial variations in their labor market behavior. Filipino and Indian immigrant wives appear to be highly influenced by their market productivity, and less restricted by their familial role, whereas Chinese, Korean and Vietnamese wives appear to be relatively constrained by their family responsibilities. Stier and Tienda (1992) later conducted a similar analysis for Hispanic immigrant wives and found that, like most other wives, Hispanic immigrant wives go to work if offered competitive wages. Furthermore, their studies suggested that the usual deterrent factors, such as the presence of young children in the household, have surprisingly little effect on Hispanic immigrant wives' labor supply.

Ethnic Communities and Household Structure. Kinship connection in the destination areas can be both a determinant of migration and a factor affecting the integration of the new immigrants in the host society. This facilitating function may be particularly important for immigrant wives. Immigrant women may reduce child care burdens by receiving help from extended household members or from neighbors in an ethnic community, or by engaging in occupations with flexible time schedules such as part-time jobs or self-employment. Ethnic groups which have stronger kinship networks or well-established ethnic enclaves may be more efficient in reducing child care costs, and therefore have higher labor force participation rates.

The supportive function of both the household and ethnic enclave is critical to the success of Cuban immigrants in the U.S. (Perez 1986). The enclave environment provides ample employment opportunities mutually attractive to both the employers and Cuban female immigrants.

The enclave easily caters to women with its traditional socio-cultural norms in the workplace, friendly recruiting efforts through relatives or friends, and free or low-cost child care. Furthermore, Cuban immigrant households tend to have more workers, greater incidence of multigenerational living, and lower fertility. All these factors contribute to the higher level of female labor force participation and earnings than the other Hispanic groups.

Southeast Asian refugees tend to maintain large households due to both high fertility level and multi-family living arrangement. Bach and Carroll-Seguin (1986) found that the presence of children limit the economic activities of both refugee men and women. As a household strategy, refugee men may sometimes stay home to care for children while their wives work. In addition, he type of sponsorship is found to influence the economic adaptation of Southeast refugee. In general, Southeast Asian refugees sponsored by the ethnic networks are less likely to be in the labor force than those sponsored by American families (Bach and Carroll-Seguin 1986). Comparing refugees with similar levels of education, those post-1979 refugee women sponsored by relatives have significantly lower market activity rates than those sponsored by American families.

The presence of kin in the host country is often said to help facilitate the economic adaptation of immigrants. Although maintaining close ties to families and ethnic communities could hinder the assimilation of the individual new immigrants (Dumon 1989), Nauck (1989) finds no evidence to support this hypothesis. In fact, pooling the resources in a migrant household often increase the chances for better economic performance. Mullan (1990) contends that social network at destination constitute a "destination specific capital," and new immigrants often benefit from it in many ways.

In general, the effects of participation in the ethnic enclaves on immigrants' socioeconomic adaptation is still under debate. One view holds that ethnic enclaves help economic adjustment because ethnic ties provide networks of social support and facilitate the learning of new skills (Perez 1986; Portes and Bach 1985). The other view contends that ethnic firms exploit the recent arrivals by paying low wages and hiring migrants for jobs which are menial, dead-end and have poor working conditions. The differences in findings may be an consequence of defining "ethnic enclave" by the geographical concentration of co-ethnics or by the ethnic identity of the employers.

Opportunities in the Receiving Society. The timing of entry is an important structural factor in circumscribing the conditions which the new immigrants encounter upon arrival. Changing opportunity structures are likely to generate different adaptation experiences for groups who arrive at different historical times (Tienda 1983; 1984). Tienda and colleagues (1984) found an wider difference between native-born and immigrant women in the industrial and occupational allocations in 1980 than in 1970. On the one hand, the proportion of immigrant women in the least-skilled and low-paying jobs increased over the 10-year period. On the other hand, more and more native-born women were moving away from these jobs and move up occupational ladder. Hispanic immigrant women were found to be particularly vulnerable to this process.

Briody (1987) points to the effects of timing of arrival on Mexican immigrants' type of employment. Those arriving after 1975 are more likely to take agricultural jobs and fare worse than the pre-1975 arrivals. Similarly, Bach and Carroll-Seguin (1986) obtains a significantly lower labor force participation among the post-1980 Southeast Asian refugees, even after controlling for other sources of variations. Apart from the usual structural interpretation, as rational actors, different kinds of immigrants may be drawn to the U.S. in responding to the different demand produced by the U.S. domestic economy in historical times.

This section reviews literature that identify determinants of immigrant women's labor force participation in the U.S. These determinants can be summarized into five groups: (1) cultural heritage; (2) human capital factors; (3) ethnic communities in the receiving country; (4) household structure; and (5) opportunities in the receiving country. The next section describes how migration factors may contribute to the differential labor market performance of immigrant men.

2.3.2 Migration Selectivity and Differential Adaptation

As described in the previous section, immigrants demonstrate different levels of economic adaptation due to the fact that they immigrated with different demographic characteristics and face different structural environments in the U.S. However, the national-origin differences remain after controlling for the observed differences. This section reviews literature addressing the effects of migration selectivity on the immigrant men's earnings along the unobserved dimension on the immigrants' economic adaptation.

The human capital model of immigrant adaptation has relied on the notions of skills transferability and self-selection in explaining the economic performances of immigrants across national-origin groups and over time (Chiswick 1986). In particular, three hypotheses are central to the argument of the model. First, due to the high costs involved, international migration is most rewarding for the most able. Hence, the economic status of immigrants progresses over time. As soon as they gain enough U.S. specific human capital, their economic performances will surpass the native-born. For white immigrants, the crossover occurs in 13-15 years (Chiswick 1978; 1980b). Second, refugees fair worst initially among immigrants, but the differential narrows with duration of residence. Third, human capital acquired before immigration has a smaller effect on economic status in the destination for refugees than economic migrants. Fourth, like refugees, tied-movers tend to possess less transferable skills and therefore earn less than economic migrants (Chiswick 1986).

Economists have made several notable contributions regarding how the migration process may lead to the well-documented differences in earnings of immigrant men across groups of various national origin in the U.S. based on human capital models (Chiswick 1978; Borjas 1985b; 1987 1990; 1991a; 1991b; Jasso and Rosenzweig 1986a; 1988; 1990a; 1990b). In particular, this line of research argues that since individuals will move to wherever their skills are valued most, country-level factors will determine the human capital characteristics of immigrant flows. This selectivity on human capital is eventually reflected in their labor market performances, and consequently the impacts of the country-level factors are embedded in the observed country-of-origin effects. At one extreme, Borjas argued that "there is no such thing as *the* effect of Asian ethnicity or race on immigrant earnings," (1991, p.64).

Migration selectivity literature differentiates three types of migration selectivity: (1) selectivity by choosing a particular migration pattern rather than other pattern; (2) selectivity by choosing the U.S. as destination rather than any other country; and (3) selectivity by choosing to stay in the U.S. rather than returning to the home country.

Selectivity by Migration Pattern. People who choose to migrate to join their relatives at the destination may have fewer qualities than those migrating on their own. On the one hand, the family provisions reduce the cost of migration through providing information and supports in time of need. On the other hand, a rational family strategy would be to send the most able member in order to obtain the U.S. visa, and then support the subsequent migration of the rest of the family. This implies that later links in the immigration chain may be relatively unskilled.

Empirical studies, however, obtain mixed results regarding the above hypothesis. Using data from the 1970 and 1980 census, Borjas and

Bronars (1990) identified three links: male relatives arriving prior to the male immigrant, the immigrant himself, and male relatives arriving after the male immigrant. They finds that on average, an immigrant male of the first link on average has less education and lower earnings than an immigrant male of later links. Similarly, they compared immigrant husbands who immigrated prior to their wives with those who immigrated after their wives, and found that the former group is less successful than the later. By hypothesizing tied migrant status for married women, Chiswick (1980a) found that those immigrant women who married prior to immigration tended to have significantly lower earnings, the earnings disadvantage being particularly apparent for Asian immigrant women who married U.S. servicemen. This may imply that if female immigrants are married before immigration, they are likely to be constrained by joint decision making within the family, and hence to be negatively selected.

Selectivity by Return Migration. Just as countries are making a decision on who are "the chosen people," prospective immigrants are making a decision on which country is the best place to be. Borjas (1991c) furthers the selectivity argument by explicitly considering choices of alternative destination. He contends that receiving countries are in fact competing for the best immigrants through the terms outlined by their immigration policies. As a result, successful immigrants of a particular country probably differ from immigrants of other countries in a systematic way. His empirical study utilizes censuses from Canada, Australia, and the United States, the major immigrant-receiving countries in the world, and concludes that selectivity does vary depending on the terms offered by the receiving countries.

Selectivity by Return Migration. Not all immigrants achieve what they hope for in the receiving country. The most unsuccessful and disappointed immigrants most likely to emigrate again. As Jasso and Rosenzweig (1986) point out, the foreign-born population in the U.S. are the "survivors" of both migration and emigration processes and are the most likely to succeed in the labor market. Using data from two U.S. censuses, they confirm the significance of both migration selectivity and emigration selectivity in explaining the variations in earnings among immigrants. Chiswick (1986), however, find little evidence of selective emigration. In addition to its importance in current earnings differential, emigration selectivity may also account for the fact that immigrants progress at different paces (Bronfrenbrenner 1982; Jasso and Rosenzweig 1982).

Country-Specific Factors. Migration selectivity apparently varies by country of origin. According to the human capital model, people are rational decision-makers seeking to maximize gains. In the migration context, people move to where their skills are best rewarded. As countries differ in national resources and economic status, they are likely to reward people of various level of skills differently. Accordingly, a higher expected gain is necessary to attract persons with high earnings in their home country.

Borjas (1987; 1989; 1991a) and Jasso and Rosenzweig (1986a; 1988; 1990a; 1990b) describe the relationship between the economic performance of immigrants and characteristics of their country of origin as follows. First, immigrants from countries where persons of given characteristics are able to earn relatively high income will, on average, have relatively high earnings in the United States. Second, migrants from locations associated with high migration costs will, on average, have relatively high earnings in the U.S. Third, immigrants from countries with a favorable environment and institutions will on average have high U.S. earnings. Fourth, since only immigrants from a country with little and poor information will be attracted to the U.S. by misconception, they are likely to have lower mean realized earnings than other immigrants in the United States. Fifth, immigrants who find it costly to return to their origin countries have strong incentives to invest in training in the receiving country and are likely to perform well in the labor market.

The theory, however, provides little indication as to what variables best describe the opportunity costs of migration, the direct costs of migration, and the quantity and quality of information available in the origin country about the destination. Controlling for differences in demographic characteristics among immigrants, Borjas (1987) and Jasso and Rosenzweig (1986a) found that higher level of economic development in the country of origin, as measured by the country's per capita Gross National Product (GNP), is associated with higher immigrant earnings. Borjas (1991a) further shows that it is the income inequality of the home country relative to that of the U.S., instead of the per capita GNP, that determines the type of selection in human capital. He explains that persons of high quality in a country with relatively low income inequality will find it more rewarding to immigrate to the United States, where his/her skills is valued at a higher rate. The political conditions in the sending countries also affects the sorting process. As skills persons are likely to flee Socialist systems and unlikely to return, immigrants from Socialist countries are found to claim higher earnings than otherwise similar immigrants.

Jasso and Rosenzweig's empirical study (1986a) was carried out separately for the Western and the Eastern Hemisphere. Their findings indicate that country variables reduce substantially more country-of-origin differences for their Western Hemisphere sample than the Eastern Hemisphere sample. In particular, their findings suggest that the low earnings of Mexican male immigrants can mostly be explained by the distance and per capita income factors. They attribute the differences in the results to differential immigration policies applying to the immigrants by hemisphere up to 1978.

This section discusses various aspects of migration selectivity and its impact on the immigrant men's earnings capacities in the U.S. Immigrant men migrating to join relatives or wives have higher earnings than independent immigrant men. The variations in earnings by groups can largely be explained by a number of macro-level country-of-origin factors, which represent the costs and gains associated with migration for immigrant men.

Summary of Chapter. This chapter reviews literature on general migration theories, male versus female migration determinants, evidence on migration selectivity, labor force participation of immigrant women in the U.S., and male migration selectivity and earnings. A number of conclusions may be drawn from the discussion. First, despite the fact that migration theories vary in the major forces of migration, they have come to the consensus that migration process is dynamic in nature, and an integration over individualistic and macro-level analysis is extremely important. Second, family/household and migration networks play an important role in motivating female migration, as well as in selecting particular types of female immigrants. In particular, female migrants tend to be more concentrated in certain age groups and educational levels than male migrants. Third, comparing between males and females, significant gender differences exist with respect to the motivation of migration and likelihood of participating in migration. Fourth, selectivity of migration tend to be related to the expected costs and benefits associated with migration. Factors indicating high net migration gains tend to attract above average migrants since they can absorb high costs and their move tend to incur high gains. Fifth, women migrating for marriage purposes or to join their husbands or relatives tend to be less selective than independent migrants. Sixth, immigrant wives in the U.S. appear to be rather actively participating in the labor market. Considerable country-of-origin variations may be attributed to the differences in their levels of fertility, English abilities, levels of education, ages, and household structures.

The discussion on migration selectivity point to the possibility that migration decision may exert an impact on the immigrants' subsequent labor market adaptation. Empirical investigation along this line have mostly focused on male experiences. In spite of ample evidence on gender-specific migration factors, the linkage between female immigration selectivity and their labor market performance is virtually non-existent. To fill this gap, this study aims to contribute to the understanding of female immigration selectivity, and provide an empirical examination on its impact on Asian and Hispanic immigrant wives' labor supply and earning potentials.

This chapter has focused on the migration process in a fairly general context. In reality, migration selectivity and migrant adaptation is highly impacted by the immigration legislation and socioeconomic conditions in the receiving countries. As this research deals with young Asian and Hispanic immigrant women in the U.S., it is essential to take into account the U.S. immigration policy and its consequences on contemporary immigration to the U.S. To do so, the next chapter will describe the legislative changes in the U.S. immigration history and the patterns of female immigration from Asia, Mexico, Caribbean and Latin America to the U.S.

3

Immigration Policy, Family Reunification, and National Origin

The United States has been one of the major immigrant-receiving countries in the world for the past few centuries. Over time, it has established and modified numerical limitations to regulate its immigrant flows by favoring some while excluding the others. Despite various changes in the legislation, the immigration policies have consistently differentiated prospective immigrants based on their race/national origin, kin connections in the U.S. and labor market qualifications (Keely 1983; Tienda 1983). Over time, the immigrant flows have witnessed shifts in national origin composition, as well as quantitative and qualitative fluctuations. To provide a background of policy issues pertaining to U.S. immigration in general, this chapter describes the legislative changes of U.S. immigration policy and its impacts on the labor market qualities of immigrants.

One of the important consequences of the family reunification policy is the increasing female immigration to the U.S. since the late 1960's, especially from both Asia and Latin America[1]. This chapter emphasizes how potential female immigrants respond and take advantage of the family reunification provisions. This chapter also describes the implications of the legislative changes on the prevalence and features of Asian and Hispanic immigrant women over time. Section 3.1 highlights the historical evolution of the U.S. immigration policy prior to 1965. Section 3.2 details the Immigration and Nationality Act of 1965 and the legislative changes in the post-1965 era. The discussion underscores national origin and family connections as a salient component shaping the contemporary Asian and Hispanic immigration. Section 3.3 addresses the impact of the family reunification policy on the quantitative and qualitative dimensions of the post-1965 immigration flows.

3.1 IMMIGRATION POLICY BEFORE 1965

The principal issues underlying the making of the United States immigration policies have concerned the following: first, what countries should be given priority to send immigrants; second, how many visas should be allocated to each country given a fixed array of countries; and third, who should be admitted given the country-specific quota. The application of the legislation often reflects mixed influences from concerns over the foreign policy, domestic socioeconomic conditions, and human rights (Tucker et al. 1990; Keely 1983; Briggs 1992).

The U.S. imposed virtually no restriction on immigration until 1875. Since then, a list of excludable people has been gradually compiled on the grounds of economic and occupational status, health status, mental conditions, literacy and misconduct, etc. For instance, the Immigration Act of 1917 imposed a literacy test and an eight dollar head tax on those intending to immigrate to the U.S. During the early twentieth century, the exclusion based on race or national origin in the legislation was created and implemented in light of the economic competition of cheap labor from the third world along with racial and ethnic bias (Briggs 1992; Reimers 1992). The discriminatory clauses were lifted in the post-war period in response to a foreign policy consideration and the civil right movement in the 1960s (Reimers 1992; Tucker et al. 1990).

This section outlines the major changes of the U.S. immigration policy prior to 1965. It focuses on legislation that impacted directly on immigration from Asia and Latin America.

3.1.1 Immigration Legislation Pertaining to Asians and Hispanics

Legislation Excluding Asians. The first law excluding immigrants on the basis of national origin was the Chinese Exclusion Act, enacted in 1882, which barred further immigration of Chinese laborers. In 1908, the United States signed the Gentlemen's Agreement with the Japanese government to restrict the labor immigration from Japan. The early immigrants from China, Japan, and the Philippines were predominantly single or married men who had left their wives in their home countries to work as laborers. However, historical records show varying sex-ratios among these groups in the early twentieth century. The Chinese Exclusion Act had included women in its definition of labor and hence, allowed very few Chinese women to enter the United States. On the contrary, the Gentlemen agreement defined women as family immigrants, not labor immigrants, and consequently, a considerable number of Japanese women did come with or join their husbands (Reimers 1992). The balanced sex ratio enabled family establishment and growth of ethnic business for the Japanese American community at the turn of the century (Nee and Wong 1985). Apart from the contribution of policies, the employers viewed the presence of Japanese women on the plantation as a positive factor in stabilizing their labor force, while those recruiting Chinese laborers used them primarily as migratory laborers.

In 1917, the U.S. banned immigration from the Far East and South Asia by creating an Asiatic Barred Zone (Reimers 1992; Xenos 1989). To restrict overall immigration and to limit immigration from certain areas, the annual ceiling for immigration was set at 358,000 in 1921, and in 1924 the ceiling was further reduced to 150,000 for immigrants from the Eastern Hemisphere (Briggs 1992). Under the numerical limitation, the 1921 legislation specified the annual quota for each country to 3 percent of the number of people coming from the same country as compiled in the 1910 census. The base of the country quota was changed to the 1890 census in 1924 and again to the 1920 census in 1929. In seeking to affect the racial and national origin composition by favoring the immigrants from Western and Northern Europe, the Immigration Act of 1924 is also known as the National Origin Act (Briggs 1992). As part of the 1924 legislation, the Oriental Exclusion Act banned virtually all immigrants from Asia, except Filipinos (Reimers 1992). However, the Filipino immigration to the U.S. was also greatly restricted by the Filipino Exclusion Act enacted in 1934, which set an annual quota of fifty (Briggs 1992).

Immigration of Asian Immigrant Women. In the early twentieth century, the majority of Asian immigrant women were of three types: wives and children joining their husbands, wives of the American servicemen, and students or scholars. The 1920s legislation allowed spouses and minor children of citizens to enter as nonquota immigrants (Reimers 1992). A significant number of Chinese women came to join their husbands[2]. In 1940 the sex ratio of Chinese in the United States was reported to be around three men to one women (Mark and Chih 1982). It was estimated that from 1948 to 1952, 90 percent of the Chinese immigrants were women joining their spouses in the U.S. (Mark and Chih 1982). This influx of immigrant Chinese women greatly raised the sex ratio of the Chinese American communities.

The close military ties between the United States and the Philippines and Korea after the Second World War explained the moderate growth of immigration from these two countries during this period. From 1945 to 1965, an estimated total of 71,100 immigrant women from Japan, Korea and the Philippines immigrated as wives of American servicemen abroad (Reimers 1992, p.365).

Loose Control over Western Hemisphere Immigration. In contrast to the exclusion of immigrants from Asia, the quota system established by the Immigration Act of 1924 did not apply to the Western Hemisphere (Briggs 1992). Consequently, most third world immigration during the post-war period came from the western hemisphere. In particular, Mexico was the leading single source of immigration to the U.S. during that period. Mexican immigration to the U.S. was interrupted by the Great Depression during the 1930s, but renewed in the 1940s. In 1942 the Bracero program was created to recruit temporary and seasonal workers from Mexico to work in agriculture. The program was finally terminated in 1964. Until then, over four million temporary workers were brought to the U.S. (Reimers 1992), and many of them overstay the duration of the program. Because of the recruitment efforts of the Bracero program, the majority of Mexican immigrants in this period were unskilled male workers.

Prior to 1965, immigration from the Caribbean and Latin America constituted about 20 percent of the western hemisphere's total (Reimers 1992). Cubans, as legal immigrants and political refugees, entered the U.S. in large number after 1959, and made up the majority of the immigrant flow from the Caribbean countries. Female immigration was prevalent among Cuban immigrants since refugees tended to move in family units, and for some period, emigration out of Cuba was extremely difficult for men of military age (Perez 1986b). In the same period, immigration from the Dominican Republic, El Salvador, and Colombia was largely pushed out by political upheaval and poverty.

To summarize, Asian immigration to the U.S. before 1965 was largely banned or discouraged. Among the few Asian immigrants who came in during this period, most of them are male and laborers. Asian immigrant women immigrated primarily as wives of U.S. servicemen or to join their immigrant husbands. In contrast, Hispanic immigrants were not subject to the quota system during the same period, and the majority of Hispanic immigrants were male Mexican workers.

3.1.2 The Immigration and Nationality Act of 1952

The Immigration and Nationality Act of 1952, which continued the selective national-origin quota system and the prevailing ceiling on immigration from the Eastern Hemisphere, made several major changes from the 1920s legislation (Briggs 1992). First, all of the exclusion against Asian immigration were lifted. Second, it instituted a priority system to distribute visas within the quota allotments assigned to each country. Third, the preference system introduced in the 1952 law gave its first priority to needed professional and skilled labors. The other three lower level preferences went to immigrants with family connections. Overall, half of the visas were reserved for the needed professional and skilled labor category. Fourth, a passive labor certification provision was enacted to exclude aliens if the Secretary of Labor certified that "there was not a shortage of labors and that their entry will adversely affect wages and working conditions in this country," (U.S. Congress 1987, p.57). Under the 1952 Act, immigration from the Western Hemisphere was still exempt from any numerical limitations.

The 1952 Immigration Act created a preference system in which skills and family connections are of prime priorities. Nonetheless, it still maintained the discriminatory national-origin quota system instituted in the 1920s, which led to a fundamental change in the 1965 amendments.

3.2 THE 1965 AND POST-1965 AMENDMENTS

The 1965 Amendments of the Immigration and Nationality Act overhauled the discriminatory system and gave equal quota regardless of national origin. It lays the cornerstone of contemporary U.S. immigration policies. The amendments in the post-1965 era mainly modify the legislation with regard to the refugees and illegal immigrants issues. This section first describes the legislative details pertaining to the family reunification component of the law. Second, it gives a brief account on the subsequent amendments. Third, the volume and composition of the post-1965 immigration flows are described.

3.2.1 The 1965 Amendments

The 1965 amendments is by far the most influential piece of immigration legislation in the United States, and its major provisions were still in effect until the 1980s. First, it abolished the national-origin quota system. Second, the prevailing four preference categories were expanded to seven categories, with primary emphasis on family reunification. Third, for the first time in the immigration history of the United States, the Western Hemisphere immigration were subject to an overall ceiling. Fourth, each country from the Eastern Hemisphere was given a 20,000 quota, which suggested that immigrants were given a equal chance regardless of their country of origin within the hemisphere. Fifth, the current passive labor certification provision was modified so that prospective foreign workers had to obtain the labor certification prior to their entry. The new labor certification provision also applied to all immigrants from the Western Hemisphere other than immediate relatives of adult U.S. citizens and permanent resident aliens.

However, the new system, actually fully effective in 1968, treated immigrants differently depending on their hemisphere of origin and kinship ties to the U.S. residents. First of all, the legislation imposed a 170,000 ceiling for the Eastern Hemisphere and a 120,000 ceiling for the Western Hemisphere. Visas for the Western hemisphere immigrants were issued on a first-come first-served basis regardless of country origin or kinship ties. In contrast, immigration from Eastern Hemisphere was subject to a country quota of 20,000 annually. Prospective immigrants from the Eastern Hemisphere were exempt from any numerical limitation if they were immediate relatives (spouses, unmarried minor children, and parents) of adult American citizens. Otherwise, the Eastern Hemisphere immigrants could obtain visas based on more distant family ties or occupational skills. Table 3.1 summarizes the qualification and the proportion of visas made available to each preference category.

Within each preference category, visas were granted on a first-come first-served basis, subject to the country quota. If a country reached its maximum total of 20,000 in a given year, for the next year the preference proportions would apply to the 20,000 country ceiling instead of the hemisphere or worldwide ceiling (U.S. congress 1987). This modification was specifically designed to protect lower preference applicants from being squeezed out in countries with high demand of third preference visas (Keely 1983). The remaining 6 percent of visas of the preference total were designed as a refugee category. From 1957-1980, the official definition of refugees included "those fleeing from Communist-dominated countries or the Middle East because of persecution, and the victims of a 'catastrophic natural calamity' in any Eastern Hemisphere country," (U.S. Congress 1987, p.56). Refugees were to be admitted on a conditional basis, with immigrant status available after two years of residence.

Table 3.1 Preference Categories in the Immigration and Nationality Act of 1965

Designation	Qualification
P1-1	Unmarried adult children of U.S. citizen
P1-2	Their children
maximum slots	20% of the hemisphere ceiling in any fiscal year
P2-1	Spouses of resident aliens
P2-2	Unmarried adult children of resident aliens
P2-3	Children of P2-2 visa holders
maximum slots	20% of the hemisphere ceiling, plus any numbers not required for the first preference
P3-1	Members of the professions and artists and scientists of exceptional ability
P3-2	Their spouses
P3-3	Their children
maximum slots	10% of the hemisphere ceiling
P4-1	Married children of U.S. citizens
P4-2	Their spouses
P4-3	Their children
maximum slots	10% of the hemisphere ceiling, plus any numbers not required by the first three preference categories
P5-1	Brothers and sisters of U.S. citizens
P5-2	Their spouses
P5-3	Their children
maximum slots	24% of the hemisphere ceiling, plus any numbers not required by the first four preference categories
P6-1	Skilled and unskilled workers in short supply
P6-2	Their spouses
P6-3	Their children
maximum slots	10% of the hemisphere ceiling

Sources: Korean Immigrants and U.S. Immigration Policy: A Predeparture Perspective, p.13; U.S. Immigration Law and Policy, 1952-1986, p.120.

However, due to the numerical limitation in the seventh preference, a large number of refugees in fact entered under the parole provision of the Immigration and Nationality Act.

The 1965 amendments took a major step in shifting the selection criteria of this country's immigrants from national-origin to family reunification. While maintaining the spirits of the 1965 amendments, the succeeding amendments of the following three decades have contributed to the formation of a unified and expanded immigration system.

3.2.2 The Amendments after 1965

In the 1970s, two relatively minor modifications occurred in the immigration law to reach a unified quota system. In the 1980s, two pieces of legislation were enacted to deal with the intensified refugee and illegal immigrant problems. Finally, based on the existing system, the Immigration Act of 1990 expands preferences system and numerical quota on immigration. This section first describes the legislation, and secondly depicts the numbers and characteristics of the post-1965 female immigrants.

1970s Amendments. In the late 1970s, two pieces of legislation took steps to eliminate the differential criteria applied to the Western and the Eastern Hemisphere immigrants. First of all, the 1976 amendments extended the 20,000 country quota and the seven-preference system equally to the Western Hemisphere. Apparently, the imposition of 20,000 country quota on the Western Hemisphere countries worked to the least advantage of Mexico. Second, the 1978 amendments combined the separate ceilings of the two hemispheres and created a worldwide unified ceiling of 29,000. This provision eliminated the favorable conditions of the Western Hemisphere due to its higher number of per capita visas under the separate ceiling. Since 1978, immigrants from the two hemispheres were on equal grounds competing for the available visas. The preference system remained intact except for the tightened restrictions on foreign medical professionals through the Health Professions Educational Assistance Act of 1976 (U.S. Congress 1987).

1980s Refugee Act. The 1980 Refugee Act separated the admission of refugees from the legal immigration legislation system. The new refugee legislation revised the definition of "refugee" to conform with humanitarian principle in the U.N. definition. Specifically, "Refugee status is based on 'persecution or a well-founded fear of persecution on account of race, religion, nationality, membership in a particular social group, or political opinion,'" (U.S. Congress 1987, p.81). Under the 1980 provision, refugees were admitted either through the normal flow subject to an annual ceiling, or emergency admission following a Presidential determination and consultation with the Congress (U.S. Congress 1987). Refugees may adjust to a permanent resident status after one year of residence, outside of any numerical limitations under the legal immigration system. Meanwhile, the 1980 Act modified the world wide ceiling to 27,000, exclusive of refugees. The 6 percent slots previously specified as the refugee quota were then added to the second preference.

1986 Immigration Reform and Control Act. The 1986 Immigration Reform and Control Act (IRCA) addresses the "control of illegal immigration by employer sanctions for the employment of unauthorized aliens, legalization of some undocumented aliens, and the legal admission of alien agricultural workers," (U.S. Congress, 1987, p.105). IRCA provides legalization of status for aliens who can prove that they have been continuously residing in the U.S. since before January 1, 1982, or that they worked in certain approved seasonal agricultural sectors in the United States for at least 90 days between May 1, 1985 and May 1, 1986 (Reimers 1992). Since the original IRCA legislation was aimed at individual illegal immigrants, the family fairness program was begun in early 1990 to allow most undocumented spouses and minor children of newly legalized aliens to remain in the United States while waiting to be sponsored (Woodrow 1990).

Immigration Act of 1990. The major provisions of the Immigration Act of 1990 reflects the growing concerns over the immigrants' human capital endowments, potential economic contribution and national-origin composition. Overall, the Immigration Act of 1990 maintained the humanitarian spirits of the law it replaced, welcoming immigrants bringing their families. Apart from that, the new legislation did significantly raise the number of visas available to employment-based immigration. However, Briggs asserts that the effects of increased employment-based immigration was simply illusive and criticizes the dominant criteria based on family reunification rather than human capital endowments (Briggs 1992).

One of the new attributes of the 1990 act is its wider basis of eligibility than the previous law. As an effort to balance the national origin composition of the immigrant flows, the new diversity immigrant category made available 40,000 visas to immigrants from countries which were under-representative as a result of the 1965 provisions. The 40,000 visas are to be granted through a lottery process on an annual basis, rather than any family and employment basis. In addition, 10,000 visas were made available to investor immigrants.

To summarize, the 1976 and 1978 amendments together institute a unified country quota system in the U.S. immigration law. The 1980 Refugee Act and the 1986 Immigration Reform and Control Act specifically deal with the refugee and illegal immigration respectively. The 1990 Immigration Act has expanded the categories and limits of legal immigration of those specified by the 1965 amendments.

3.2.3 Immigration in the Post-1965 Era

After the passage of the Immigration and Nationality Act, the immigration from Asia has expanded dramatically, while the trend of Hispanic immigration has continued and accelerated. This section summarizes the volumes and trends of the Asian and Hispanic immigration to the U.S. with a major emphasis on gender composition of the immigrants by country of origin.

Legal Asian Immigration. In the 1955-64 period, the Asian immigrants constituted about 8 percent of the total U.S. immigrants admitted in that period, while in the 1980s, Asians constituted 44 percent of the total immigrants (INS 1989). Chinese and Japanese are the first Asian groups to immigrate to the U.S. in significant number. Filipinos started migration to the U.S. mainly in the early twentieth century; Korean started around 1950s. Few Indian and Vietnamese immigrants were present in the U.S. prior to 1965.

Table 3.2 summarizes the sex ratio of selected immigrant cohorts from 1978 to 1990 by selected Asian countries.

Table 3.2 Sex Ratios* of the Asian Immigrant Cohort.

	1978	1982	1986	1990
Philippines	68.7	71.1	69.3	68.0
India	116.9	99.7	102.1	100.9
Vietnam	114.8	136.8	130.0	92.4
Korea	63.0	67.8	74.2	81.2

* *defined as the number of males every one hundred females*

Source: Statistical Yearbook of the Immigration and Naturalization Service, 1979, 1983, 1987 and 1991.

The table shows that the Filipino and Korean immigrants are predominantly females, while the Indian and Vietnamese immigrants are predominantly male.

Legal Hispanic Immigration. Immigrants from other countries in the Americas constitute about 42 percent of the total U.S. immigrants admitted in both 1955-64 and during the 1980's. The percentage of Mexican immigrants has been fairly constant over the three decades; however, the significance of immigration from Canada is replaced by immigration from the Caribbean and other countries in the Americas (INS 1989). The timing of the immigration of the Hispanic population is closely related to the distance between the sending country and the U.S. Mexican immigration has a long history dated back to nineteenth century. The Caribbean immigration started in the 1950s; other Hispanics started in early 1970s.

The sex ratio of the Hispanic immigrant cohorts are summarized in Table 3.3.

Table 3.3 Sex Ratios* of Hispanic Immigrant Cohorts.

	1978	1982	1986	1990
Mexico	100.0	130.9	132.2	137.2
Cuba	85.5	95.0	126.2	123.2
El Salvador	66.0	na	na	103.4
Dominican Rep.	92.6	90.2	94.5	101.9
Colombia	70.6	84.6	84.5	95.5

* *defined as the number of males every one hundred females*
Source: Statistical Yearbook of the Immigration and Naturalization Service, 1979, 1983, 1985, and 1991.

The table shows that Mexican immigration is predominantly male. Cuban immigration consists of more females in the early years, while shifting to more males in the recent years. Immigration from Central and South America is predominantly female.

Refugees. As part of legal immigration, the bulk of Cubans, Vietnamese, Laotians and Cambodians entered the U.S. as political refugees in the last few decades. Although admitted under the same category, refugees are in fact quite diverse in terms of their demographic characteristics by their timing of arrival.

While the earlier waves of Cuban refugees were generally of professional, technical, or entrepreneurial backgrounds, the refugees departing Cuba in the early 1980s seemed to be of lower levels of education and skill. They tended to be young working class males (Reimers 1992). In total, an estimated 800,000 Cuban refugees were admitted from 1960 to 1984. About 3,500 Cuban refugees were admitted under the emergency provision in 1980 under the Refugee Act (U.S. Congress 1987). Cuban immigrants are disproportionally older and female-dominated in the 1960s and 1970s (Perez 1986). The Cuban immigrant population in general shows a higher degree of three-generational living arrangements, with the elderly least likely to be found institutionalized or living alone.

With only a few thousand present in the U.S. prior to the early 1970, the vast majority of Vietnamese immigrants came to the United States as refugees or families of refugees starting in 1975. The Vietnamese refugee population is generally subdivided into three groups according to their timing of arrival, background prior to fleeing Vietnam, and modes of resettlement by the U.S. (Gold 1992). The 1975-77 cohort is frequently described as an elite class, with relatively highly educated, professional backgrounds, some western connections back in Vietnam, and usually came as an intact family (Kelly 1977; Gold 1992). The post-1978 Vietnamese have more diverse backgrounds, consisting of people fleeing by boat and ethnic Chinese. Vietnamese classified in the former group are largely young men with low educational attainments and skills in Vietnam. It was reported that men outnumbered women in this group by 24 percent (Gold 1992). The latter group is characterized as an entrepreneurial class. The high sex-ratio, or scarcity of Vietnamese women appeared to limit the process of family building in the United States for this group (Gordon 1987), which to a certain extent resembles the Chinese case in the early twentieth century (Gold 1992). In general, Vietnamese have high fertility rates, large households, and low median ages (Gold 1992). Refugees of the first wave had an average household size of 5.1 persons; only slightly more than 10 percent of them came alone; 62 percent came in households of over five persons (Kelly 1986). The household size is 7.6 persons among the Hmong and 6.9 among Laotians.

Undocumented Aliens. In addition to legal immigration, substantial illegal immigrants have entered and worked in the U.S. without proper documents in recent decades (hence, the term "undocumented aliens.") It was estimated that the vast majority of illegal aliens in the 1970s were Hispanics, with 60 percent from Mexico, 30 percent from other Western

Hemisphere countries, and only 5 percent were Asians (Massey 1981, p.61). Many illegal Mexican immigrants were former Braceros or had gained migration information from them, and were found to be very similar to the Braceros in many ways (Reimers 1992). They were mostly single young males of rural background. Nonetheless, it is generally believed that they were not from the poorest section of Mexican population (Garcia 1980; Reimers 1992).

The illegal status and the transitory nature of this population made it difficult to obtain representative and reliable information about them. Data based on those apprehended by the U.S. immigration officers at the border tend to count more Mexicans than their fair share. Interviews conducted in the sending countries are limited to only returned illegal migrants (Reimers 1992). Additional estimation methods include (1) comparing Mexican nationals counted in Mexico census with legal Mexican migration to the U.S., taken into account of fertility and mortality rates; (2) comparing immigrants counted in the U.S. census and legal Mexican immigrants recorded by INS; (3) comparing age-specific death rates between the whole U.S. and states with large number of illegal aliens; (4) interviews with unapprehended illegal immigrants in the U.S.; and (5) information collected from legal immigrants in the U.S. who formerly worked illegally here in the U.S. (Hill 1985; Massey 1981). While estimates of illegal migrants in the U.S. vary considerably, a more consistent estimate of the 1970s have ranged from 3 to 6 millions (Massey 1981; Tienda 1983). Slightly over 2 million undocumented residents was reported living in the United States in 1980 based on the 1980 census (Warren and Passel 1987). The figure goes to 3 million in June 1986 (Woodrow, Passel, and Warren 1987).

In the absence of accurate data, Massey (1981) inferred two major implications regarding the gender composition and patterns of migration of undocumented population from the existing research findings. First, females are systematically underrepresented in the apprehensions statistics and their participation in the illegal migration to the U.S. was on the rise, with a mean around 33 percent. Second, family undocumented migration is relatively common among Western Hemisphere nations, except that the Mexican undocumented population are disproportionally young male.

In summary, the post-1965 immigration is characterized by high volume of Asian and Hispanic female immigrants. Over time, Asian and Hispanic female immigrants have entered the U.S. as legal immigrants, refugee, or undocumented aliens. In particular, family reunification is one of the major channel and motivation of female immigration. The next section describes the utilization of the family reunification and its labor market consequences.

3.3 FAMILY REUNIFICATION IN ACTION

The 1965 amendments of the Immigration and Nationality Act creates mass waves of family immigrants from Asia and Latin America. Concerns emerged over the potential unmanageable entrance of immigrants through family reunification, the diverse backgrounds the new immigrants bringing with them, the decreasing level of skills of the new immigrant flows due to the emphasis on family reunification and the prevalence of illegal immigration. These concerns were rooted in the fear of the unmeltable new immigrant groups due to their inability or unwillingness to assimilate to the American mainstream culture. The decreasing quality of the new immigrants and the refugees' dependence on the welfare system cast the fear that new immigrants will burden rather than contribute to the U.S. economy.

This section addresses three issues pertaining to the family reunification legislation. First, does the family reunification policy create a snowball effect, so that the immigration flows expedites uncontrollably? Second, how is the legislation utilized; do female immigrants have a distinct migration patterns from their male counterparts? Third, does the admission category under which the immigrants enter the U.S. effect their subsequent labor market performance?

3.3.1 The Immigration Multiplier

The U.S. immigration policy encourages chain migration[3]. The presence of a relative in the U.S. not only provides legal access to immigration but also provides information and support for settlement. Hypothetically, a new immigrant could sponsor his/her relatives unlimitedly as soon as he/she naturalize to be a U.S. citizen according to the family reunification provisions. In reality, people may not utilize the provisions even if they are qualified. The question leads to thriving research interests in estimating the actual immigration multiplier[4].

Jasso and Rosenzweig (1986b) found that the actual chain effects of family reunification is substantially lower than the hypothetical potential multiplier. They suggested three factors that possibly deter a full utilization of the family provisions . First, due to the numerical limits, it sometimes takes ten or twenty years to successfully sponsor siblings.

Second, not every eligible legal immigrant eventually naturalizes. Third, some people decide not to migrate even if they are immediately qualified. The estimated immigration multipliers are highest among immigrants entering under occupational preferences, with 1.19 new visas induced by each original male immigrant within the first decade after arrival, 1.17 for each female immigrant. Their findings further suggest that the type of entry visas of the original immigrants and their origin country characteristics determine the magnitude of immigration multiplier. The sibling preference to unite with American citizens appears to contribute most to the immigration multipliers. Immigrants from countries with lower GNP, close proximity to the U.S., not centrally planned, and lower literacy rates tend to have lower naturalization rates.

Jasso and Rosenzweig's study triggered debates and further interests regarding immigration multiplier. Goering (1987; 1989) contended that their analysis fails to incorporate country and preference category ceilings, which may differentially suppress visa demand across origin countries. It was pointed out that their data from the 1960s and 1970s were unlikely to be representative of immigration trends in the 1980s (Passel and Woodrow 1987; Borjas 1990; Liu et al. 1991). As pointed out by the authors, their analysis, constrained by data, is unable to distinguish between the intention to migrate and the availability of relatives in the home country. As noted by Arnolds et al. (1989), the demographic factors at home countries circumscribed the availability of kin. Among their study sample of people applied for visa to the U.S. in Korea and the Philippines in 1986, Koreans had almost one third fewer relatives than Filipinos due to fewer siblings and children.

Several studies continued to investigate immigration chain effects through other dimensions. John Heinberg and colleagues (GAO 1988; Heinberg et al. 1989) found no evidence of uncontrollable chain migration likely in the future using General Accounting Office (GAO) data linking petitioners to a sample of exempt immediate relative immigrants in the 1980s. This conclusion was based on two observations. First, 64 percent of the petitioners were native-born sponsoring their spouses, implying a majority of the immigrants are not part of a chain migration. Second, considerable delays in petitions among foreign-born is observed, which varies across origin countries. Asian countries appear to naturalize and petition in relatively shorter periods, and they are more likely to petition for parents than other countries. In addition, they found that native sponsors tend to be young, mostly male and petitioning for spouses, whereas immigrant sponsors tend to be older, predominantly female, and petitioning for parents.

On the contrary, Jasso and Rosenzweig (1989) reported a much higher sponsorship rate of the foreign-born than that of the natives after reanalyzing the GAO data. Furthermore, immigrant sponsors tend to petition as soon as they are able to do so. They found that native-born citizens sponsored over 80 percent of the foreign born spouses in 1985, the majority of which came from the Philippines and Mexico. The sponsorship of parents are most prevalent among Asian countries, with the Philippines responsible for 20 percent of the petitions for parents. Other studies also suggest the importance of sponsoring parents as an emerging pattern since early 1970s and as a rational strategy to reunite more family members among Filipino immigrants (Liu et al. 1991; Arnold et al. 1989). In all, that Asian countries appear to be most able and willing to take advantage of the family reunification provisions is confirmed.

Warren (1988) examined the extent to which recently legalized aliens under the 1986 Immigration Reform and Control Act (IRCA) are likely to sponsor their relatives. His estimates suggest fewer than 300,000 additional relatives mostly through the second preference category under the effect of IRCA, largely due to the historically low naturalization rate of Mexican immigrants.

Woodrow and Parage (1991) examined the numerical presence of kin in the United States of the foreign-born population with the November 1989 Current Population Survey supplement, . Their results show 62 percent of the immediate relatives of the naturalized citizen population reside in the United States, as compared to 39 percent of the alien population. By region of origin, 62 percent of the immediate relatives of the Mexico-born population live outside the United States, as compared to 57 percent of the Caribbean-born, 57 percent of the Central American-born, 58 percent of the South American-born, 41 percent of the European-born and 52 percent of the Asian-born population.

In summary, the actual migration multiplier is far smaller than theoretically hypothesized. Three major factors contribute to the deflated migration multiplier. First, considerable immigrants delay naturalization after they are qualified to do so. Second, not all qualified people decide to immigrate to the U.S. Third, numerical limits in the preference categories appear to effectively slow down the immigration of certain types of immigrants. The next section documents the actual utilization of the provisions.

3.3.2 Modes of Entry

Family reunification not only encourages immigration, but also encourages certain types of immigration. Dodging and colleagues (1986) found that the nature of family ties in the U.S. significantly affect the migration patterns. Their analysis shows that nearly two-third of immigrants with both immediate and less immediate family ties plan to move with someone, while three-fifth of immigrants with more distant family ties report intention to migrate alone.

Migration pattern may differ by gender in responding to the family reunification legislation. Donate and Tyree (1986) hypothesize three ways foreign women may be more likely to immigrate to the U.S. than foreign men: (1) entering as spouses of American men; (2) as mothers of American citizens; and (3) as health workers, such as nurses. Their study utilized the immigrant cohort of 1979 of the Immigration and Naturalization Service (INS) and found that these migration patterns explain considerable variations in sex ratios among immigrant groups. They suggest that the relative status of women to men in the origin population, political stability, and the distance from the U.S. may account for the remaining variations.

Houstoun and her colleagues (1984) found substantial gender differentials in the utilization of the family reunification provisions by analyzing immigrants entering the U.S. between 1972 and 1979. Females are less likely to enter as unmarried daughters than males as unmarried sons, while much more likely to enter as spouses than males. In contrast, males are much more likely to enter as skilled and unskilled workers than females. Despite the fact that immigrant women are much less likely to report an occupation at immigration, women constitute 43 percent of the principle immigrants entering as professionals. Nonetheless, they are also more likely to enter as beneficiaries in this category. Gurak and Gilbertson (1989) obtained similar findings that Dominicans and Colombians immigrant parents are more likely to sponsor male children than female children. Caces and colleagues (1985) suggest that Filipino women are more likely than men to migrate under the auspices of relatives.

The family reunification legislation clearly favors the immigration of married women over single women, given comparable ages. Houstoun and her colleagues (1984) suggested that a high percentage of immigrant women migrating to the U.S. were married at the time of migration. Among the 1972-79 cohorts under 50, foreign-born women were more likely to be married than native-born women, and this difference is much pronounced for the 20-24 age group. Similarly, of the 1979 cohort of female immigrants 18 and older, Tyree and Donate (1986) reported 73 percent are married, despite the relative youth of the population. Nonetheless, among immigrant women from the Caribbean, only 58 percent are married. Southeast Asia, South and Central America also send a relatively higher proportion of single women than the rest of the sending areas. Based on information from a 1981 New York survey, both Colombians and Dominicans are more likely to begin their current marriage in the United States than in their homeland (Gurak 1987). This implies a high percentage of Colombians and Dominicans migrating while single. Furthermore, given the older age structure of the former group, Colombians are more likely to be married prior to migration.

Borjas and Bronars (1990) analyzed the migration patterns of household members by comparing the timing of immigration among them with the 1970 and 1980 census data. Of those 1970-74 cohorts who were married at the time of migration, 16 percent were following either their spouse or children to the U.S., and 15 percent followed by their spouse or children in the subsequent five-year interval. Their study shows a higher percentage of immigrants entering the U.S. with a kin connection over time (Borjas and Bronars 1990). Over 14 percent of the 1960-1964 cohort had relatives present in the U.S. at the time they immigrated. The corresponding figure went up to nearly 27 percent for the 1975-1979 cohort. 14 percent of the 1960-64 cohort sponsored an immigrant in the subsequent period. The corresponding figure went up to 23 percent for the 1970-1974 cohort. Over 60 percent of the 1960s and 1970s cohorts reside with relatives who immigrate in the same five-year interval as themselves.

The preference system clearly draw different kinds of immigrants with respect to gender, marital status, age, level of education and occupation. In addition to demographic selectivity, immigrants may also be differentially selected by their categories of admission along unobserved dimensions. The next section examines how these selectivity affect the contemporary immigrants' labor market performance in the U.S.

3.3.3 Labor Market Implications

In the last two decades, concerns have been raised over the labor market qualifications of immigrants who were admitted based on kin connections instead of occupational preferences. Briggs (1992) argues forcefully that the immigration policies adopted since 1965 have recruited predominantly unskilled labors, which not only ignores the continuing transformation of the domestic economy and needs for skilled labors but also deteriorates the working condition of native unskilled labors. His argument assumes that immigrants admitted through family connection are less skilled than those screened by occupational preferences and thus unlikely to meet the immediate demand of the U.S. labor market. This section summarizes the research findings pertaining to migration selectivity of immigrants.

Keely (1975; 1971) examines the occupational composition of the post-1965 immigrants using the annual reports of Immigration and Naturalization Service (INS). He finds a significant number of Mexican and Caribbean women entering the U.S. as live-in-maids, in which category, labor certificates were easy to obtain. Overall, Mexicans were likely to enter based on family relationship. Asian and Caribbean immigrants tended to enter as professionals or relatives of citizens through the preference system. Labor certification requirements appeared to depress immigrants entering in sales or clerk category, most of whom traditionally came from Northern Europe. He notes that the majority of skilled immigrants in fact entered outside of the third preference category (preference over professionals) in the 1966-1973 period, relying mainly on family relations. Among those who did enter through the third preference category, most of them came from Asian countries.

In addition to the observed characteristics of immigrants, several studies have addressed the issues of unobserved "quality" of immigrants. The discussions focus on (1) changes of immigrant quality over time; and (2) the policy elements that contribute to the changes. Using the 1970 and 1980 censuses, Borjas (1990) found evidence of decreasing quality (measured by years of education and earnings) for male immigrants of recent cohorts. Comparing the most recent 5-year immigrant cohorts of the 1940, 1960, 1970 and 1980 censuses with their comparable natives, and he found that the difference between the skills (education) and labor market characteristics (percent in labor force, percent unemployed, annual hours worked, hourly wage rate) of natives and immigrants is growing over time. The 1970 cohort had a substantially lower labor force participation rate, higher unemployment rate, and worked fewer hours than the 1950 and 1960 cohorts. The differences remain even after controlling for demographic differences. Borjas (1990) argues that recent immigrants are less skilled than the earlier cohorts since most of them are admitted through kinship ties instead of occupational selection and had come from predominantly less-developed countries.

Empirical evidence, however, paints a mixed picture concerning the migration selectivity of male immigrant. Regardless of their mode of entry, men who immigrated with relatives are more skilled and have higher earnings than their independent counterparts based on analyses of the census data (Borjas and Bronars 1990). A direct test of the relationship between the immigrant's labor market performances and his/her category of entry was conducted by a joint project through the Urban Institute and the Rand Corporation (Sorensen, et al. 1992). Utilizing information on the Alien Address Registration forms provided by the INS, the authors found that employment-preference legal aliens earn more than family-preference counterparts. Otherwise, they found no other major differences between these two groups. As acknowledged by the authors, immigrants entering under employment-preference could be drawn by cultural and family ties, whereas those entering under family-preference could be motivated by economic reasons. In a recent study based a 1977 cohort of male immigrants who eventually naturalized,, Jasso and Rosenzweig (1995) argued that, as a result of screening by their sponsors, family immigrants are at least as selective as occupational immigrants. They found that although family immigrants are less-skilled than occupational immigrants at the time of admission, the differences narrowed substantially over time.

Much of the uncertainty surrounding the issue stems from the lack of a longitudinal study of a representative sample of immigrants. Studies of immigrant selectivity using cross-sectional data rely on the assumption that recent cohorts will fare the same as the earlier cohorts as their duration of stay increases. The results are subject to biases if in fact cohort quality changes considerable over time (Borjas 1985a). Emigration selectivity presents another empirical difficulty that threatens to bias the findings even with a longitudinal data set. As those who don't adjust well in the U.S. are likely to return to their home country or migrate elsewhere, family immigrants may do so at a different rate from that of occupational immigrants (Jasso and Rosenzweig 1982; 1995). Furthermore, household surveys such as census data can only captures the migration history of those who remain in the same household and hence may underestimate the extent of family chain migration (Borjas and Bronars 1990).

This section describes the labor market skills of the post-1965 immigrants. Evidence suggests that recent immigration cohorts tend to be less skilled than the early cohorts. This may be attributed to the following. First, recent immigrants are more likely to enter through family reunification than early immigrants. Second, recent immigrants, the majority coming from developing countries, tend to have less transferable skills in the U.S. than early immigrant cohorts. Empirical evidence on whether family reunification provisions select less qualified immigrants than occupational preferences do is inconclusive.

Summary of Chapter. This chapter portrays the development of the U.S. immigration legislation. Prior to 1965, Europeans constituted the bulk of immigrants as a result of national origin quota and discriminatory acts against Asian. The enactment of the 1965 amendments of the Immigration and Nationality Act eliminated these discriminatory components in the policy and instituted a preference system that give priorities to family reunification and occupational skills. Accordingly, the post-1965 era has witnessed overwhelmingly Asian and Hispanic immigrants coming to join their families in the U.S. A majority of them are female.

The review of literature reveals variations in the specific utilization of the family reunification provisions by their demographic characteristics. The concerns that immigrants entering through family connections are less skilled than those admitted through occupational qualifications do not seem to bear out by the empirical data. The review of literature shows that, in spite of the significance of female migration to the U.S. in recent decades and gender-specific factors in migration process, very few studies has been done looking into the economic adaptation experiences of immigrant women in the U.S. This research aims to contribute to the understanding of the phenomenon of female immigration to the U.S. and the selectivity implications of family reunification for Asians and Hispanics. Next chapter presents the conceptual framework, lays out the empirical questions and research design that aims to answer these questions.

NOTES

1. As pointed out by Houstoun and her colleagues (1984), the immigration to the U.S. has been characterized by female-predominance since 1930.

2. The earthquake of 1906 in San Francisco destroyed the official birth records, and many Chinese claimed citizenship as "long-time Californians," (Nee and Nee 1973). This event increased the number of Chinese eligible for sponsoring family members.

3. The migration of one family member triggers the migration of other family members.

4. i.e., the number of future admittances attributable to the admission of one immigrant today.

4

Research Design

This study examines whether the family reunification emphasis in the U.S. immigration policy give rise to selectivity among the Asian and Hispanic immigrant wives. The selectivity, operated through both the observed and unobserved dimensions, is hypothesized to affect the immigrant wives' labor supply decisions and their earnings potentials. This chapter hypothesizes on the relationship between immigration selectivity and the immigrant wives' labor supply and earnings potentials, and specifies empirical models and procedures to test the hypotheses. As this study examines the labor market performance of immigrant wives, the neoclassical married women's labor supply theory constitutes the theoretical foundation for this study.

A central component in the theory and estimation of married women's labor supply is the explicit treatment of the self-selection bias in earnings and hours of work resulting from wives' decisions to participate in the market work. In addition to this well-documented source of self-selection bias, this chapter shall illustrate how immigrant women's immigration selectivity, measured by their marital status and migration patterns, constitutes another source of self-selection bias. Failure to control for these characteristics will result in confounded estimates of country-of-origin and cohort effects.

This chapter first provides a brief review of the theory, methodology, and a discussion of measurement problems. Next, the chapter demonstrates the immigration selectivity arguments drawing implications from the immigration literature. Theoretical hypotheses regarding the effects of immigration selectivity on immigrant wives' labor supply are derived. Next, the empirical model for this study is specified based on the conceptual framework. To develop tools to operationalize the study, empirical hypotheses are listed and corresponding test statistics are formulated.

4.1 MARRIED WOMEN'S LABOR SUPPLY

This research analyzes the impact of selectivity at immigration on the labor market performances of Asian and Hispanic immigrant wives based on the well-established neoclassical labor supply theory. Over the last few decades, the development of the married women's labor supply theory, estimation techniques, and empirical research are in fact interrelated. This section first gives a brief account of the neoclassical theory on married women's labor supply. Next, it provides a discussion of the measurement issues with respect to empirical studies. Finally, it gives a brief account on the nature of self-selection bias, and estimation schemes suggested in the literature to correct for the bias. Theoretical hypotheses and previous research findings on the effects of important variables are summarized.

4.1.1 Theoretical Framework

The role of the family and the allocation of time constitute the two major components in married women's labor supply theory (Killingsworth and Heckman 1986). A family is assumed to maximize its representative utility function subject to a pooled budget constraint[5]. In the equilibrium, a wife will allocate her time between work and leisure according to her relative market productivity compared to that of other household members (in most cases, the husband), and her productivity at home (Becker 1965; 1981). Biologically and culturally, women are the major providers of services at home. The cost of hiring someone to do the wife's job while she is participating the paid work has been suggested as a measure of the value of her home production (Zick and Bryant 1983). Therefore, her labor supply decision is determined not only by her own taste and labor market productivity, but also her family responsibilities, the resources available in the household and the market productivity of other family members.

Heckman (1974) explicitly modelled this relationship by postulating that a married woman will enter the labor force if her value of time spent at market work (market wage rate) exceeds her value of time spent at housework (reservation wage rate)[6]. Specifically, the model takes the following form (Zick and Bryant 1983):

$$(4.1) \quad W = X\beta + u_1,$$

$$(4.2) \quad W^{*} = Z\alpha + H\gamma + u_2,$$

where W is a woman's market wage rate (or the offered wage),
W^* is her reservation wage rate (or the asking wage),
X is a vector of market productivity determining characteristics,
H is her observed hours of work,
Z is a vector of home production determining factors,
α, β, and γ are corresponding coefficient parameters,
u_1 and u_2 are random error terms.

This model states that the reservation wage is dependent on the number of hours worked. The more hours she works, the higher her reservation wage becomes (Heckman 1974; Killingsworth and Heckman 1986). If a woman is free to choose the number of work hours and she works in the market, she will choose hours to equate the marginal value of nonmarket time to the marginal value of market time. This implies that for working wives, their observed hours of work can be expressed as a function of determinants in both offered wage and asking wage equations. Thus, for wives with $W=W^*$, the observed hours of work equation takes the following form:

$$(4.3) \quad H = (1/\gamma)\ (X\beta - Z\alpha + u_1 - u_2),$$

The above presents a static model of married women's labor supply. From a life-cycle perspective, a woman makes decisions on her human capital accumulation through education, training and work experiences which enhance her competitiveness in the labor market, and hence raise her wage rates in the long-run. However, she also makes marital and fertility decisions that will intervene with her human capital acquisition process (Mincer and Polachek 1974; Killingsworth and Heckman 1986). Given everything else constant, married women will have a higher reservation wage than single women. Similarly, women with young children at home will have a higher reservation wage than those who don't. These life-cycle events clearly interrupt the woman's human capital accumulation process, and lower her market productivity.

4.1.2 Measurement Issues

The above conventional theory gives no explicit guideline for the time dimension appropriate for the model. A comprehensive discussion concerning the appropriate measurement of the labor supply, the wage, and the property income variables is provided by Killingsworth (1983).

Labor Supply Variables. Empirically, hours of work may be measured by the number of hours worked in the reference year[7], the number of weeks worked in the year, or the number of hours worked in the reference week, and most studies use these measures interchangeably. While Hanoch (1980) demonstrates that weeks of work and hours of work are not perfect substitutes, Killingsworth (1983) pointed out that the choice of an appropriate measure of labor supply really depends on the relevant time dimension specified in the utility functions. He further suggested that any flexible "short period" compatible with the relevant stock variables, i.e., wage and unearned income, will be appropriate for a static model. labor force participation and hours of work.

Labor supply may be measured continuously (the hours of work variable) and discontinuously (the labor force participation variable). There are three major circumstances when a discontinuous measure may be a necessary addition to the hours of work measure (Heckman, Killingsworth, and MaCurdy 1981; Killingsworth 1983). First, firms may find it most efficient to have a fixed work schedule for everyone, such that the job offer is "take-it-or-leave-it." In other words, there are no continuous options for individuals with different maximized number of work hours. Second, there may be fixed costs involved in starting a job, such as transportation expenses. These costs make it not worthwhile to work under a certain number of hours $\bar{H}$. Thus, the hours of work variable will never have values from zero to a lower limit $\bar{H}$. Third, individuals may not be able to obtain the wage offer that they desire due to disequilibrium in the market in the short run[8], or imperfect information, and hence remain unemployed in the market. Killingsworth (1983) suggests that the possibilities of unemployment sets an upper limit $\bar{H}$ in the observed work hours. Thus, the values beyond $\bar{H}$ will never be observed for the hours of work variable.

Frequently, there are no hours of work or wage information for unemployed people. Potential problems may arise by dropping the unemployed people based on their reported employment status in a one-week reference period. Suppose that the weekly hours of work observed is representative of the underlying behavior for that particular individual plus a random error term, then there will be no problem. However, if those reporting unemployed in a given week tend to work less during the year, which is most likely the case, then excluding these unemployed people will result in selection biases.

Wife's Wage Variable. A few measures of the market wage rate have been used in empirical studies, such as the hourly earnings in the reference week, weekly earnings in the reference week, or annual earnings in the reference year (Killingsworth 1983). If hours of work is entered in the wage calculation as the denominator, any potential measurement error will contaminate the wage measure as well. This may create an artificial correlation between the observed wage and hours of work if the bias is in one direction (Borjas 1980; Killingsworth 1983). Furthermore, there ought to be consistencies between the time frames of both the denominator and the numerator in the wage calculation, and between the wage and hours variables to implement meaningful estimation.

Another wage measurement problem stems from the fact that the wage is missing for wives who are not working. Early studies confronting this problem often utilized an "predicted" or "imputed" wage strategy (killingsworth 1983). Thus, an ordinary least squares (OLS) regression is estimated on the work-only sample. The obtained parameters estimates are then used to predict the wage of the non-workers, or sometimes, the whole sample. The former practice would imply a sole purpose of imputing missing wage information for non-workers, while the latter attempts to eliminate any potential correlation between the random errors in the wage equation and the hours equation. Nevertheless, this imputed wage measurement still suffers from the sample selection bias to be discussed in section 4.1.3. Recent research employs a similar imputed wage strategy by including an extra selection-bias correction term in the estimation of the wage variable.

Nonlabor Income. Nonlabor income refers to all sources of income except employment-related income. It enters a married woman's labor supply function as a measure of her family wealth status, or material resources available to her. To obtain a "pure" income effect independent of the error term in the hours equation, any element that is related to the wife's labor supply decision has to be excluded from the measure. Killingsworth (1983) pointed out the difficulties of finding a pure nonlabor income measure that is truly independent of employment.

In practice, property income plus all earnings of other family earners (usually only the husband) is used as a measure of the nonlabor income, assuming that the wife's employment will not affect the earnings of the other family earners. Alternatively, one has to include all the wage rates of the other family members, which imposes an empirical problem since not all the other members work and have observed wage rates. Furthermore, it requires a concrete definition of the relevant decision unit, be it a nuclear family, family or household.

To summarize, a few empirical issues arise as to how to properly measure hours of work, wage, as well as nonlabor income in the labor supply estimation. The empirical problems stem from the fact that the neoclassical labor supply theory is ambivalent in the appropriate time dimension and unit of decision-making. The review suggests the importance of defining the hours of work, wage, and nonlabor income in a coherent way with respect to the time dimension of measurement and unit of decision-making. Another set of empirical issues arises from the non-random observation rule, i.e., only a sub-set of sample report wage and hours of work information. The next section describes the potential bias resulting from this observation rule, and econometric techniques to remedy for the potential bias.

4.1.3 Self-Selection Bias in Labor Supply

Three major estimation schemes have been suggested and utilized in the married women's labor supply literature: (1) the OLS regression; (2) the Tobit regression; and (3) the selection bias-corrected regression (Killingsworth 1983). Empirical studies adopting the first approach are often labelled as the first-generation studies, while the last two as the second-generation. The second-generation studies explicitly deal with the self-selection problem by incorporating the selection rule of working versus non-working in the theoretical model and empirical specification. This section first illustrates the nature of the self-selection problems heavily discussed in the second-generation literature. Next, it describes the Tobit and sample selection-bias corrected regression procedures in correcting for the sample selection bias.

Nature of Sample Selection Bias. One unique feature in the empirical studies of married women's labor supply confronts the fact that a significant number of women choose not to work. It imposes serious empirical problems since the estimation will be biased if the worker-only sample is used. If the full sample is to be used, one has to deal with the missing observations in the hours of work and the wage variable.

Selection bias occurs when estimating a female labor supply equation without taking into account the fact that those who report zero working hours and missing earnings may have systematic smaller or negative error terms (or less taste for work). In other words, the sample is not randomly selected, and the selection rule is endogenous to the behavior of interests, in this case, labor supply. Given similar demographic characteristics, wives who work are more likely to have higher wages and stronger preferences over work than wives who don't work. In statistical terms, the sample selection bias arises due to the fact that the error term is correlated with variables in the equation. This violates the basic assumption for least square estimates to be unbiased.

Correction for Sample Selectivity Bias. The estimation of married women's labor supply addresses two problems: missing wages and hours information for non-workers, and sample selectivity bias due to non-random missing. Two estimation techniques are most frequently employed to deal with these problems (Killingsworth 1983; Maddala 1983). First, the Tobit analysis essentially models the labor supply as one equation, i.e., the hours equation, and explicitly deals with the censor problem[9] (Wales and Woodland 1980; Killingsworth 1983). A Tobit regression takes the following form:

$$(4.4) \quad \begin{aligned} H^* &= X\beta + \varepsilon, \\ H &= 0, \qquad if \ H^* \leq 0, \\ H &= H^*, \qquad if \ H^* > 0, \end{aligned}$$

where H^* is the underlying latent hours equation,
H is the observed hours,
ϵ is normally distributed with mean zero and variance σ^2,

The Tobit estimation uses information from both workers and non-workers. The maximum likelihood method is used to solve for the parameters. The first part of its likelihood function specifies the probability of working H hours given working at all (Killingsworth 1983). The second part of the likelihood function specifies the probability of non-working.

To allow for the endogeneity of wage in the labor supply model, Heckman (1974) extends the Tobit regression to a system of simultaneous equations, i.e., the hours of work equation (equation (4.4)), the market wage equation (equation (4.1)) and the reservation wage equation (equation (4.2)). This estimation scheme utilizes the maximum likelihood method and is often referred to as full-information maximum likelihood (or Heckit) method. In the Tobit likelihood expression, the part representing workers is based on a univariate normal distribution. In the Heckit likelihood, the part representing workers is a bivariate normal distribution. Thus, the Heckit procedures utilize all available data, including the market wage information. However, it is less popular in practice due to its computational difficulty integrating over a bivariate density function (Wals and Woodland 1980).

A second procedure in the labor supply estimation, namely the selection bias-corrected regression, gets around the selectivity problem through an explicit estimation of the selectivity factor. By utilizing the decision rule in labor force participation and the assumption that ϵ is normally distributed as specified in equation (4.4), the selectivity factor, known as the inverse of mills ratio, may be estimated using the whole sample. Specifically, the inverse of Mills ratio takes the form of the following.

$$(4.5) \qquad \lambda = \frac{\phi(-x\beta)}{1-\Phi(-x\beta)},$$

where ϕ is the probability density function of a standard normal distribution,
Φ is the cumulative distribution function of a standard normal distribution.

Under the normality assumption, this ratio contains an estimate of the unknown parameter in the truncated mean of the error term (u_1-u_2) in the hours equation as specified in equation (4.3). This estimate is then included in the hours of work and the wage equations for workers to control for the sample selectivity bias. Heckman (1979) described the sample selection bias as an omitted variable in the hours and wage equation, and interpreted the sample selection bias as a specification error.

In practice, the selection bias-corrected regression procedures is composed of three stages (Killingsworth 1983). In the first stage, a probit equation on labor force participation decision is estimated using both workers and non-workers. A probit regression takes the following form:

$$(4.6) \qquad \begin{aligned} &H^* = X\beta + \varepsilon, \\ &Y = 0, \quad if \;\; H^* \leq 0, \\ &Y = 1, \quad if \;\; H^* > 0, \end{aligned} \qquad and$$

$$(4.7) \qquad P_i = Pr(Y=1) = \Phi\left(\frac{\beta X_i}{\sigma}\right)$$

$$= \frac{1}{\sqrt{2\pi}} \int_{-\infty}^{\frac{\beta X_i}{\sigma}} E^{-t^2/2} dt$$

where H^* is the latent hours of work,
Y is the observed response,
ϵ is normally distributed with mean zero and variance σ^2,

t is normally distributed with mean zero and variance 1. An estimate of the inverse of Mills-ratio is then constructed for workers by the coefficient estimates obtained from the probit estimation. The second stage estimates the wage equation, including the mills-ratio to impute wages for non-workers. The third stage estimatcs the hour of work equation, including mills-ratio. A fourth optional stage enters the imputed wage into the labor force participation or hours of work equations, if one wishes to obtain parameter estimates on a "pure" wage effects on labor supply[10]. Since the wife's market wage and her labor supply are likely to be influenced by the same set of variables, multicollinearity is a common problem when the fourth stage is implemented. To cope with the multicollinearity problem, Stier (1991) suggested dropping variables that are highly significant in the wage equation, such as the wives' level of education, in the fourth stage labor force participation estimation without providing any theoretical justification.

The Tobit procedure differs from the selection bias-corrected regression procedures by imposing a restriction on the parameters. The Tobit specification models hours of work as a continuous variable with a lower limit of zero with no jump or discontinuity. In contrast, the selection bias-corrected regression procedures acknowledges the discontinuity in the labor supply schedule by comparing the wage and the reservation wage equations (Killingsworth 1983; Killingsworth and Heckman 1986). Statistically, this is reflected by the fact that the selection bias-corrected regression procedures allows for different parameter estimates in the labor force participation and the hours equations, while the Tobit regression restricts the two sets of parameters to be the same.

The previous discussion reviews the married women's labor supply theory, relevant measurement issues and its estimation techniques. The next section will illustrate sources of female immigration selectivity and hypothesize its effects on immigrant wives' labor supply.

4.2 FEMALE IMMIGRATION SELECTIVITY AND LABOR SUPPLY

This research refers the female immigration selectivity to systematic differences among immigrant women that are correlated with their labor market competencies in the U.S. Given the fact that they made a decision to immigrate to the U.S., the immigrant women are already a selective[11] group as compared to those remain immobile. Among immigrant women in the U.S., they are still systematically different by the fact that they choose to immigrate at different life-cycle stages, and utilized different categories of admission. These self-selection decisions reflect their unobserved labor market qualities, and their abilities to accumulate U.S.-specific labor market experiences. Since the unobserved qualities are likely to be systematically correlated with the country-of-origin and cohort variables in the labor supply estimation, the estimated effects are contaminated by the selectivity biases.

This section illustrates the sources of female immigration selectivity and hypothesizes its likely impact on immigrant wives' labor supply, drawing implications from the immigration literature. It also discuss the potential associations between the immigration selectivity and the immigrant wives' country-of-origin and timing of immigration.

4.2.1 Unobserved Labor Market Qualities

As pointed out above, female immigration selectivity occurs because of the choice made by immigrant women about their mode of entry to the U.S. and at which life-cycle stage they immigrated to the U.S. This section elaborates on these two arguments.

Mode of Entry. The immigration literature suggests that immigration selectivity may occur through costs and benefits calculation by the immigrant women. Immigrant wives who had expected more immigration costs tend to have more unobserved qualities, such as motivation, and risk-taking personality, which make them more competitive in the U.S. labor market than wives expecting lower costs. These unobserved qualities will enter the error term in the wife's market wage equation, u_1. Wives with more "qualities" (or higher u_1) tend to have higher offered market wages than those with less "qualities" (or lower u_1). According to the decision rule in labor supply, wives with higher u_1 are more likely to be in the labor force, and work more hours than those wives with lower u_1, given the same reservation wage rates. These qualities embedded in u_1 are not directly observable, but a strong correlation exists between these qualities and immigrant wives' modes of entry which are observable. The U.S. immigration policy gives different incentives to immigrant women based on their marital status or kin connections, and therefore plays an important role in "selecting" immigrant women in their unobserved qualities.

There are three immigration selectivity arguments documented in the immigration literature that relate unobserved qualities with mode of entry. First, Borjas and Bronars (1990) demonstrated that the position in the migration chain is an important indicator of immigrant men's observed and unobserved quality, modelling the migration decision within the family framework. To reduce costs and risks, households are likely to adopt strategies facilitating chain migration, with distinct selectivity implications for individual members of each link. Since the first migrants are likely to encounter great uncertainty and difficulty in getting admission, migrants of the first link are likely to possess more qualities than those of the latter links.

Unlike immigrant men, the majority of who are often qualified as economic migrants, the position in the migration chain has an even greater implication on immigrant women's qualities. Immigrant females joining husbands or family in the U.S. are far less likely to be motivated by the economic opportunities in the receiving country than females migrating on their own, and therefore, possess more labor market qualities. If female immigrants are married before immigration, they are likely to be constrained by joint decision made within the family, and hence to have lower qualities. The reverse may be true for women who marry after immigration.

Second, U.S. immigration policy gives priority to potential immigrant women who have husbands or immediate relatives in the U.S. Immigrant women seeking permanent stay on their own find it more difficult than those with U.S. relative sponsors. In other words, independent immigrant women encounter greater immigration costs than immigrant women migrating to join their husband or immediate relatives. Since only highly competitive persons can afford great immigration costs, the former group will be have more unobserved qualities than the latter.

Third, from a network function argument, immigrant women with husbands or family in the U.S. are more likely to gain information about the U.S. than those without any U.S. relative. As a consequence, the former group face less risk or uncertainty associated with migration, and thus are hypothesized to have fewer labor market qualities than the latter group. Since low costs motivate immigrants with fewer unobserved qualities, they tend to be less competent in the U.S. labor market.

The above three lines of argument all imply that (1) immigrant women who were married at the time of migration will have fewer unobserved labor market qualities than immigrant women who were single at the time of migration; (2) immigrant wives migrating to join their husbands or migrating with their husbands will have fewer labor market qualities than wives migrating before their husbands; and (3) immigrant women sponsored by their immediate relatives will have fewer labor market qualities than independent immigrant women.

Life-Cycle Stage at Migration. The human capital theory identifies the labor market experiences as one of the crucial determinants of earnings (Mincer 1974). Empirically, it is often measured by the number of years after schooling for men, assuming a continuous work life disrupted only by education. For a woman, such a measurement is apparently inappropriate since she is likely to have a discontinuous work schedule due to family responsibilities, childbirth and child-rearing activities. Long (1980) suggests using the number and age of children as a proxy for the depreciation by such activities in the estimation of women's earnings. When applying this conventional framework to immigrant wives, one needs to consider explicitly the interaction of timing of immigration and life-cycle stage.

Specifically, immigrant women who are single at the time of migration are not constrained by marriage, child-bearing or child-rearing activities, and may be better able to pick up U.S.-specific skills than married women. Similarly, immigrant women without children are not constrained by reproductive activities and maybe better able to adapt to the U.S. labor market then their counterparts. Given the same duration since immigration, immigrant women who start their reproductive years after immigration are likely to suffer from greater disruption effects on labor supply than those have completed or started their reproductive stage before migration.

To summarize, marital status at migration and migration patterns represent the immigrant wives' unobserved labor market qualities through different migration motivations and processes of accumulating U.S.-specific experiences. Based on the above arguments, several hypotheses emerge. First, immigrant women who are married at the time of migration possess fewer labor market qualities and therefore less competitive in the U.S. labor market, less likely to be in the labor force, and work fewer hours than their single counterparts. Second, immigrant wives migrating to join their husbands or migrating with their husbands possess fewer labor market qualities than immigrant wives migrating before their husbands. Third, immigrant wives who are sponsored by immediate relatives possess fewer labor market qualities than independent immigrant wives. The effects of sponsorship on immigrant wives' labor supply may vary by types of sponsoring relatives.

4.2.2 National Origin and Immigration Cohort

The previous section establishes arguments identifying marital status and migration patterns as important factors determining immigrant wives' labor supply. This section presents arguments that these characteristics at migration will explain a significant portion of national-origin and cohort differences in immigrant wives' labor supply. By arguing correlation between the underlying unobserved labor market qualities, it demonstrates a potential source of self-selection bias in the country-of-origin and cohort effects in the labor supply estimation.

Female Immigration Selectivity and Country-Of-Origin. Female immigrant selectivity may confound the country-of-origin effects on immigrant wives' labor supply. Groups may demonstrate different labor market behavior simply because of differences in the marital status and migration patterns as specified in the previous section. Macro-level characteristics of the countries of origin appear to contribute to these differences.

In particular, distance of the origin country from the U.S., social or cultural differences in attitudes toward female immigration in the origin countries, familial roles of women in the origin countries, and socioeconomic connections between the origin countries and the U.S. are all possible factors that encourage/deter a particular kind of female immigration to the U.S. Immigrant wives from bordering countries such as Mexico are likely to wait for more years before following their husbands than wives from Asian countries do. It has been widely documented that Caribbean and Latin American countries have a tradition of female immigration, particularly among single females. Therefore, immigrant wives from the Caribbean and Latin America are more likely to be single at the time of migration than those from Asian countries. Family-sponsored immigration is more likely to be prevalent from countries have strong historical ties with the U.S. than from other countries.

Female Immigration Selectivity and Immigrant Cohort. The immigrant wives who immigrated in a particular time period may be likely to have utilized a particular mode of entry. Three factors may have contributed to this first level of selectivity. First, the implementation of the 1965 Immigration and Nationality Act apparently had drawn more family immigrants to the U.S. than occupational immigrants. Consequently, female immigrants are more likely to immigrate through family reunification than early immigrants. In addition, cumulative immigration over time may be a second factor that explains the trend. From the network migration thesis, the presence of immigrants in the U.S. may trigger further immigration from the same origin country. As a result, recent female immigrants are likely to have sponsors in the U.S. before they immigrate. Third, there may be socioeconomic changes that happen in the origin countries that encourage/hinder a special type of female immigration to the U.S., such as rapid economic development and urbanization. As independent female immigration becomes more socially acceptable in recent years, contemporary female immigrants are more likely to immigrate as single than early female immigrants.

These three conflicting factors predict different trends in the mode of entry of immigrant women. If it is more difficult for single women to immigrate to the U.S. in the early years than recent years, single immigrant women of earlier cohorts will be more selective than single immigrant women immigrated in recent years. Similarly, if it is more difficult for married women to immigrate to the U.S. in the early years than recent years, married immigrant women of earlier cohorts will be more selective than married immigrant women who immigrated in recent years.

To summarize, this section illustrates female immigration selectivity by origin country and immigration cohort. Since marital status and migration patterns carry information on immigrant wives' unobserved labor market qualities, potential correlation between country-of-origin and the unobserved qualities, and immigration cohort and the unobserved qualities are likely to be present. This correlation creates selection biases in the country-of-origin and immigration cohort estimates in the immigrant wives' labor supply equations. The discussion leads to three empirical questions: (1) whether marital status at migration and migration patterns are important factors explaining the labor supply among female immigrants; (2) whether the national-origin differences can be explained by this differential composition at the time of migration; and (3) whether the cohort effects can be explained by this differential composition at the time of migration.

This section illustrates the potential significance of female migration selectivity on immigrant wives' labor supply based on migration literature. Major empirical questions are derived. The next section specifies the empirical models.

4.3 EMPIRICAL MODELS

The objective of this empirical study is to (1) investigate the significance and magnitude of marital status at migration and migration patterns variables in the immigrant wives' labor supply estimation; and (2) evaluate the selectivity bias on the country-of-origin and cohort effects. As this study aims to evaluate the three aspects of the immigrant wives' labor market performance, i.e., labor force participation, hours of work, and earnings, the selection bias-corrected regression procedures, as described in section 4.1.3 are preferable. Specifically, the empirical model for this study estimates a reduced-form labor force participation equation, hourly earnings equation, and hours of work equation. Due to the potential correlations between the error terms in the wage and the hours of work equations, a reduced-form specification will actually end up with including exactly the same set of variables in all three equations.

4.3.1 Model Specification

The empirical model is specified as follow.

$$H^* = \alpha + \beta S + \delta O + \eta W + \zeta D + \gamma X + \epsilon, \tag{4.8}$$

where H^* is the latent hours of work,
S is a vector of variables representing migration selectivity,
O is a vector of dummy variables representing country of origin,
W is a vector of dummy variables representing period of immigration,
D is a vector of dummies variables representing year of survey,
X is a vector of all other control variables,
ϵ is a vector of disturbance terms normally distributed with mean zero and variance σ^2,
α is a vector of constant parameters,
β, δ, η, ζ, and γ are vectors of corresponding coefficient parameters.

The labor force participation regression takes on the value of 1 if $H^*>0$, and 0 otherwise. The hours of work regression takes on positive values if $H^*>0$, and 0 otherwise. The hourly earnings regression takes on positive values if $H^*>0$, and missing otherwise. The estimation of the probability of being in the labor force utilizes the probit regression technique. The estimations of the hourly earnings and hours of work utilize the OLS regression technique.

4.3.2 Variables Constructed

The current study employs the June 1986, 1988 and 1991, and the November 1989 CPS supplements to address the empirical questions. Since the marital history information are only asked of females age 18-44, each sample includes Asian and Hispanic[12] immigrant women age 18-44, married with husbands present at the time of survey. There are 703 observations in the 1986 sample, 564 in the 1988 sample, 823 in the 1989 sample, and 829 in the 1991 sample.

As indicated in equation (4.8), the variables in the regression analyses include the (1) selectivity variables; (2) the country-of-origin variables; (3) the immigration cohort variables; (4) the year of survey variables; and (5) variables that control for market conditions, individual human capital, and family characteristics. Variables in groups (1) to (4) represent the migration experiences of the immigrant wives, and are the main focus of this study. The group (5) variables represent both market wage factors and reservation wage factors. This section describes the regression variables constructed.

Labor Supply and Wage. The CPS directs its labor force participation questions towards activities the week before survey. It classifies the following three types of people as "in the labor force": (1) at work in the reference week; (2) with a job, but not at work; and (3) unemployed, but actively seeking for employment. The earnings and hours of work questions are asked only of salaried and wage workers in a private industry or any level of the government. This study imputed these information for the self-employed immigrant wives, the self-employed husbands, the unemployed immigrant wives and unemployed husbands using auxiliary information from the March supplements, to be described in section 5.3. Earnings and hours of work questions refer to usual weekly earnings and hours of work obtained from the primary (or longest) job.

Specifically, the vector of dependent variables are defined as follows. First, a binary dummy variable indicates whether in the labor force or not in the reference week. Second, a continuous variable measures usual weekly hours of work. Third, a continuous variable measures log usual hourly earnings. The hourly earnings variable refers to hourly wages for hourly workers, and hourly earnings[13] for non-hourly workers.

Marital Status and Migration Patterns (S Variables). The marital status at migration variable is constructed by comparing the immigrant wife's year of first marriage and her year of immigration[14]. The set of migration patterns variables are assigned based on the year of immigration of both the immigrant wife and her husband. Furthermore, a set of combined marital status and migration patterns variables are defined as migrating single, migrating married preceding the husband, migrating married following the husband, migrating married during the same five-year interval as the husband. Wives who married and immigrated in the same period are classified in the married group, since they are likely to have immigrated for marriage reasons.

Sponsorship of Immediate Relatives (S Variables). The immigration of immediate relatives, including parents, siblings, and in-laws carry similar implications to those of husbands. Two sets of variables are constructed using the information available in both the November 1989 and June 1991 CPS supplements.

First, the percentage of immediate relatives currently living in the U.S. is calculated to indicate the extent to which family reunification has occurred. Holding everything else constant, it is hypothesized that the higher percentage of immediate relatives in the U.S., the more likely an immigrant woman is sponsored by the relatives. Or from the migration network argument, the more relatives in the U.S., the lesser the immigration risks. Both arguments suggest that this variable will have a negative effect on immigrant wives' earnings and labor supply. Second, the number of the woman's own immediate relatives and the number of her husband's immediate relatives are separately calculated to indicate the help/responsibilities provided/imposed by these relatives.

Country-Of-Origin Differences (O Variables). Substantial country-of-origin effects have been documented in previous research on Asian immigrant wives (Stier 1991) and Hispanic immigrant wives (Stier and Tienda 1992). To capture differences caused by racial/ethnic origin, O variables consist of a variety of specification, i.e., a set of national-origin dummies O_c, a set of region of origin dummies O_r, or simply a racial/ethnic dummy O to be included in separate regressions. The subscript c in the country-of-origin dummies O_c indicates China[15], Colombia, Cuba, Dominican Republic, El Salvador, India, Japan, Korea, Mexico, the Philippines, Southeast Asian refugee countries[16], all other Hispanic countries, and all other Asian countries. The subscript r in the region of origin dummies O_{rc} indicates Mexico, Central America, Spanish-speaking Caribbean, South America, East Asia, Southeast Asia and South Asia. The racial/ethnic dummy O differentiates between Asian immigrant wives and immigrant wives of Hispanic origin. The labor supply model is also estimated separately for Asian and Hispanic immigrant wives, in which case the corresponding country-of-origin variables are O_{ac} and O_{ac} respectively.

Cohort Effects (W Variables) and Period Effects (Y Variables). The length of stay in the U.S. has been shown to have significant positive effects on immigrant men (Borjas 1980; Chiswick 1980), while having mixed effects on immigrant women (Long 1980; Stier 1991; Stier and Tienda 1992). Since the acquisition of U.S.-specific experiences for immigrant wives is often interrupted by family responsibilities, the assimilation effects for women are not as straightforward as for men. Borjas (1985) pointed out that the length of stay variable obtained from the cross-sectional data is in fact composed of both assimilation effects and cohort effects. Furthermore, his research (1985; 1987; and 1990) showed substantial decreases in the qualities (measured by educational attainment and earnings) of immigrant men over time using several census data. Thus, the effects of this set of variables on immigrant wives' labor supply and wage can't be determined on a priori basis.

Based on information on the period of immigration, W_t variables are constructed as a set of cohort dummies to distinguish among those immigrating prior to 1970, in 1970-1974, in 1975-1979, in 1980-1984, and those during 1985-1991. When estimated separately for Asian and Hispanic immigrant wives, the corresponding country-of-origin variables are W_{at} and W_{ht} respectively.

The year-of-survey variable measures both design effect and period effect. First, there appear to be systematic differences and similarities across supplements. Surveys covering the same topic, and/or conducted in adjacent years tend to be homogeneous in many ways. The June 1986 and 1988 supplements show pronounced similarities in both survey design and variable specifications, while considerable similarities are found between the November 1989 and June 1991 supplements. Second, economic fluctuations over the five-year period may contribute to the differences by survey years. The 1990 recession may have dampening effects on immigrant wives' labor supply in 1991, as compared to those of previous years. To capture effects specific to the timing of survey, or a single survey design, D_y variables represent each sample included.

Other Control Variables (X Variables). The other independent variables, labelled by X, included in the model are factors hypothesized to contribute to either the market wage rates, the reservation wage rates, or both (Killingsworth and Heckman 1986; Becker 1981). Specifically, they include (1) factors that specify the constraints/motivations from the family/household faced by the immigrant woman; (2) variables that specify individual ability; and (3) variables indicating regional/local economic opportunities/constraints.

According to the time allocation theory, the labor supply decision of married women is highly responsive to her husband's earnings capacity. Specifically, the husband's earnings affects the wife's labor supply through the family budget constraints (income effects) and relative opportunity costs (substitution effects). Assuming the wife's home production a normal good, as the family's unearned income increases so does the demand for the wife's home time (Zick and Bryant 1983). As a proxy of the family unearned income, the higher the husband's income, the less likely the wife will enter paid work. The cross-substitution effect of the husband's wage on the wife's labor supply is undetermined from the theory, depending the degree of substitutability or complementarity between both spouses (Zick and Bryant 1983). This study specifies a set of linear spline[17] variables representing the husband's weekly earnings. For a detailed treatment on the specification and interpretation of splines function, see Poirier (1976). In addition, a number of dummy variables are also constructed to indirectly capture the husband's wage effect and earning capacities, such as the educational attainment of the husband, his racial/ethnic origin, and his nativity status. It was hypothesized that having a husband who immigrated in recent years increases the demand for the wife's earnings, and thus increases her likelihood of going to work (Stier and Tienda 1992).

The presence of young children in the household creates the demand for a wife's time at home. Thus the more young children at home, the higher her reservation wage. In addition, the more births a woman has, the more likely her work schedule is disrupted, and thus the lower her market wage offers is likely to be (Long 1980; Montgomery and Trussell 1986). Holding reservation wage constant, the lower the wife's market wage offer is, the less likely she will be in the labor force, and the fewer hours of work she will supply. The presence of other adults in the household may facilitate the entry of wives into the labor force by sharing the household responsibilities (Tienda and Angel 1982; Tienda and Glass 1985). Therefore, the empirical estimation includes variables indicating the number of children under 6 in the household, the number of children between 6 to 17 in the household and the number of other adults in the household.

The variables indicating the wife's personal abilities include her educational attainment, her English-speaking ability (only available from the 1989 sample) and her age. Education level is an indication of productivity both in the market and at home (Killingsworth and Heckman 1986). In the short run, it captures a woman's opportunities costs of being at home. In the long run, it shapes the perception of the woman about market work (Bean and Tienda 1987). The more education a wife has, the more likely she will be in the labor force. The immigrant wife's English-speaking ability represent a major components of the immigrant wife's human capital stock. Nonetheless, the immigrant wife may choose to enter an occupation or work place which requires little English-speaking ability, such as an ethnic enclave. In general, the effect is hypothesized to be positive. In the human capital specification, age enters the earnings function in both linear and quadratic forms (Mincer 1974). This study specifies a age spline to allow for a possible nonlinear earnings profile. The relationship between age and labor supply is less straightforward, depending on her life-cycle stage.

Two sets of variables are included to represent the forces of regional or local labor markets: the region of residence dummies and the metropolitan statistical area (MSA) dummies. Immigrants in the U.S. have been largely concentrated in the west and south regions of the country. The concentration of immigration in a particular area may be highly correlated with the availability of jobs.

Table 4.1 presents a list of the working definitions and abbreviations of all the variables described above.

4.4 MAJOR QUESTIONS, EMPIRICAL HYPOTHESES, AND TESTS

This section first reiterates major research questions. Next, it lays out empirical hypotheses addressing these questions. Finally, relevant hypothesis tests are described.

4.4.1 Empirical Hypotheses

Based on the empirical model, four specific empirical questions emerge. First, do immigrant wives differ in labor supply by country-of-origin, cohort, or year of survey even after controlling for demographic differences? Second, do immigrant wives differ in their labor supply by marital status at migration and migration patterns? Third, do the

Table 4.1 Definition and Abbreviation of Regression Variables

	Operational Description
dependent variables: labor supply or hourly earnings	
L_p	dummy, in the labor force
L_e	continuous, log usual hourly earnings in 1991 dollars
L_h	continuous, usual hours of work per week
independent variables:	
dummies, marital status and migration patterns, (omitted group is married at migration and immigrated before husband)	
S_1	single at the time of migration
S_2	married at migration and immigrated after the husband
S_3	married at migration and immigrated with the husband
continuous, the extent of family reunification in the U.S.	
S_4	percentage of immediate relatives in the U.S.
S_5	percentage of in-laws in the U.S.
continuous, number of immediate relatives living in the household	
S_6	number of own immediate relatives in the household
S_7	number of in-laws in the household
dummies, origin countries, (omitted group is Mexico for Hispanics, and the Philippines for Asians)	
O_1	immigrated from China
O_2	immigrated from India
O_3	immigrated from Japan
O_4	immigrated from Korea
O_5	immigrated from Laos, Cambodia, or Vietnam
O_6	immigrated from all other Asian countries
O_7	immigrated from Colombia
O_8	immigrated from Cuba
O_9	immigrated from Dominica Republic
O_{10}	immigrated from El Salvador
O_{11}	immigrated from all other Hispanic countries
dummies, region of origin, (omitted group is the Spanish-speaking Caribbean)	
O_{r1}	immigrated from central America
O_{r2}	immigrated from south America
O_{r3}	immigrated from Mexico
O_{r4}	immigrated from east Asia
O_{r5}	immigrated from southeast Asia
O_{r6}	immigrated from south Asia
dummy, racial/ethnic origin, (omitted group is Hispanics)	
O	Asian immigrant wives

Table 4.1 (continued)

	Operational Description
dummies, immigration cohort, (omitted group is immigrated before 1970)	
W_1	immigrated between 1970-1974
W_2	immigrated between 1975-1979
W_3	immigrated between 1980-1984
W_4	immigrated between 1985-1991
dummies, year of survey, (omitted group is surveyed in 1991)	
D_1	surveyed in 1986
D_2	surveyed in 1988
D_3	surveyed in 1989
dummies, region of residence, (omitted group is the West)	
X_3	Northeast
X_4	Midwest
X_5	South
dummies, MSA status, (omitted group is not identified)	
X_6	in MSA and in central city
X_7	in MSA, not in central city
X_8	not in MSA
dummies, husband's education, (omitted group is wives with college-educated husbands)	
X_9	husband has less than 7th grade education
X_{10}	husband has high school education
dummies, wife's educational attainment, (omitted group is wives with college education)	
X_{11}	wife has less than 7th grade education
X_{12}	wife has high school education
continuous, number of children or other adults in the household	
X_{13}	number of children age less than 6 in the household
X_{14}	number of children age 6-17 in the household
X_{15}	number of other adults in the household
splines, wife's age	
X_{16}	less than 30 years old
X_{17}	ages between 31 to 44
dummies, husband's nativity status, (omitted group is wives of established immigrants)	
X_{18}	husband U.S.-born
X_{19}	husband immigrated within the last 2 years
splines, the husband's usual weekly earnings	
X_{20}	earns less than \$170 per week (or \$4. 25 per hour) in 1991 dollars
X_{21}	earns \$170-\$400 per week (or \$4. 25-\$10. 0 per hour) in 1991 dollars
X_{22}	earns more than \$400 per week (or \$10. 0 per hour) in 1991 dollars

differences in the characteristics at migration explain country-of-origin differences? Fourth, do the differences in the characteristics at migration explain cohort differences?

To answer these research questions, 19 hypotheses are formulated. Hypotheses 1 to 10 address research question 1 and 2, while Hypotheses 11 to 19 address research question 3 and 4. Hypotheses 1 to 5 test whether there is racial/ethnic or country-of-origin differences in the immigrant wives' labor supply. Hypotheses 6 through 8 test whether there is cohort difference in the immigrant wives' labor supply. Hypotheses 9 test whether there is difference in the immigrant wives' labor supply by the timing of survey. Hypotheses 10 test whether there is difference in the immigrant wives' labor supply by their marital status at migration and migration patterns. Hypotheses 11 through 19 test whether the marital status at migration and migration patterns significantly contribute to the country-of-origin, cohort, and period effects as specified in Hypotheses 1 to 9. Specific hypotheses are presented as follow:

1. O_c=0 for all c, c=1-11, i.e., there is no difference in the immigrant wives' labor supply by country-of-origin.
2. O_{rc}=0 for all c, c=1-6, i.e., there is no difference in the immigrant wives' labor supply by region-of-origin.
3. O=0, i.e., there is no difference in immigrant wives' labor supply between Asian and Hispanics.
4. O_{ac}=0 for all c, c=1-6, i.e., there is no difference in labor supply among Asian immigrant wives.
5. O_{hc}=0 for all c, c=7-11, i.e., there is no difference in labor supply among Hispanic wives.
6. W_t=0 for all t, t=1-4, i.e., there is no difference in immigrant wives' labor supply by immigrant cohorts.
7. W_{at}=0 for all t, t=1-4, i.e., there is no difference in Asian immigrant wives' labor supply by timing of immigration.
8. W_{ht}=0 for all t, t=1-4; i.e., there is no difference in Hispanic immigrant wives' labor supply by timing of immigration.
9. D_y=0 for all y, y=1-3; i.e., there is no difference in immigrant wives' labor supply by source of data or year of survey.
10. S_j=0, j=1-3; i.e., there is no significant differences in immigrant wives' labor supply by marital status at migration and migration patterns.

11. The country-of-origin effects can't be changed by controlling for marital status at migration and migration patterns.
12. The region-of-origin effects can't be changed by controlling for marital status at migration and migration patterns.
13. The racial/ethnic effects can't be changed by controlling for marital status at migration and migration patterns.
14. The country-of-origin effects among Asian immigrant wives can't be changed by controlling for marital status at migration and migration patterns.
15. The country-of-origin effects among Hispanics can't be changed by controlling for marital status at migration and migration patterns.
16. The cohort effects can't be changed by controlling for marital status at migration and migration patterns.
17. The cohort effects among Asian immigrant wives can't be changed by controlling for marital status at migration and migration patterns.
18. The cohort effects among Hispanic immigrant wives can't be changed by controlling for marital status at migration and migration patterns.
19. The period effects can't be changed by controlling for marital status at migration and migration patterns.

This section states the specific hypotheses to be tested in the empirical study. The next section describes the test procedures.

4.4.2 Hypothesis Testing

To implement tests, the following techniques and steps are taken. Hypotheses 1 to 10 require joint tests on more than a single parameter; therefore, F-tests are used to test the linear restrictions in both hourly earnings regression and hours of work regression; and likelihood ratio tests are used to test the non-linear restrictions in the labor force participation probit regressions. Specifically, the two test statistics can be expressed as (Gujarati 1988):

$$\text{(4.9)} \quad \textit{the F statistic} \quad F(J, N\text{-}K) = \frac{(RSS_{*}-RSS)/J}{RSS/(N\text{-}K)} \quad \textit{or in matrix forms}$$

$$= \frac{(e_{*}'e_{*}-e'e)/J}{e'e/(N\text{-}K)} \quad \textit{or}$$

$$= \frac{(R^2-R_{*}^2)/J}{(1-R^2)/(N\text{-}K)}$$

where RSS_{*} is the residual sum of squares from the restricted regression,
RSS is the residual sum of squares from the unrestricted regression,
J is the number of linear restrictions,
N is the sample size,
K is the number of regressors,
R^2 is the R squared from the unrestricted regression,
R_{*}^2 is the R squared from the restricted regression.

$$\text{(4.10)} \quad \textit{the likelihood ratio test} \quad \lambda = -2(lnL^{*}-lnL)$$

where $\ln L^{*}$ is the log likelihood evaluated at the restricted estimates,
lnL is the log likelihood evaluated at the unrestricted estimates.

The unrestricted regressions are estimated by including all variables of interest. The restricted regressions are estimated by excluding the set of dummy variables restricted under the null hypothesis. The F-test measures whether there is a significant reduction in the residual sum of squares by including the variables tested, while the likelihood ratio test measures whether there is a significant increase in the log likelihood.

Hypotheses 11 to 19 test whether including marital status at migration and migration pattern variables in the regressions will result in significant changes in the estimates of country-of-origin, cohort or period effects. The evaluation should not depend on the base-groups chosen in the regression estimation. Two measures are developed to accomplish this goal. First, F tests are conducted for Hypothesis 1 to 9 separately for regressions with and without marital status and migration patterns. Qualitative conclusions regarding the effects of marital status at migration and migration patterns variables may be drawn by examining the magnitude of increases in F statistics before and after including these variables. Second, each regression being tested is estimated separately before and after including marital status at migration and migration patterns variables. Assuming zero mean effects for the base-groups, the weighted standard deviations of both the before and after coefficient estimates are then obtained. As the standard deviation captures the mean distance from the mean, it is a base-group-free measure of the country-of-origin, cohort and period effects. The differences between the before and after estimates then provide a quantitative measure of the impact of marital status at migration and migration pattern on the estimation of the country-of-origin, cohort and period effects.

4.4.3 Regression Strategies

Given the empirical questions and hypotheses to be tested, this section recaps the availability of data and summarizes the actual empirical procedures undertaken.

The selectivity variables of interests in this study are marital status and migration patterns, family reunification variables, and the number of immediate relatives in the household. Nonetheless, not all the information required is available in all samples. Marital status and migration patterns variables can be defined exactly in the 1986, 1988, and 1991[18] supplements. In the 1989 sample, no marital history information was collected. Therefore, marital status at migration is unknown. The variables defined in relation to immediate relatives are only available in the November 1989 and June 1991 samples. Nonetheless, a variable counting the number of other adults in the household is constructed for every sample.

Table 4.2 summarizes the regressions estimated and their relevance to questions of interests. The labor supply model is first estimated using single samples. This will enable the control for variations due to the economic conditions in the survey year (period effect) and noises specific to a particular survey design. The estimation is repeated for the pooled sample, given the assumption that the differences across survey years are constant over individuals. Separate estimations are conducted by region-of-origin, race/ethnicity, country-of-origin, immigration cohort, and age at immigration, provided the sample size is not less than 100. These estimates allows regression parameters to be different by the sorting variables.

Table 4.2 Regression Estimated and Variables of Interests

Year of Sample	N	Universe	Variables
Single Sample			
1986	703	all	marital status, migration patterns,
1988	564	all	marital status, migration patterns,
1989	823	all	migration patterns, family reunification, number of kin in household
1991	829	all	marital status, migration patterns, family reunification, number of kin in household
Pooled Sample			
1986, 88 & 91	2096	all	marital status, migration patterns, period effect
1989 & 91	1652	all	family reunification, number of kin in household, period effect
By Region of Origin			
1986, 88 & 91	642	Mexico	marital status, migration patterns, period effect
1986, 88 & 91	360	East Asia	marital status, migration patterns, period effect
1986, 88 & 91	369	southeast	marital status, migration patterns period effect
1986, 88 & 91	151	south Asia	marital status, migration patterns, period effect
1986, 88 & 91	181	south America	marital status, migration patterns, period effect
1986, 88 & 91	163	central America	marital status, migration patterns, period effect
1986, 88 & 91	152	the Caribbean	marital status, migration patterns, period effect

Table 4.2 (continued)

Year of Sample	N	Universe	Variables
By Country of Origin			
1986, 88 & 91	180	China	marital status, migration patterns, period effect
1986, 88 & 91	186	Philippines	marital status, migration patterns, period effect
1986, 88 & 91	142	India	marital status, migration patterns, period effect
1986, 88 & 91	116	Korea	marital status, migration patterns, period effect
By Race/Ethnicity			
1986, 88 & 91	1159	Hispanics	marital status, migration patterns, period effect
1986, 88 & 91	937	Asians	marital status, migration patterns, period effect
By Age at Migration			
1986, 88 & 91	825	by age 21	marital status, migration patterns, period effect
1986, 88 & 91	1271	after age 21	marital status, migration patterns, period effect
By Immigration Cohort			
1986, 88 & 91	291	prior to 1970	marital status, migration patterns, period effect
1986, 88 & 91	784	1970-1979	marital status, migration patterns, period effect
1986, 88 & 91	1021	1980-1991	marital status, migration patterns, period effect

Note: The universe include all Asian and Hispanic immigrant women aged 18-44, married with husband present at the time of survey.

For each specification, three regressions are estimated, namely, the probit regression for labor force participation, the OLS regression for hourly earnings, the OLS regression for hours of work.

Summary of Chapter. This chapter gives a brief account of the conventional married women's labor supply theory, its measurement and estimation issues. The review suggests the importance of consistency in defining the time frame of the labor supply and wage variables. It also suggests Tobit and selection bias-corrected regression procedures to correct for the sample selection bias due to the endogenous work decision.

To demonstrate the links between migration selectivity and immigrant wives' labor market performance, the migration selectivity implications derived from the migration literature are integrated into the conventional framework. Specifically, three hypotheses are derived. First, immigrant wive migrating while single tend to be more committed to the labor force and obtain higher hourly earnings than their married counterparts. Second, wives migrating before their husbands are more likely to be in the labor force and make higher earnings than those migrating with or following their husbands. Third, immigrant women sponsored by relatives in the U.S. may be less successful in the U.S. labor market.

Based on the conceptual model and theoretical hypotheses, this chapter specifies the empirical questions, empirical model, empirical hypotheses, and regression and test procedures. This study employs the selection bias-corrected regression procedures due to its less restricted assumption in the parameters than Tobit technique. The empirical procedures involves (1) estimating a labor force participation probit regression; (2) derive the inverse of mills ratio λ; (3) estimate the hourly earnings OLS regression with λ included; and (4) estimate the hours of work OLS regression with λ included.

To examine the significance of migration selectivity, the selectivity variables, i.e., marital status at migration, migration pattern, and family reunification, are included in all three regression estimations. To take into account the fact that immigrant wives of given characteristics may exhibit different labor supply behaviors by country-of-origin, cohort, and year of survey, all three regressions are estimated separately along these dimensions. In addition to the regression analysis, hypotheses testing are formulated to examine if there are significant country-of-origin, cohort, period differences in the immigrant wives' labor supply and earnings using a base-group free strategy. The same strategy is applied to test if the selectivity variables significantly bias the country-of-origin, cohort, and period effects in the immigrant wives' earnings and labor supply.

Given the research design, the next chapter proceed to describe the source of empirical data for this study, and imputation procedures undertaken to clean the data.

NOTES

1. A representative utility function may be arrived at through compromises and bargaining between the individual family members, as well as intra-family resource transfers.

2. The reservation wage is defined as the highest wage level an individual is indifferent between working or non-working. In other words, the wage level at which an individual desires to work exactly zero hours. It represents a wage threshold in individual's work decision.

3. In most cases, the reference year refers to the calendar year before the survey year. similarly, the reference week refers to the calendar week before the survey week.

4. The disequilibrium may comes from the fact that individuals are not always informed of all possible offers, or they are not perfectly mobile. This is more realistic than the perfect competition assumption in the conventional theory.

5. A censored sample is defined when the dependent variable is truncated at some point, while all the independent variables are available for everyone in the sample. A truncated sample is defined when both dependent and independent variables are not observed for some portion of the sample.

6. On the other hand, if one's research question does not require a direct estimate of the market wage effect, putting all the variables that affect the market wage in the regression will still be controlling for the market wage, through these variables.

7. This term means significant deviations from the characteristics of the average population.

8. For the purpose of this study, Asian and Hispanic immigrants are defined by race, Hispanic origin and place of birth questions. Persons who are Asians and born in Asian countries are defined as Asian immigrants. Persons who are of Hispanic origin, and born in either Mexico, the Caribbean, central or south America are defined as Hispanic immigrants.

9. i.e., usual weekly earnings divided by usual hours worked per week. This number may differ from hourly wage due to tips and overtime pay.

10. The age at first marriage may give an inaccurate account of the marital status at migration for immigrant women whose first marriage were dissolved before immigration.

11. Chinese from China, Taiwan, and Hong Kong are grouped together due to ambiguous national identity for Chinese from these areas.

12. This category includes immigrants from Southeast Asian countries including Laos, Vietnam, and Cambodia, the vast majority of whom are either refugees or family of refugees.

13. Spline variables allow the slopes of the specific effect to change at particular knots.

14. obtained through matching information from the June 1990 and 1992 samples and imputation procedures, to be described in section 5.2 and 5.3.

5

Sources of Data and Imputations

Issues of immigration and immigrant adaptation have been a central debate in the U.S. over the last few decades. The evaluation on the selectivity implications of family reunification remains inconclusive in the literature due to the complexity of the question and the lack of data documenting both the immigrants' immigration and economic adaptation experiences. Specifically, information identifying the migration selectivity of the immigrants is often not available in the household-based censuses and surveys, whereas the adaptation information is not available in the administrative records of the Immigration and Naturalization Service (INS). In coping with this empirical difficulty, this study utilizes a merged file from the Current Population Survey (CPS) supplements. The selectivity measurements for immigrant women, marital status at migration and migration patterns, are obtained through matching observations across samples.

This chapter first describes and contrasts three major sources of immigration data, i.e., the census, the administrative records of the INS, and the CPS supplements. Next, it documents the design of sample selection for the purpose of the current study. Due to the nature of the data set, substantial imputations have been conducted to maximize its usefulness. This chapter gives a comprehensive account on the imputation procedures and rationales. To demonstrate effects of imputation, summary statistics before and after imputations are presented. The extent of imputation is demonstrated by the corresponding imputation rates. Finally, the resulting sample statistics of the empirical data for this study are presented and discussed.

5.1 IMMIGRATION DATA

This study aims to explore the significance of immigration selectivity on the young Asian and Hispanic immigrant wives' labor market performance. For this purpose, an ideal data should contain reasonably detailed information on marital history, fertility history, immigration history and work history of the immigrant wives' family with sufficient number of Asian and Hispanic sample size that permits meaningful statistical inferences. In practice, no data sources exist in the U.S. that meet such criteria. Most immigration data are cross-sectional with very little retrospective information and the scope of the data-collection is often limited to either the individual or the household.

Three major sources of immigration data are reviewed here: the U.S. census, the administrative records of the INS, and the Current Population Survey (CPS) supplements. The INS official records provide useful information on the immigration status of legal aliens; however the information was collected only at the time of entry or change of legal status on an individual basis. The census and the CPS supplements collect detailed household demographic information but very little immigration information.

This section describes the features of each data source, and provides a comparison on their pros and cons as a potential source of empirical test for the current research.

5.1.1 Census of the United States

The public-use micro samples (PUMS) of the decennial censuses provide snap-shot images of immigrants' economic activities as well as limited information on immigration status. The long-form questionnaire, the sources of PUMS data, asks a detailed array of questions on income and earnings of all adults in households, as well as moderate information on labor force participation and hours of work. In the 1990 census, the PUMS 5 percent sample contains over 12 million persons and over 5 million housing units (USDC 1992).

The advantages of using PUMS are threefold. First, it contains large sample sizes that permit meaningful comparison of sub-groups, such as individual origin countries or immigration cohorts. Second, being a household survey, it provides demographic and social-economic information on all the other household members of the immigrants at the time of survey. Third, the census gives a current count of the foreign-born population, which includes both legal and illegal migrants. This feature may be a plus for studies referring to all immigrants, i.e., legal or illegal. However, it may be considered a drawback if one's research interests require knowledge of immigrants' legal status.

In addition, the following features limit the application of census data on immigration research. First, it does not have information on immigrants' mode of entry or legal status. Second, the universe of immigrant population in the census is in fact the "survivors" of return immigration by the foreign-born. If the emigration of immigrants is not random with respect to the variable of interest, the census will be a biased representation of the original immigrants. In other words, if those who immigrated while single faring poorly in the U.S. are more likely to emigrate and do so more quickly than similarly unsuccessful married counterparts, the estimation of the effects of marital status at migration on immigrant wives' labor supply will be biased. Third, it contains no information on family members who are not living together with the respondents. This feature poses serious constraints on the ability of modelling the migration decision as a family/household decision. Fourth, the timing of immigration question is ambiguous in that it leaves immigrants to decide on the starting point of their "permanent stay." In answering the question "when did you come to the U.S. to stay?" people may give the year of first entry or the year of gaining legal status (Jasso and Rosenzweig 1990a).

To summarize, the Census contains the largest sample of immigrants in the U.S. and thus constitutes the most popular source for evaluating the immigrants' adaptation experiences by subgroups. Nonetheless, the 1990 census did not collect the immigrants' marital history information and thus unable to capture the selectivity effects of the most recent immigration cohorts. Hence, this study turns to other potential sources of immigration data.

5.1.2 Administrative Records of INS

The second source of immigration data is the administrative records of the Immigration and Naturalization Service. In particular, INS has published the public-use tapes containing annual immigrant records since 1972 (Houstoun et al. 1984). This data source records legal immigrants' class of admission, port of entry, and basic demographic data for each entry cohort. However, four drawbacks limit its use. First, no follow-up information is provided. Hence, characteristics of the immigrants at the time of immigration can't be matched with their subsequent adaptation experiences. Second, the information is reported on an individual basis, and the role of a spouse or other family members can not be evaluated by this type of data. Third, this data set includes only legal immigrants, not those entering without proper documents. Fourth, since the main focus of these records is on immigration data, very limited demographic items are obtained. Occupation is the only information related to labor market characteristics.

The INS occasionally gathered immigration data for certain purposes or under special request. For instance, the Immigrant Cohort of 1971 records obtained the naturalization experiences of the 1971 cohort of legal immigrants who subsequently naturalize (Jasso and Rosenzweig 1982). The cohort data provide an excellent opportunity for disentangling the age, cohort and assimilation effects on the socioeconomic progresses of a specific group of immigrants. Nonetheless, it also suffers from an individual based design, and lacks information on earnings, education, and family and household structure (Jasso and Rosenzweig 1990a).

In summary, the INS records provide invaluable information on legal immigrants' status at migration. Nonetheless, information regarding their family/household composition and their subsequent economic performance is virtually nonexistent. Therefore, this source of data is not suitable for the purpose of evaluating immigrants' adaptation experiences.

5.1.3 Current Population Survey Supplements

The Current Population Survey (CPS) is a large-scale household survey that collects current labor force information on the noninstitutional population in the U.S. each month. In the 1980s, each CPS sample consist of approximately 71,000 housing units or other living quarter; 57,000 of them, containing about 114,500 adults, are interviewed (USDC 1993). Designed to supplement labor force information between the decennial census years, the basic CPS contains a detailed array of questions related to labor market activities surveyed on a monthly basis. In addition, the March survey collects detailed demographic information, as well as income and labor force experiences referring to the year before the survey. For each month except March, the CPS has a set of supplemental question addressing specific issues such as fertility, marital history, school enrollment, immigration, child care, displaced workers, etc. Certain topics are collected biennially or intermittently. Immigration data have been collected five times in the past 10 years, along with marital history and fertility data. The 1983 April, the 1986 June, the 1988 June, the 1989 November, and the 1991 June supplements are the five CPS supplements that collected immigration data since 1980.

The five CPS supplements have a rich collection of demographic and economic data on immigrants which are not available in any other large nationally-representative data set. Its sample rotation scheme, to be described in the next section, provides opportunities to match up background information over supplements and time-varying information over time. Moreover, its specialization in labor force information makes it a better sources to investigate issues related to labor supply than other surveys. The questionnaire was designed to define each labor force category through a series of questions. For every civilian adult, detailed job-search activities were inquired regardless of their labor force status. However, due to its small sample size as compared with the Census, the ability to examine underlying forces by subgroups is seriously hindered. A second constraint of the CPS supplements for this study is that no income information is available except a categorical family income variable.

Other potential sources of data, such as the Survey of Income and Program Participation (SIPP) or Panel Study of Income Dynamics (PSID), or National Longitudinal Study (NLS) all suffer from relatively small sample sizes, and in most cases, immigrants can't be identified at all. Furthermore, these sources do not contain immigrants entering the U.S. in the late 1980s or early 1990s.

The review of sources of immigration data show a lack of combined information between immigration history and immigrants' socioeconomic achievements in the U.S. for the purpose of evaluating immigration policy. The crucial information required in this study includes marital status at migration, fertility information, immigration history of other immediate relatives, and a considerable amount of information on labor force participation and earnings. This study uses the June 1986, 1988 and 1991, and November 1989 CPS supplements as the major sources of data. The April 1983 supplement is excluded due to the fact that marital history information is available only for less than 50 percent of the sample.

In fact, each CPS supplements contain incomplete marital history, hours of work and earnings information. The sample selection procedure involves matching individual over CPS supplements to draw important information from other survey month or year by utilizing its sample rotation scheme. The following section describes the rotation scheme operated by the CPS, and the methods by which CPS immigration supplements and relevant information are put together for this study.

5.2 SAMPLE SELECTION

Although all the five CPS supplements collected immigration data, the availability of critical information, such as fertility, marital history, and earnings varies depending on the year and month of collection. Nonetheless, the "4-8-4" rotation scheme of the CPS provides opportunities of recovering a substantial amount of information. Specifically, the CPS sample is divided into 8 rotation groups, where the household is the unit of rotation. Each new rotation group was entered the sample for four consecutive months, excluded for eight months, returned for another four months, and then was retired from the CPS sample (USDC 1978).

Each month, there are two out-going rotation groups, one of which has finished its first-run interview and leaves for 8 months, the other leaving the sample permanently. To replace the departing-rotation groups, two rotation groups enter the sample, one of which will be interviewed for the first time, the other starting its second-run interview. Each month, 75 percent of the households in the sample had been interviewed last month, and 75 percent of the households in the sample will be interviewed next month. Similarly, each month, 50 percent of the households had been interviewed exactly one year before, and the other 50 percent of the households will be interviewed the same month in the following year. As a rule of thumb, there is a 75 percent month-to-month overlapping, a 50 percent overlapping every other month, a 25 percent overlapping every two month, and a 50 percent year-to-year overlapping.

To make the best use of the rotation scheme, information is pulled from months with overlapping rotation groups. Approximately, one half of the April 1983 CPS can be matched with the June sample of the same year to obtain age at first marriage, fertility and birth expectation information. One half of the June 1986 CPS sample can be matched with the June 1985 CPS to obtain marital history data. Similarly, one half of the June 1991 sample can be matched with the 1990 June sample and the other one half with the June 1992 sample to obtain marriage and fertility history data. The June 1985 and 1990 CPS supplements collected detailed information on marital history with a wider coverage than the fertility supplement[1]. Due to a major change in the CPS sampling frame from 1970 to 1980, it is virtually impossible to do any matching between the June 1985 and the June 1986 samples for the public-use files (USDL 1988).

The CPS non-March surveys inquire about labor force information referring to the work activities last week. Among those wage and salaried workers in the reference week, only the out-going rotation groups are asked about their usual weekly earnings and hourly wage, if paid by the hour. It was so designed to avoid possible negative effects on the future cooperation of the households (Donovan and Norwood 1982). Due to the highly sensitive nature of the questions, if asked, these questions may jeopardize the responses of other labor force questions. The sample rotation scheme ensures that over a four month period, the whole sample will have been asked the usual earnings and hours of work questions. This will still enable the Bureau of Labor Statistics to compile quarterly earnings information in a timely fashion. Theoretically, the other 75 percent of each non-March sample may be matched with the samples of the following three consecutive months to obtain earnings and hours of work information for individuals[2].

Table 5.2.1 demonstrates the potential matching of the CPS supplements for the purpose of this study and information gained through the matches.

Based on this analysis of data, this study utilizes a merged file from the 1986 June supplement, the 1988 June supplement, the 1989 November supplement, and the 1991 June supplement[3]. Each participating sample is viewed as being drawn from the super-universe[4]. The merged data set is then treated as a repeated cross-sectional design, and all the statistics reported in the following are weighted up to represent the respective population at a given point in time. Only young Asian and Hispanic immigrant wives aged 18-44 are included in each sample, for the marital history and fertility questions were only asked of women aged 18-44. The age limitation in the data essentially focuses the study on the selectivity and labor market experiences of young Asian and Hispanic immigrant wives in their reproductive years.

5.3 IMPUTATIONS AND CLEANING

By recovering the missing information based on the observed data or external sources of information, imputation procedures try to make the best use of the available data. There are three types of missing values that need to be imputed in this study. First, respondents sometimes fail to complete the entire questionnaire. In the CPS, variables such as earnings,

Table 5.2.1 Variables of Interests and Sources of Matching

	age at first marriage	earnings and hours of work	immediate relatives
April 1983	Not collected this month. 50% of the sample may be matched with June 1983 sample.	Collected for 25% of the sample Will match the other 75% with - May 1983 (25%) - June 1983 (25%) - July 1983 (25%)	Not collected this month. No matching is possible.
June 1986	Collected for women aged 18-44.	Collected for 25% of the sample Will match the other 75% with - July 1986 (25%) - August 1986 (25%) - September 1986 (25%)	Not collected this month. No matching is possible.
June 1988	Collected for women aged 18-44	Collected for 25% of the sample Will match the other 75% with - July 1988 (25%) - August 1988 (25%) - September 1988 (25%)	Not collected this month. No matching is possible.
November 1989	Not collected this month. No matching is possible.	Collected for 25% of the sample. Will match the other 75% with - December 1989 (25%) - January 1990 (25%) - February 1990 (25%)	Collected for all adults.
June 1991	Not collected this month. 100% match with - June 1990 (50%) - June 1992 (50%)	Collected on 25% of the sample. Will match the other 75% with - July 1991 (25%) - August 1991 (25%) - September (25%)	Collected for all adults.

Note: Immediate relatives refer to parents, siblings and children.

hours of work and age at first marriage are imputed by the Census Bureau, while most of the other missing variables are left unallocated (USDC 1993). Second, the matching procedures documented in previous section seek to recover information which is not asked in the particular immigration supplement. Meanwhile, the procedures also create non-match missing values due to the fact that some individuals drop out of the sample in subsequent surveys. Third, earnings and hours of work data are only obtained for wage and salaried workers. Those who are self-employed or unemployed thus have missing earnings and hours of work information.

This section gives a brief account of the reason why imputations were needed, the principles guiding the choice of imputation techniques and describes procedures undertaken to clean the data.

5.3.1 Methods of Imputation

In the presence of missing survey data, assumptions are always needed in utilizing the data no matter what procedure is adopted (Kalton 1983). The decision to throw out the observations containing missing items has an implicit assumption that those observations with missing data have the same variable distribution as those without missing data. Every imputation procedure also requires assumptions. However, they attempt to do so by utilizing the available information from the respondents. It provides the means to quantify the losses and gains in biases and efficiency associated with each alternative procedures. One of the major problems with imputation is that it treats the pseudo data as if they were the actual data (Rubin 1987). The direct application of the imputed values tend to underestimate the standard errors of the imputed variables, since it fails to take into account the variability due to unknown missing values[5].

The major methods of imputation include non-response adjustment (weights), mean value imputation, cold-deck and hot-deck imputation and model-based imputation (Kalton 1983; Johnson et al. 1989). Variations are found by the ways the class variables and choice of residuals are defined (Kalton and Kasprzyk 1986).

This study imputes its missing values through consistency edit, mean imputation within classes, the hot deck procedure and the regression imputation. The consistency edit uses other relevant information in the same data set. Through logical editing, some or all of the missing information may be recovered. The mean imputation within classes procedures first divides the total sample into classes (cells) according to a number of important covariates. It then assigns the mean values of the donors to each recipient in the same class. This procedure assumes a deterministic model, where the respondents and non-respondents are homogeneous within each cell. The hot deck procedures assign values from otherwise similar individuals from the observed sample. Cells of donors and cells of recipients are defined according to a few important covariates. A random procedure is then implemented to draw donors, and assign the donor's value to the recipient. This procedure relies on the assumption that data are randomly missing within each cell.

The advantage of a hot-deck imputation over the other methods are as follows (Kalton and Kasprzyk 1986; Johnson et al. 1989). First, the hot-deck procedure always gives feasible values since the imputed values are taken directly from the observed sample. Second, the distribution of the observed sample is likely to be preserved. Third, there is no need to specify a model to describe underlying behavior. However, the hot-deck procedure has limited capacities in multiple control of the correlation between covariates. As the number of control variables increases, the risk of having fewer donors than recipients in a particular cells increases. Furthermore, for the imputation of a continuous variable, the hot-deck method is limited in its ability to utilize the quantitative relationship between covariates.

The regression imputation is a model-based imputation. This procedure assumes an explicit relationship between the imputed variable and a set of important covariates. For each variable of interests, a regression model is estimated. Missing values are then replaced by the predicted values plus a normal random error term from the models. The advantage of adopting a regression strategy is twofold. First, it allows for multiple control by including as many variables on the right-hand side as possible. Thus, it is likely to preserve more correlations than the hot deck procedure. Second, it is appropriate for the imputation of continuous variables since the regression model explains the quantitative relationship between the dependent variable and the independent variables.

The above discussion illustrates the choices between various types of imputation methods. The strategies developed for the imputations for this study take into account the types of variables to be imputed, sources and the nature of missing, and the relevance of the variables in the empirical analysis. The missing data imputed in this study include: immigration information, family income, English-speaking abilities, earnings, hours of work, kin information and age at first marriage. The following sections describe the details of the imputation procedures.

5.3.2 Imputation of Immigration Data

This section describes imputation procedures undertaken to clean and impute the wife's country of birth, the wife's timing of immigration, the wife's citizenship status, the husband's country of birth, the husband's timing of immigration, the husband's citizenship status, and the parents' countries of birth. Similar hot deck procedures were applied to all four samples, i.e., June 1986, June 1988, and June 1991, as well as November 1989 supplements. Immigration information was cleaned for all Asian and Hispanic wives. In each step, small cells were collapsed to ensure that the number of donors exceed the number of recipients.

To preserve the relationship between the wife's own immigration information, as well as the relationship between the wife's immigration status, her husband's, and her parents' immigration status, data were imputed for four subsamples. The first set of imputation dealt with the missing immigration information of husband's and wife's for the subsample of young immigrant wives who reported valid countries of birth. The variables used to form the cells are the wife's country of birth, employment status and age, and her husband's nativity status.

The second set of imputation dealt with the husband's and the wife's immigration information for the subsample of wives reporting to be foreign-born, but failing to report their countries of birth. The variables used to form the cells are the wife's racial or ethnic origin, employment status and age, and her husband's nativity status.

The third set of imputation dealt with missing country of birth for wives who did not respond to this question, and their timing of immigration and citizenship status if foreign-born. The variables used to form the cells are the wife's racial or ethnic origin, employment status and age, and her husband's racial ethnic origin.

The fourth set of imputation dealt with the remaining missing immigration information of husbands and parents of native-born Asian and Hispanic wives. The variables used to form the cells are wife's racial or ethnic origin, employment status, education attainments and age, and her husband's racial or ethnic origin.

Table 5.3.1 summarizes imputation rates for the four samples. Tables 5.3.2 and 5.3.3 present the percentage distributions of the wife's timing of immigration, her country of birth, and the husband's timing of immigration.

Since this study is mainly concerned with the wife's behavior and its association with the behaviors of other family members, major efforts

Table 5.3.1 Number of Missing Observations in the Hot Deck Imputation of Immigration Information, Corresponding Imputation Rates in Parentheses

Year of sample	1986	1988	1989	1991
Number of Missing Observations and Rate of Imputation by Imputation Step				
total imputation	201 (7.8)	260 (11.7)	395 (16.3)	519 (19.9)
1st step imputation	94 (7.2)	96 (8.8)	189 (13.7)	207 (14.0)
2nd step imputation	20 (1.5)	10 (0.9)	14 (1.0)	14 (0.9)
3rd step imputation	64 (2.5)	110 (5.0)	133 (5.5)	231 (8.8)
4th step imputation	23 (1.9)	44 (4.2)	59 (6.4)	67 (7.0)
Number of Missing Observations and Rate of Imputation for Each Immigration Variable				
wife's timing of immigration	123 (4.8)	166 (7.5)	187 (7.7)	314 (12.0)
wife's citizenship status	89 (3.5)	136 (6.1)	161 (6.6)	291 (11.1)
wife's country of birth	84 (3.3)	120 (5.5)	147 (6.1)	245 (9.3)
husband's timing of immigration	115 (4.5)	150 (6.8)	170 (7.0)	291 (11.1)
husband's citizenship status	75 (2.9)	120 (5.4)	150 (6.2)	251 (9.6)
husband's country of birth	80 (3.0)	115 (5.2)	138 (5.7)	232 (8.9)
father's country of birth	100 (3.9)	151 (6.8)	163 (6.7)	271 (10.3)
mother's country of birth	99 (3.9)	156 (7.1)	156 (6.4)	270 (10.3)
wife's reported family income	13 (0.5)	25 (1.1)	194 (8.0)	163 (6.2)

Source: June 1986, 1988, and 1991, and November 1989 Current Population Survey Supplements.

Table 5.3.2 Percentage Distribution of the Wife's Timing of Immigration, Country of Birth, and the Husband's Timing of Immigration Pre- and Post-Imputation

Year	1986		1988		1989		1991	
imputation	pre	post	pre	post	pre	post	pre	post
Wife's Timing of Immigration								
US-born	48.1	47.0	48.9	47.2	40.0	38.1	38.5	36.9
< 1960	4.6	4.6	4.1	4.2	4.2	4.5	3.4	3.6
1960-64	4.1	4.4	4.0	4.3	3.8	3.8	2.9	3.1
1965-69	5.6	5.8	6.9	7.0	6.0	6.2	5.3	5.2
1970-74	9.3	9.7	8.1	8.4	8.8	8.9	7.6	7.9
1975-79	12.8	13.2	9.2	9.7	11.4	11.7	10.7	10.7
1980-81	6.4	6.4	7.0	7.3	6.7	7.1	7.3	7.7
1982-84	6.1	5.9	5.4	5.5	6.3	6.4	5.4	5.5
1985-86	3.0	3.0	3.7	3.6	5.3	5.6	5.4	5.5
1987-89			2.7	2.7	7.4	7.7	9.5	9.8
1990-91							3.9	4.1
Husband's Timing of Immigration								
US-born	52.5	52.0	55.5	54.3	46.2	44.6	43.7	42.8
1960	5.5	5.5	4.9	5.3	4.5	4.6	4.5	4.7
1960-64	3.7	3.8	3.0	3.2	3.6	3.5	2.8	2.8
1965-69	5.3	5.3	5.1	5.0	5.6	5.8	5.7	5.7
1970-74	9.2	9.5	7.4	7.7	7.9	8.3	6.8	7.1
1975-79	11.4	11.5	8.7	8.9	10.7	11.1	10.5	10.7
1980-81	5.4	5.4	6.3	6.5	7.0	7.5	8.1	8.1
1982-84	4.8	4.7	4.2	4.4	5.6	5.6	4.4	4.5
1985-86	2.2	2.2	2.8	2.8	3.7	3.8	4.4	4.6
1987-89			2.0	2.0	5.1	5.4	6.6	6.7
1990-91							2.3	2.2

Source: June 1986, 1988 and 1991, and November 1989 Current Population Survey Supplements.

Table 5.3.3 Percentage Distributions of the Wife's Timing of Immigration, Country of Birth, and the Husband's timing of Immigration Pre- and Post-Imputation

Year of sample	1986		1988		1989		1991	
pre/post imputation	pre	post	pre	post	pre	post	pre	post
US-born	47.3	47.1	47.8	47.2	39.3	38.1	37.4	37.0
China	4.9	4.8	4.3	4.4	5.7	5.7	5.8	5.9
Colombia	1.5	1.6	1.4	1.4	1.5	1.6	1.4	1.5
Cuba	4.4	4.4	4.9	4.7	4.1	4.2	4.3	4.0
Dominican Republic	1.3	1.2	1.4	1.4	1.3	1.4	1.6	1.6
El Salvador	1.5	1.5	1.4	1.4	1.5	1.6	2.8	2.9
India	2.9	3.0	3.5	3.5	2.9	3.1	3.7	3.6
Japan	2.1	2.1	2.3	2.5	2.5	2.6	2.3	2.1
Korea	3.3	3.4	3.3	3.4	3.7	3.6	4.1	4.1
Laos	1.3	1.2	1.0	0.9	0.7	0.7	0.9	0.9
Mexico	15.1	15.1	13.0	13.2	19.1	19.0	18.8	19.2
Philippines	4.3	4.2	5.8	6.1	4.9	5.2	5.3	5.4
Vietnam	2.6	2.7	2.2	2.3	2.2	2.4	2.2	2.2
all others	7.4	7.4	7.7	7.3	10.6	10.8	9.3	9.6

Source: June 1986, 1988, and 1991, and November 1989 Current Population Survey Supplements.

were made to preserve the correlations between the wife's and family members' information. Wherever applicable, the imputation was always carried out in a sequential fashion: impute the wife's missing values first, and then all the husband, children and other relatives information are imputed conditional on the wife's characteristics. The timing of immigration for children in the household were imputed by a simple hot deck procedure, which uses the wife's country of birth and her timing of immigration as class variables. Since the reporting status on children's citizenship, nativity status and timing of immigration information are highly correlated, these variables were imputed together. Overall, the imputation was done on 220 (21.7 percent out of non-US born children) children's records of the sample of Asian and Hispanic wives for the 1989 sample and 403 (31.6 percent) for the 1991 sample.

5.3.3 Imputation of Family Income and English-Speaking Ability

The family income variable in the CPS non-March supplements is a categorical variable. The imputations of missing family income for the 1989 and 1991 sample were incorporated in the imputation of immigration information, as described in the above section. The 1986 and 1988 missing family income were imputed by a simple hot deck procedure, using the wife's nativity status, her employment status, and age; the husband's employment status, his age; and the size of the household. The missing information in the 1989 and 1991 samples appeared to be highly correlated with the missing immigration information. The hot deck procedure incorporating family income in the immigration imputation was done to help preserve the correlation between these two sources of information.

The measurement of wife's English-speaking ability in the 1989 sample was imputed through a hot deck procedure that includes the wife's country of birth, her timing of immigration, employment status, and age to define cells. The imputation of the husband's English-speaking ability used the husband's country of birth, his timing of immigration, employment status, age, and the imputed wife's English-speaking ability. This step of imputation was only carried out on immigrant wives. The percentage distribution before and after the imputation for these two variables are summarized in Table 5.3.4.

Table 5.3.4 Number of Missing Observations in the Hot-Deck Imputation of the Wife's and the Husband's English-Speaking Abilities, Percentage Distribution in Parentheses

Imputation Status	Before	After
Wife's English-Speaking Ability		
speak English only	126 (8.4)	131 (8.7)
speak English very well	268 (17.8)	288 (19.2)
speak English well	327 (21.8)	354 (23.6)
speak little English	435 (29.2)	475 (31.6)
no English at all	237 (15.8)	252 (16.8)
Number Imputed=109, Imputation Rate=7.3%		
Husband's English-Speaking Ability		
speak only English	66 (4.9)	78 (5.8)
speak English very well	305 (22.6)	322 (23.9)
speak English well	362 (26.8)	386 (28.6)
speak little English	399 (29.6)	438 (32.5)
no English at all	118 (8.7)	124 (9.2)
Number Imputed=99, Imputation Rate=7.3%		

Source: November 1989 Current Population Survey Supplement.

5.3.4 Imputation of Earnings and Hours of Work for Wage and Salaried Workers

This section describes the imputation of the following labor force data: family usual weekly earnings, wife's usual weekly earnings, her usual hourly earnings, and usual hours of work, and husband's usual weekly earnings, his usual hourly earnings, and usual hours of work. As described previously, these variables were asked only to salaried and wage workers who are either in the private sector or the government, and are in the out-rotation groups. Since the Bureau of Labor Statistics have cleaned these items in the public-use files, this imputation is conducted on those who should have a valid entry but actually don't, because of non-match. The rate of matched records are as follow: 67.0 percent for the 1986 sample, 68.7 percent for 1988 sample, 67.7 percent for 1989 sample, and 70.0 percent for 1991 sample. The little discrepancies of these actual matching rates from the theoretical 75 percent match shows an encouraging sign for matching observations over consecutive months for the CPS sample.

Topcoding. The CPS topcoded the weekly earnings information based on a list of hourly wage and usual hours of work, so that their products would not exceed an annualized wage of $100,000, or $1923 per week consistently throughout the four survey years. In addition, the usual hours of work variable was topcoded at 99. No attempt was taken to adjust for the potential bias created by topcoding. However, since the 1986 and 1988 samples in fact also topcoded the weekly earnings at $999, this created inconsistencies when comparing across the four samples. The higher earnings groups (over $999/week) from the 1989 and 1991 samples formed the pool of donors. The $999 code in the 1986 and 1988 samples were replaced by the values[6] of randomly chosen donors given the same number of usual hours of work. This hot deck procedure attempted to map the upper tail distribution from the 1989 and 1991 samples to the 1986 and 1988 samples. There were 83 high-earnings wives or husbands in 1986, 105 in 1988, 108 in 1989 and 203 in 1991.

Earnings and Hours of Work. The imputations of earnings and hours of work were carried out through regression imputations. The imputation was basically carried out sequentially: thus, first family weekly earnings, next husband's weekly earnings, next husband's hourly earnings, next wife's weekly earnings, and finally wife's hourly earnings. The imputed information from the preceding regression was entered in the current regression. The number of usual work hours for either husband or wife was obtained through dividing weekly earnings by hourly earnings respectively. Furthermore, if there were only two earners in the household, then the wife's weekly earnings was automatically entered as the residual of family weekly earnings minus husband's weekly earnings. Tables 5.3.5, 5.3.6, 5.3.7 and 5.3.8 summarize means, minimums and maximums of the imputed variables before and after the imputation for the 1986, 1988, 1989 and 1991 samples respectively. The variables included in the regressions, their coefficient estimates and R^2 statistics for the regressions are presented in appendix A.

5.3.5 Imputation of Earnings and Hours of Work for the Self-Employed and the Unemployed

As described earlier, the CPS collects usual earnings and hours of work information of wage and salaried workers in the reference week. Self-employed and unemployed people are ineligible for these questions as it is difficult to access their wage rate and work schedule. The CPS defines a self-employed worker as someone who works either in his/her own incorporated business or profession, or in his/her own unincorporated business or profession or on his/her own farm (USDC 1984). This definition does not include people working in a family enterprise without pay, since this group is considered "not working." An unemployed worker can be of any the following three category. (1) Someone who was not working and did not have a job during the reference week, and has made explicit efforts looking for a job during the last four weeks. (2) Someone who has been temporarily laid off from a job and is waiting to be recalled. (3) Someone who was waiting to report to a new job in 30 days.

Since both self-employed and the unemployed workers are likely to have very distinct earnings capacities and work schedules, dropping them out of the sample may create serious biases. In particular, the unemployed people may be those who have lower wage offers and fewer hours of work if offered a job, as compared to the wage and salaried workers. Hence, using the wage and salaried worker sample to impute for these two groups would be inappropriate.

This study utilizes information from the corresponding subsamples of self-employed and unemployed people from the CPS March 1987 supplement, March 1989, March 1990 and March 1992[7] to impute earnings and hours of work information for the immigrant samples. The relevant CPS March work experience supplement questions for the imputation are number of hours worked, number of weeks worked during last year at all jobs, and the type of workers for the longest job worked last

Table 5.3.5 Weighted Mean Characteristics Before and After Imputation and Imputation Rates, 1986

Variable	Imputation Rate	Mean	Minimum	Maximum
Before imputation				
family weekly earnings		578.0	50.0	2523.0
wife weekly earnings		282.9	40.0	1223.0
husband weekly earnings		405.0	40.0	1923.0
wife hourly earnings		7.3	2.0	60.0
husband hourly earnings		9.7	1.8	45.7
wife usual hours of work		38.0	5.0	72.0
husband usual hours of work		41.1	10.0	99.0
After imputation				
family weekly earnings	13.4	586.0	50.0	2523.0
wife weekly earnings	8.8	286.9	40.0	1585.9
husband weekly earnings	12.4	402.6	40.0	1923.0
wife hourly earnings	8.8	7.3	2.0	60.0
husband hourly earnings	12.4	9.6	1.8	45.0
wife usual hours of work	8.8	38.7	4.0	99.0
husband usual hours of work	12.4	41.4	7.0	99.0

Source: June, July, August, and September 1986 Current Population Survey Supplements.

Table 5.3.6 Weighted Mean Characteristics Before and After Imputation, 1988

Variable	Imputation Rate	Mean	Minimum	Maximum
Before imputation				
family weekly earnings		625.7	30.0	2824.0
wife weekly earnings		291.7	34.0	1500.0
husband weekly earnings		445.1	30.0	1923.0
wife hourly earnings		7.8	2.0	42.8
husband hourly earnings		10.6	1.0	48.0
wife usual hours of work		36.7	10.0	60.0
husband usual hours of work		41.7	10.0	99.0
After imputation				
family weekly earnings	11.9	625.5	30.0	2824.0
wife weekly earnings	8.7	291.7	34.0	1500.0
husband weekly earnings	9.9	436.2	30.0	1923.0
wife hourly earnings	8.7	7.8	2.0	42.8
husband hourly earnings	9.9	10.4	1.0	48.0
wife usual hours of work	8.7	36.7	10.0	60.0
husband usual hours of work	9.9	41.8	10.0	99.0

Source: June, July, August, and September 1988 Current Population Survey Supplements.

Table 5.3.7 Weighted Mean Characteristics Before and After Imputation, 1989

Variable	Imputation Rate	Mean	Minimum	Maximum
Before imputation				
family weekly earnings		694.9	14.0	3500.0
wife weekly earnings		319.5	20.0	1500.0
husband weekly earnings		461.4	14.0	1923.0
wife hourly earnings		8.3	1.7	37.5
husband hourly earnings		10.9	1.0	64.1
wife usual hours of work		37.1	4.0	99.0
husband usual hours of work		41.4	4.0	98.0
After imputation				
family weekly earnings	10.3	706.1	18.0	3500.0
wife weekly earnings	7.4	324.6	20.0	1500.0
husband weekly earnings	9.3	461.6	14.0	1923.0
wife hourly earnings	7.4	8.2	1.7	37.5
husband hourly earnings	9.3	10.8	1.0	64.1
wife usual hours of work	7.4	38.4	3.0	99.0
husband usual hours of work	9.3	41.9	4.0	98.0

Source: November and December 1989, and January and February 1990 Current Population Survey Supplements.

Table 5.3.8 Weighted Mean Characteristics Before and After Imputation, 1991

Variable	Imputation Rate	Mean	Minimum	Maximum
Before imputation				
family weekly earnings		703.1	40.0	3600.0
wife weekly earnings		325.0	30.0	1923.0
husband weekly earnings		483.1	20.0	1923.0
wife hourly earnings		8.6	1.6	50.0
husband hourly earnings		11.4	1.6	54.9
wife usual hours of work		37.0	5.0	70.0
husband usual hours of work		41.2	10.0	99.0
After imputation				
family weekly earnings	10.2	709.4	40.0	3600.0
wife weekly earnings	4.7	327.1	30.0	1923.0
husband weekly earnings	9.5	482.0	20.0	1923.0
wife hourly earnings	4.7	8.5	1.8	50.0
husband hourly earnings	9.5	11.2	1.6	54.9
wife usual hours of work	4.7	37.8	4.0	99.0
husband usual hours of work	9.5	41.8	10.0	99.0

Source: June, July, August, and September 1991 Current Population Survey Supplements.

year. In addition, the imputation procedures utilizes the earnings information[8] from the March income supplement, which collected detailed sources of annual income of the year prior to the survey. A weekly earnings measure was obtained through dividing the total yearly earnings by the number of weeks worked last year. It was expected that this measure will approximate the usual hourly earnings as defined in the earnings and hours of work questions in the non-March supplements.

As a guideline for the imputation, it was assumed that the underlying earnings capacity and labor supply of an individual is unobserved randomly in each time period. The imputation sought to use the observed information assuming that their unobserved earnings capacities and hours of work will be realized during at least one of the time periods specified. For those self-employed and unemployed who can be matched with the following three months and who are eligible to answer the earnings questions, i.e., they have changed to another class of worker within four months, their corresponding answers in other months are assigned. The usual weekly earnings and hours of work information was assigned.

The imputation for both self-employed and unemployed workers employs the means imputation within classes method. For the self-employed persons, the mean log weekly earnings were obtained within each class defined by sex and race/Hispanic origin among the pool of married couples. A normal random error term was added to the mean log earnings to spread out the distribution. The same error term was applied to the hours of work imputation, assuming that earnings and hours of work are positively correlated. The usual hours of work for the self-employed workers are taken directly from the answer to the monthly labor force questions. Since almost all the self-employed people did work during the reference week, their hours worked during the last week was assigned as their usual hours of work. Note that there is a slight difference between the usual number of hours worked, and the number of hours worked during the last week. The former asks the total number of hours worked last week at all jobs, while the latter asks the usual, as defined by the respondents, number of hours worked per week at the primary job held last week.

For the unemployed workers, those who reported usual weekly earnings and hours of work in the following three months were assigned the values reported in the observed month. To impute the remaining missing earnings and hours of work information for unemployed workers, the donors for the class mean imputation include married couples who reported unemployed during the reference week, and reported non-zero total yearly earnings and number of weeks worked last year in the March CPS. Since this group of workers did not report any work hours even for the reference week in the immigration supplements, both earnings and hours of work information were imputed. The mean log weekly earnings, as so calculated for the self-employed workers, and weekly hours of work plus random error terms were assigned to the unemployed workers in the immigration supplements from the corresponding classes, defined by race and sex.

The imputation was carried out onto the sample of Asian and Hispanic immigrant women aged 18 to 44 and their husbands from the June 1986, June 1988, November 1989 and June 1991 supplements. Overall, there are 12 self-employed wives and 33 self-employed husbands in 1986, 19 wives and 24 husbands in 1988, 22 wives and 48 husbands in 1989, and 19 wives and 38 husbands in 1991 assigned earnings values through the classes mean imputation. For the self-employed imputation, the corresponding number of donors from the March CPS are 155 wives and 4322[9] husbands in 1987, 148 wives and 4017 husbands in 1989, 190 wives and 4321 husbands in 1990, and 191 wives and 4130 husbands in 1992. There are 24 unemployed wives and 17 unemployed husbands in 1986, 13 wives and 13 husbands in 1988, 25 wives and 17 husbands in 1989, and 35 wives and 15 husbands in 1991 who receive imputed earnings and hours of work through the classes mean procedure. The corresponding number of self-employed donors from the March CPS are 93 wives and 1080 husbands in 1987, 69 wives and 714 husbands in 1989, 95 wives and 827 husbands in 1990, and 119 wives and 1227 husbands in 1992.

To summarize, the March CPS provides the observation on earnings and hours of work over a one year period, while the non-March supplements provide observation over a week. The imputation of earnings and hours of work utilizes the realized information through these two sources of the same kind of workers. Nonetheless, if those unemployed workers with unobserved earnings and hours of work who are persistently out of work over the one-year reference period are also more likely to be low-wage workers and work for fewer hours if offered a job, this imputation procedure will still be biased upward for unemployed workers.

5.3.6 Imputation of Kin Information

This section describes the imputation of three types of kin information: (1) how many of immediate relatives an immigrant wife has;

(2) whether these relatives are currently living in the U.S.; and (3) how many immediate relatives are living in the household. The imputation to be described in this section was applied to the 1989 and 1991 samples, since the information was only collected in these two years.

Consistency Check. The 1989 November and 1991 June CPS supplements included a block of questions on the number and residence of immediate relatives to evaluate the current state and the potential of family immigration to the U.S. Each adult respondent was asked to identify (1) if he/she has any living immediate relative[10], and if yes, how many for each type of relative; (2) if any of these relatives are currently living outside U.S., and if yes, how many for each type of relative; and (3) if any of these relatives have ever been in the U.S., and if yes, how many for each type of relative. This research utilized only the first two sets of information. Assuming respondent will answer to all four types of relatives, if answer at all, zero value was assign to any non-response in any category of relatives[11]. However, for those who indicated having a particular type of relative, the missing value was not replaced, and remained to be imputed. After the editing check, the number of missing values for each variables of interests are listed in Table 5.3.9.

Number of Relatives and Relatives Outside U.S.. The number of immediate relatives and relatives living outside U.S. was imputed based on a hot deck procedure. First, the number of living immediate relatives was imputed using the wife's country of birth, her timing of immigration, age, and employment status. Second, the number of relatives living outside U.S. was imputed based on the number of living relatives. Table 5.3.10 summarizes the percentage distribution of the imputed kin information before and after the imputation.

Number of Relatives in the Household. The presence of parents, in-laws and children in the household was identified through the wife's parent's code, the husband's parent code and the children's parents code respectively. However, the identification of brothers or sisters in the household were done by checking a relationship code (individual respondent's relation to the householder) and the number of kin reported in the immigration questions. A pool of potential brothers and sisters were obtained through the relationship code. This pool of candidates was then screened through checking the consistency of the kin information reported between the respondent and the candidates. Those who met these two criteria were than assigned as a brother or a sister to the respondent. This procedure identified 204 siblings and siblings-in-law for 148 Asian and

Table 5.3.9 Summary of the Number of Missing Values on Kin Information, Imputation Rates in Parentheses

Year of sample	1989	1991
Total Missing Imputed	388 (16.0)	369 (14.1)
Number of Wife's Living Relatives		
parents	69 (2.8)	78 (3.0)
brothers	63 (2.8)	81 (3.0)
sisters	64 (2.6)	76 (2.9)
children	60 (2.5)	72 (2.8)
Number of Wife's Relatives Living Outside U.S.		
parents	257 (10.6)	96 (3.7)
brothers	255 (10.5)	94 (3.6)
sisters	255 (10.5)	87 (3.3)
children	260 (10.7)	286 (10.9)
Number of Husband's Living Relatives		
parents-in-law	89 (3.7)	138 (5.3)
brothers-in-law	97 (4.0)	144 (5.5)
sisters-in-law	93 (3.8)	143 (5.5)
husband's children	91 (3.8)	138 (5.3)
Number of Husband's Relatives Living Outside U.S.		
parents-in-law	237 (9.8)	158 (6.0)
brothers-in-law	238 (9.8)	154 (5.9)
sisters-in-law	236 (9.7)	152 (5.8)
husband's children	240 (9.9)	261 (10.0)

Source: November 1989 and June 1991 Current Population Survey Supplements.

Table 5.3.10 Percentage Distributions of Kin Information Before and After Imputation.

Year	1989				1991			
connection	wife's		husband's		wife's		husband's	
imputation	pre	post	pre	post	pre	post	pre	post
Number of Living Relatives								
no parent	29.2	29.3	30.9	30.9	30.1	30.2	32.7	32.8
1 parent	27.1	27.1	28.1	28.2	24.1	24.2	26.3	26.2
2 parents	43.7	43.6	41.1	40.8	45.8	45.6	41.1	41.0
no brother	23.4	23.1	22.5	22.4	24.2	23.9	23.2	23.1
1 brother	23.5	23.5	23.8	23.9	22.7	22.6	22.9	23.0
2 brothers	19.7	19.8	19.1	19.2	20.3	20.3	20.6	20.8
3 brothers	15.1	15.3	13.6	13.4	13.4	13.5	12.4	12.2
4+ brothers	18.3	18.4	21.0	21.1	19.5	19.6	20.9	20.8
no sister	24.1	23.8	22.8	23.0	24.8	24.6	24.8	24.6
1 sister	22.5	22.4	23.2	23.3	22.4	22.2	23.0	22.9
2 sisters	18.6	18.9	20.0	20.0	18.8	19.0	21.4	21.7
3 sisters	12.3	12.3	15.0	14.9	13.8	13.8	12.1	12.2
4+ sisters	22.4	22.6	19.0	18.8	20.2	20.4	18.6	18.5
Number of Relatives Currently Living Outside U.S.								
no parent	72.4	73.4	75.3	76.0	72.9	72.9	77.3	77.1
1 parent	11.1	11.1	10.8	10.6	10.4	10.3	9.9	9.9
2 parents	16.5	15.5	13.9	13.5	16.8	16.8	12.8	13.0
no brother	70.5	71.3	72.6	72.9	69.0	68.6	72.0	71.8
1 brother	10.2	9.9	10.6	10.6	10.9	11.2	10.1	10.2
2 brothers	7.7	7.4	7.0	6.7	8.4	8.4	7.1	7.2
3 brothers	5.8	5.8	4.7	4.7	5.0	5.0	4.7	4.6
4+ brothers	5.8	5.6	5.2	5.1	6.7	6.8	6.0	6.1
no sister	69.2	69.7	71.6	72.0	68.7	68.3	71.6	71.2
1 sister	11.0	10.6	10.8	10.8	11.9	11.9	10.5	10.6
2 sisters	8.2	8.0	7.1	7.0	7.6	7.9	7.1	7.3
3 sisters	4.9	4.9	5.2	5.0	5.3	5.2	4.8	5.0
4+ sisters	6.8	6.7	5.3	5.2	6.5	6.7	5.8	5.9

Source: November 1989 and June 1991 Current Population Survey Supplements.

Hispanic wives in 1991, and 191 siblings and siblings-in-law for 139 wives in 1989.

5.3.7 Imputation of Age at First Marriage

This section describes the imputation procedures for the age at first marriage information in the June 1991 sample. This information was not asked for in 1991, but obtained through matching the information from the June 1990 and 1992 supplements since the marital history and fertility information questions were asked to females age 15-44 in 1990 and 1992. The 1990/91 matched 63.5 percent of the respondents who were in the 1991 sample for the second round of the rotation while the 1991/92 matched 65.6 percent of the respondents who were in the 1991 sample for the first round of the rotation. The total matching rate is approximately 64.6 percent.[12]

The attrition of the sample over time is most likely to be highly correlated with the event of marital disruption. The unmatched sample may not be a random sample with respect to age at first marriage, in which case the imputation using the matched sample as donors would not be appropriate. However, it is plausible to assume that the underlying attrition mechanisms were constant over the three years. To put it differently, respondents who were in the 1991 sample for the first run, and could not be matched with the 1992 sample were expected to resemble people who were in the 1990 sample for the first run, and could not be matched with the 1991 sample. Similarly, respondents who were in the 1991 sample for the second run, and could not be matched with the 1990 sample were expected to resemble people who were in the 1992 sample for the second run, and could not be matched with the 1991 sample.

Given this assumption, the imputation of the non-matched "age at first marriage" information was carried out through regression imputations. A regression on age at first marriage[13] was estimated using the ordinary least squares (OLS) technique for young Asian and Hispanic wives who were in 1990 sample for the first run and not matched with the 1991 sample. A predicted value of the age at first marriage was then assigned to a comparable 1991/92 non-matched wife in the 1991 sample for the first run. An OLS regression was estimated on young Asian and Hispanic wives who were in the 1992 sample for the second run and not matched with the 1991 sample. A predicted value of the age at first marriage was then assigned to a comparable 1991/92 non-matched wife in the 1991 sample for the second run. Overall, 618 (35.4 percent) young

Asian and Hispanic wives in 1991 were given imputed age at first marriage information as a result of this procedure. The variables included in the regressions, their estimated coefficients, and R^2 statistics for the regressions are included in appendix A. The weighted mean age at first marriage is 22.5 (270. 1 months) before imputation, and 22.4 (269.3 months) after imputation.

Section Discussion. This section describes the imputation procedures undertaken in this study. Less than 20 percent cases were imputed for most variables. In particular, the imputation rates of dependent variables for this study, earnings and hours of work, are below 10 percent in all four samples. Nonetheless, over 30 percent of the 1991 sample are imputed for the age at first marriage variable, which is the crucial information in the measurement of the marital status at migration variable for the 1991 sample. The high imputation rate may reduce the precision of the estimate on the selectivity variables.

The use of pseudo data in the analysis relies on the assumption that the respondents are similar to the non-respondents in the uncontrolled dimensions. However, since the survey observations often drop out of the sample for reasons such as economic hardship, mobility, or changes in life-cycle status, respondents and non-respondents are very likely to be systematically different from each other. The strategy developed to impute age at first marriage incorporated the fact that women dropping out of sample in one year may be a result of changes in marital status. Evidence based on the June 1990, 1991 and 1992 CPS supplements suggests that those non-matched young wives over one year tend to be younger and have shorter marriage duration. The imputation of immigration information, family income, English-speaking abilities, and kin information explicitly treat respondents and non-respondents as the same. Estimates may be biased if certain immigrants are more likely to refuse to participate in the survey. In particular, new immigrants may be less likely to participate since they may be uncomfortable and unfamiliar with the survey. The high non-response rates for the immigration status of children and information on the residence of immediate relatives may result on high variability in the estimates of kin effects.

The imputation on earnings and hours of work overlook the fact that those non-matched may be at both extremes of the earnings distribution since a lot fewer respondents drop out over one to three month period than those over one year. The imputation of earnings and hours of work for self-employed and unemployed utilizes information based on similar self-employed and unemployed people obtained from the March

CPS. Potential biases may occur due to the fact that March CPS measures earnings on an annual basis, while the non-March supplement employs a usual weekly earnings/hours concept. Furthermore, since the March CPS do not collect immigration information, failure to control for immigration status in the imputation may distort the correlation between immigration status, earnings and hours of work for these two groups of people.

This section describes and summarizes the imputation procedures undertaken for the CPS supplements under study. The imputation procedures enhance the usefulness of the data, although the interpretation of the data requires cautions in case non-responses are not missing randomly with respect to the variables of interests. The next section presents the sample statistics.

5.4 DESCRIPTIVE STATISTICS OF THE SAMPLE

This section describes the sample statistics pertaining to the young Asian and Hispanics wives in the U.S. Table 5.4.0 summarizes the weighted percentage of young Asian and Hispanic immigrant wives in the labor force, their hourly earnings, weekly earnings and hours of work by their marital status at migration and migration patterns. Young immigrant wives migrating while single appear to work fewer hours and earn higher hours earnings than any other groups. Young immigrant wives who migrated before their husbands are most likely to be in the labor force and also enjoy relatively high hourly earnings. Those migrating following their husbands are least likely to be in the labor force. Nonetheless, among those in the labor force, they work more hours than any other group, and this compensates for their relative low hourly earning capacities. These descriptive statistics show evidence of differential labor market performances by the young immigrant wives' marital status at migration and their migration patterns.

As the regression analyses in this study were conducted separately by racial/ethnic origin and timing of immigration, the means of the regression variables provides opportunities to compare the demographic characteristics along these dimensions. Tables 5.4.1 to 5.4.15 summarize the young immigrant wives' labor market and demographic characteristics by the year of survey, country-of-origin, region-of-origin and timing of immigration for both the pooled whole sample[14] and the pooled employed sample. Since the general patterns and trends are similar between the pooled whole sample and the pooled employed sample, the following discussion is mainly directed to the pooled whole sample unless otherwise

Table 5.4.0 Labor Force Participation, Earnings, and Hours of Work by Marital Status at Migration and Migration Patterns

Marital Status and Migration Pattern	Mean	N
Labor Force Participation Rate		
single at migration	64.2%	749
migrating before husband	78.3%	111
migrating with husband	56.1%	794
migrating after husband	53.5%	748
Hourly Earnings		
single at migration	$9.2	491
migrating before husband	$9.1	85
migrating with husband	$8.6	457
migrating after husband	$8.7	419
Weekly Earnings		
single at migration	$345.2	491
migrating before husband	$348.8	85
migrating with husband	$323.5	457
migrating after husband	$342.7	419
Hours of Work		
single at migration	37.1	491
migrating before husband	38.1	85
migrating with husband	38.0	457
migrating after husband	39.4	419

Source: June 1986, 1988 and 1991, and November 1989 Current Population Survey Supplements.
Note: Figures in parentheses are the number of observations.

Table 5.4.1 Weighted Mean Earnings and Hours of Work, in 1991 Dollars

Variable	N	Mean	Standard Deviation
1986 (59.5% wives in the labor force)			
family weekly earnings	804	728.8	467.7
wife weekly earnings	495	351.4	233.1
husband weekly earnings	787	510.7	337.6
wife hourly earnings	495	9.1	6.0
husband hourly earnings	787	12.0	7.0
wife weekly work hours	495	38.5	12.7
husband weekly work hours	787	41.8	10.6
1988 (61.2% wives in the labor force)			
family weekly earnings	645	720.2	459.7
wife weekly earnings	401	329.9	206.6
husband weekly earnings	626	508.9	347.7
wife hourly earnings	401	8.7	4.6
husband hourly earnings	626	12.0	7.7
wife weekly work hours	401	37.3	12.2
husband weekly work hours	626	42.1	10.1
1989 (58.4% wives in the labor force)			
family weekly earnings	922	728.3	459.4
wife weekly earnings	554	355.4	235.7
husband weekly earnings	902	518.0	323.3
wife hourly earnings	554	8.7	4.8
husband hourly earnings	902	11.9	6.9
wife weekly work hours	554	39.7	14.6
husband weekly work hours	902	42.7	10.3
1991 (57.1% wives in the labor force)			
family weekly earnings	953	709.4	459.0
wife weekly earnings	556	332.0	228.7
husband weekly earnings	927	493.2	324.8
wife hourly earnings	556	8.6	5.4
husband hourly earnings	927	11.3	7.1
wife weekly work hours	556	38.1	12.0
husband weekly work hours	927	42.4	11.0
Pooled 1986, 88 and 91 (59.0% wives in the labor force)			
family weekly earnings	2402	733.4	462.0
wife weekly earnings	1452	343.4	224.4
husband weekly earnings	2340	516.2	335.3
wife hourly earnings	1452	8.9	5.4
husband hourly earnings	2340	12.0	7.2
wife weekly work hours	1452	38.2	12.3
husband weekly work hours	2340	42.2	10.6

Sources: June 1986, 1988, 1991, and November 1989 Current Population Survey Supplements; Bureau of Labor Statistics, Consumer Price Index.

Table 5.4.2 Weighted Means of Labor Force Participation Regressors by Year of Survey

Variable	1986	1988	1991	1986 1988 1991	1989	1989 1991
Region of Residence						
northeast	17.8	18.1	16.5	17.4	17.5	17.0
midwest	9.4	10.1	8.5	9.3	8.4	8.5
south	26.3	26.4	22.3	24.8	23.3	22.8
west	46.5	45.4	52.7	48.6	50.8	51.7
MSA Status						
in central city	49.8	46.6	47.7	47.6	46.1	46.9
not in central city	35.7	38.5	40.8	38.6	39.9	40.4
not in msa	6.1	5.1	3.6	5.6	4.9	4.2
suppressed	8.5	9.9	7.9	8.2	9.2	8.5
Husband's Level of Education						
less than 7th grade	22.3	18.4	20.2	20.4	22.7	21.4
7-12th grade	39.0	42.1	38.2	39.5	38.8	38.5
college education	38.7	39.5	41.6	40.1	38.5	40.1
Origin Country						
China	8.0	7.1	7.2	7.4	7.0	7.1
Colombia	3.2	2.3	2.4	2.6	2.7	2.5
Cuba	6.2	4.4	3.9	4.8	4.0	4.0
Dominican Republic	2.4	4.2	1.8	2.6	2.4	2.1
El Salvador	3.7	4.3	5.3	4.5	3.9	4.6
India	6.0	5.5	5.6	5.7	4.3	5.0
Japan	2.3	3.0	1.9	2.3	2.1	2.0
Korea	4.1	5.4	5.1	4.9	4.5	4.8
SE Asian refugees	6.8	7.0	5.0	6.1	4.7	4.8
Mexico	36.3	33.9	38.8	36.6	40.2	39.4
Philippines	6.5	9.9	8.0	8.0	6.3	7.2
other Asians	5.1	3.5	2.3	3.5	5.0	3.6
other Hispanics	9.4	9.7	12.8	10.8	12.9	12.9
Immigration Cohort						
prior to 1970	18.7	17.7	8.9	14.6	11.9	10.4
1970-74	21.3	16.1	12.1	16.2	15.0	13.5
1975-79	27.3	19.6	19.8	22.3	20.4	20.1
1980-84	27.2	33.8	23.9	27.7	26.9	25.4
1985-91	5.4	12.7	35.3	19.3	25.9	30.7
Wife's Level of Education						
less than 7th grade	23.2	21.0	21.7	22.0	23.3	22.5
7-12th grade	42.7	45.9	45.2	44.5	43.8	44.5
college education	34.1	33.2	33.1	33.4	32.9	33.0
Number of Immediate Relatives						
wife's kin	na	na	0.1	na	0.1	0.1
husband's kin	na	na	0.2	na	0.2	0.2

Table 5.4.2 (continued)

Variable	1986	1988	1991	1986 1988 1991	1989	1989 1991
Wife's Age						
30 or less	44.5	37.4	39.5	40.6	42.2	40.8
over 30	55.5	62.6	60.5	59.4	57.8	59.2
Marital Status and Migration Patterns						
single	38.1	38.9	22.9	32.3	na	na
after husband	26.0	25.2	36.7	30.0	28.4	32.6
with husband	33.4	33.0	31.8	32.7	46.0	38.8
before husband	2.4	2.9	8.6	5.0	9.2	8.9
Husband's Immigration Status						
US-born	18.5	21.8	16.8	18.7	15.0	16.6
recent immigrant	3.3	3.8	2.8	3.2	3.3	3.4
established immigrant	78.2	74.4	80.4	78.1	81.7	80.0
Husband's Usual Weekly Earnings, in 1991 Dollars						
less than $170	6.5	8.1	8.1	7.6	6.5	7.3
$170-$400	42.4	45.0	46.6	44.8	40.8	43.8
over $400	51.1	46.9	45.3	47.7	52.7	48.9
Year of Survey						
1986	na	na	na	33.5	na	na
1988	na	na	na	26.9	na	na
1989	na	na	na	na	na	48.9
1991	na	na	na	39.7	na	51.1
Number of Children/Other Adults in Household						
children 6-17	1.1	1.2	1.0	1.1	1.1	1.1
children less than 6	0.7	0.6	0.7	0.7	0.6	0.7
adults	0.4	0.4	0.6	0.5	0.5	0.6
Percentage of Immediate Relatives in U.S.						
wife's kin	na	na	0.4	na	0.4	0.4
husband's kin	na	na	0.5	na	0.5	0.5
Wife's English-Speaking Abilities						
English only	na	na	na	na	7.6	na
very well	na	na	na	na	18.9	na
well	na	na	na	na	24.4	na
little or no English	na	na	na	na	49.1	na
Husband's English-Speaking Abilities						
English only	na	na	na	na	11.6	na
very well	na	na	na	na	23.6	na
well	na	na	na	na	29.5	na
little or no English	na	na	na	na	34.7	na

Sources: June 1986, 1988, and 1991 Current Population Survey Supplements; Bureau of Labor Statistics, Consumer Price Index.

Table 5.4.3 Weighted Means of Hourly Earnings and Hours of Work Regressors by Year of Survey

Variable	1986	1988	1991	1986 1988 1991	1989	1989 1991
Region of Residence						
northeast	19.2	18.3	17.5	18.3	18.5	18.0
midwest	8.7	9.9	8.8	9.1	8.8	8.8
south	26.1	25.7	21.3	24.1	23.0	22.2
west	46.0	46.1	52.4	48.5	49.7	51.0
MSA Status						
in central city	48.0	43.7	49.3	46.7	45.7	47.5
not in central city	36.9	39.7	40.5	39.6	40.3	40.4
not in msa	4.7	5.5	3.6	4.7	4.5	4.0
suppressed	10.4	11.1	6.5	9.0	9.6	8.0
Husband's Level of Education						
less than 7th grade	19.7	18.1	17.7	18.5	19.1	18.4
7-12th grade	35.6	42.9	37.6	38.4	36.8	37.2
college education	44.7	39.0	44.7	43.1	44.1	44.4
Origin Country						
China	9.0	8.2	7.9	8.4	7.8	7.9
Colombia	4.2	2.2	2.0	2.8	2.3	2.1
Cuba	8.7	4.6	4.4	5.9	5.4	4.9
Dominican Republic	1.8	5.1	2.0	2.8	1.5	1.8
El Salvador	4.5	2.9	5.6	4.5	4.0	4.8
India	6.1	5.3	6.5	6.0	5.2	5.8
Japan	1.1	2.0	1.6	1.6	1.7	1.7
Korea	3.6	4.8	5.2	4.6	5.2	5.2
SE Asian refugees	7.3	9.6	5.5	7.3	5.9	5.7
Mexico	27.5	30.9	32.4	30.3	32.0	32.2
Philippines	9.1	12.1	12.0	11.0	9.7	10.9
other Asians	5.9	3.8	1.1	3.5	5.3	3.2
other Hispanics	11.3	8.2	13.9	11.4	14.0	13.9
Immigration Cohort						
prior to 1970	23.2	21.3	10.9	18.0	15.5	13.2
1970-74	21.7	17.8	13.4	17.4	17.9	15.6
1975-79	27.9	19.7	22.4	23.5	21.7	22.0
1980-84	23.2	30.8	25.6	26.2	24.5	25.0
1985-91	4.0	10.4	27.8	14.9	20.3	24.1
Wife's Level of Education						
less than 7th grade	16.0	19.1	18.4	17.8	19.1	18.7
7-12th grade	43.7	44.1	43.1	43.6	41.5	42.3
college education	40.3	36.8	38.5	38.6	39.4	38.9
Wife's Age						
30 or less	41.5	33.3	36.6	37.4	36.8	36.7
over 30	58.5	66.7	63.4	62.6	63.2	63.3

Table 5.4.3 (continued)

Variable	1986	1988	1991	1986 1988 1991	1989	1989 1991
Marital Status at Migration and Migration Patterns						
single	43.3	41.7	23.2	35.2	na	na
after husband	21.9	21.5	36.0	27.2	22.9	29.5
with husband	31.5	32.4	29.6	31.0	46.6	38.0
before husband	3.3	4.4	11.1	6.6	11.2	11.2
Husband's Immigration Status						
US-born	19.8	24.1	18.3	20.4	19.3	18.8
recent immigrant	12.0	8.9	11.0	2.4	12.4	4.2
established immigrant	68.2	67.0	70.7	77.2	68.3	77.0
Husband's Usual Weekly Earnings, in 1991 Dollars						
less than $170	6.8	11.4	10.8	9.6	6.9	8.9
$170-$400	39.5	45.6	43.9	42.9	40.1	42.0
over $400	53.7	43.0	45.4	47.5	53.0	49.1
Year of Survey						
1986	100	na	na	33.8	na	na
1988	na	100	na	27.8	na	na
1989	na	na	na	na	100	49.5
1991	na	na	100	38.4	na	50.5
Number of Children/Other Adults in Household						
children 6-17	1.1	1.2	1.0	1.1	1.1	1.1
children less than 6	0.5	0.5	0.6	0.5	0.5	0.6
adults	0.6	0.5	0.7	0.5	0.5	0.6
Percentage of Immediate Relatives in U.S.						
wife's kin	na	na	0.4	na	0.4	0.5
husband's kin	na	na	0.5	na	0.5	0.5
Number of Immediate Relatives in Household						
wife's kin	na	na	0.1	na	0.1	0.1
husband's kin	na	na	0.2	na	0.1	0.2
Wife's English-Speaking Abilities						
English only	na	na	na	na	10.5	na
very well	na	na	na	na	23.4	na
well	na	na	na	na	28.6	na
little or no English	na	na	na	na	37.6	na
Husband's English-Speaking Abilities						
English only	na	na	na	na	15.0	na
very well	na	na	na	na	24.1	na
well	na	na	na	na	28.0	na
little or no English	na	na	na	na	31.9	na

Sources: June 1986, 1988, and 1991 Current Population Survey Supplements; Bureau of Labor Statistics, Consumer Price Index.

Table 5.4.4 Weighted Mean Earnings and Hours of Work by Country, Pooled Sample, in 1991 Dollars

Variable	N	Mean	Standard Deviation
Cuba (72.8% wives in the labor force)			
family weekly earnings	111	717.3	363.5
wife weekly earnings	81	347.3	180.6
husband weekly earnings	110	507.8	259.1
wife hourly earnings	81	9.9	8.3
husband hourly earnings	110	11.8	4.9
wife weekly work hours	81	37.0	11.2
husband weekly work hours	110	43.1	12.2
China (66.4% wives in the labor force)			
family weekly earnings	207	883.8	487.8
wife weekly earnings	140	401.4	212.2
husband weekly earnings	200	649.7	356.1
wife hourly earnings	140	10.6	5.0
husband hourly earnings	200	14.9	7.8
wife weekly work hours	140	39.4	13.7
husband weekly work hours	200	43.0	9.1
The Philippines (81.4% wives in the labor force)			
family weekly earnings	211	1039.4	531.3
wife weekly earnings	173	472.9	265.3
husband weekly earnings	201	634.4	314.0
wife hourly earnings	173	11.7	6.1
husband hourly earnings	201	14.8	6.9
wife weekly work hours	173	39.2	7.4
husband weekly work hours	201	42.1	9.2
India (62.5% wives in the labor force)			
family weekly earnings	166	965.8	505.5
wife weekly earnings	98	397.6	302.6
husband weekly earnings	162	717.9	377.2
wife hourly earnings	98	10.2	7.0
husband hourly earnings	162	16.4	7.7
wife weekly work hours	98	37.5	9.0
husband weekly work hours	162	43.7	12.3
Korea (55.2% wives in the labor force)			
family weekly earnings	141	763.5	400.9
wife weekly earnings	86	372.9	187.5
husband weekly earnings	137	591.9	332.3
wife hourly earnings	86	9.7	6.3
husband hourly earnings	137	14.0	7.0
wife weekly work hours	86	38.6	11.3
husband weekly work hours	137	41.7	13.5

Sources: June 1986, 1988, 1991, and November 1989 Current Population Survey Supplement; Bureau of Labor Statistics, Consumer Price Index.

Table 5.4.5 Weighted Means of Labor Force Participation Regressors by Country-of-Origin, Pooled Sample

Variable	Cuba	China	Philip-pines	India	Korea	Asian Refugees
Region of Residence						
northeast	14.4	25.5	12.0	34.4	16.8	11.2
midwest	3.7	12.0	9.8	25.4	11.8	15.4
south	78.3	9.5	13.6	25.1	24.6	24.4
west	3.5	53.0	64.6	15.1	46.8	49.0
MSA Status						
in central city	49.0	46.5	41.9	23.0	42.0	50.8
not in central city	44.7	45.4	45.5	59.7	38.0	28.1
not in msa	1.6	2.0	5.3	4.0	5.2	6.9
suppressed	4.7	6.0	7.2	13.2	14.7	14.3
Husband's Level of Education						
less than 7th grade	3.8	3.8	1.6	0.0	2.5	19.8
7-12th grade	59.1	28.0	26.0	15.1	25.3	39.5
college education	40.9	68.1	74.0	84.9	74.7	40.7
Immigration Cohort						
prior to 1970	51.1	12.7	12.5	3.8	7.4	3.2
1970-74	22.1	18.2	17.9	14.3	18.0	4.7
1975-79	6.2	25.1	18.8	22.0	23.9	33.5
1980-84	26.8	24.3	32.0	33.0	26.6	49.3
1985-91	5.0	19.8	18.8	26.9	24.1	9.3
Wife's Level of Education						
less than 7th grade	3.5	7.2	1.8	0.4	2.7	22.0
7-12th grade	58.6	30.9	18.9	25.0	50.9	51.0
college education	41.4	61.8	79.3	75.0	46.4	27.0
Marital Status at Migration and Migration Patterns						
single	53.8	29.4	32.7	20.0	21.8	21.2
after husband	9.1	29.3	35.2	41.4	36.5	24.8
with husband	30.1	37.2	23.0	33.9	36.0	51.8
before husband	7.1	4.1	9.2	4.7	5.6	2.2

Table 5.4.5 (continued)

Variable	Cuba	China	Philip-pines	India	Korea	Asian Refugees
Wife's Age						
30 or less	42.0	27.1	31.2	37.9	34.8	38.2
over 30	58.0	72.9	68.8	62.1	65.2	61.8
Husband's Immigration Status						
US-born	18.4	13.5	33.7	1.8	34.7	6.1
recent immigrant	1.0	1.1	3.1	7.0	10.1	0.3
established immigrant	80.6	85.4	63.2	91.2	55.2	93.6
Year of Survey						
1986	43.0	36.1	27.3	34.9	28.5	37.3
1988	24.5	25.6	33.2	25.9	29.9	30.7
1991	32.5	38.3	39.5	39.1	41.6	32.0
Husband's Usual Weekly Earnings, in 1991 Dollars						
less than $170	4.4	6.5	7.2	3.2	8.3	8.2
$170-$400	40.6	30.2	25.1	22.9	30.3	45.7
over $400	54.9	63.3	67.8	73.9	61.4	46.1
Number of Children/Other Adults in Household						
children 6-17	0.9	1.0	1.0	0.8	0.8	1.3
children less than 6	0.5	0.4	0.6	0.7	0.6	0.8
adults	0.3	0.6	0.6	0.5	0.4	0.5

Sources: 1986, 1988, and 1991 June Current Population Survey Supplements; Bureau of Labor Statistics, Consumer Price Index.

Table 5.4.6 Weighted Means of Hourly Earnings and Hours of Work regressors by Country-of-Origin, Pooled Sample

Variable	Cuba	China	Philip-pines	India	Korea	Asian Refugees
Region of Residence						
northeast	15.5	27.4	10.3	33.6	15.9	9.9
midwest	2.1	10.8	11.2	25.3	12.5	18.9
south	80.8	9.0	12.3	23.4	24.3	24.8
west	1.6	52.8	66.2	17.7	47.3	46.4
MSA Status						
in central city	48.7	51.2	44.7	24.3	39.7	50.6
not in central city	45.9	44.3	46.2	57.9	38.2	30.9
not in msa	1.7	1.4	4.3	4.3	7.9	5.9
suppressed	3.6	3.1	4.8	13.5	14.3	12.6
Husband's Level of Education						
less than 7th grade	3.7	4.7	2.0	0.0	3.1	19.4
7-12th grade	58.3	26.1	23.6	17.2	29.9	36.0
college education	41.7	69.2	76.4	82.8	70.1	44.7
Immigration Cohort						
prior to 1970	51.8	18.0	14.0	4.3	10.1	3.5
1970-74	25.8	20.1	17.1	13.1	16.5	6.5
1975-79	8.6	19.6	20.4	25.4	32.9	38.2
1980-84	22.4	26.5	32.4	33.9	25.4	47.1
1985-91	4.1	15.8	16.1	23.3	15.1	4.8
Wife's Level of Education						
less than 7th grade	1.0	7.1	1.7	0.6	2.0	16.6
7-12th grade	55.5	29.4	17.3	23.0	50.2	53.5
college education	44.5	63.5	81.0	77.0	47.8	30.0
Marital Status at Migration and Migration Patterns						
single	54.4	30.3	35.0	20.6	22.3	23.1
after husband	8.3	26.5	28.7	43.3	41.4	21.7
with husband	30.5	39.1	25.8	29.7	27.5	52.2
before husband	6.7	4.2	10.5	6.4	8.7	2.9

Table 5.4.6 (continued)

Variable	Cuba	China	Philip-pines	India	Korea	Asian Refugees
Wife's Age						
30 or less	43.6	25.1	28.8	30.5	29.8	43.3
over 30	56.4	74.9	71.2	69.5	70.2	56.7
Husband's Immigration Status						
US-born	19.9	13.9	27.1	2.0	37.0	8.1
recent immigrant	0.0	0.7	2.8	5.8	5.4	0.4
established immigrant	80.1	85.4	70.1	92.2	57.6	91.5
Husband's Usual Weekly Earnings, in 1991 Dollars						
less than $170	4.8	9.3	7.9	5.1	11.3	6.2
$170-$400	43.7	31.5	29.1	28.0	29.6	43.4
over $400	51.5	59.2	62.9	66.9	59.1	50.4
Year of Survey						
1986	49.6	36.2	27.7	34.3	26.7	34.1
1988	21.8	27.4	30.5	24.6	29.6	36.9
1991	28.6	36.3	41.7	41.1	43.7	29.0
Number of Children/Other Adults in Household						
children 6-17	0.8	1.1	1.0	0.8	1.0	1.2
children less than 6	0.4	0.3	0.5	0.6	0.5	0.6
adults	0.4	0.7	0.7	0.6	0.4	0.5

Sources: 1986, 1988, and 1991 June Current Population Survey Supplements; Bureau of Labor Statistics, Consumer Price Index.

Table 5.4.7 Weighted Mean Earnings and Hours of Work by Region-of-Origin, Asians, Pooled Sample, in 1991 Dollars

Variable	N	Mean	Standard Deviation
Total Asians (65.5% wives in labor force)			
family weekly earnings	1073	891.4	500.3
wife weekly earnings	709	404.2	252.8
husband weekly earnings	1041	639.5	366.2
wife hourly earnings	709	10.3	5.9
husband hourly earnings	1041	14.7	7.8
wife weekly work hours	709	38.7	10.9
husband weekly work hours	1041	43.0	10.8
East Asia (58.5% wives in labor force)			
family weekly earnings	419	859.6	494.4
wife weekly earnings	257	397.9	238.0
husband weekly earnings	406	661.3	395.7
wife hourly earnings	257	10.4	6.2
husband hourly earnings	406	15.3	8.6
wife weekly work hours	257	38.6	13.3
husband weekly work hours	406	42.8	10.7
Southeast Asia, including refugees (76.2% wives in labor force)			
family weekly earnings	413	907.3	503.9
wife weekly earnings	319	413.3	251.8
husband weekly earnings	398	576.1	303.5
wife hourly earnings	319	10.4	5.5
husband hourly earnings	398	13.3	6.5
wife weekly work hours	319	38.9	8.3
husband weekly work hours	398	42.6	10.1
Southeast Asian refugees (69.8% wives in labor force)			
family weekly earnings	162	744.5	443.1
wife weekly earnings	116	331.8	192.9
husband weekly earnings	157	486.0	291.4
wife hourly earnings	116	8.5	4.3
husband hourly earnings	157	11.1	6.0
wife weekly work hours	116	38.5	9.3
husband weekly work hours	157	42.8	11.7
South Asia (61.9% wives in labor force)			
family weekly earnings	178	958.0	500.2
wife weekly earnings	103	400.4	299.7
husband weekly earnings	174	725.5	375.6
wife hourly earnings	103	10.2	6.9
husband hourly earnings	174	16.5	7.8
wife weekly work hours	103	37.5	9.7
husband weekly work hours	174	44.5	12.5

Sources: June 1986, 1988, 1991, and November 1989 Current Population Survey Supplement; Bureau of Labor Statistics, Consumer Price Index.

Table 5.4.8 Weighted Mean Earnings and Hours of Work by Region-of-Origin, Hispanics, Pooled Sample, in 1991 Dollars

Variable	N	Mean	Standard Deviation
Total Hispanics (55.0% wives in labor force)			
family weekly earnings	1329	605.8	385.1
wife weekly earnings	743	285.3	171.7
husband weekly earnings	1299	417.5	272.5
wife hourly earnings	743	7.5	4.4
husband hourly earnings	1299	9.8	5.9
wife weekly work hours	743	37.8	13.5
husband weekly work hours	1299	41.6	10.5
Central America (60.3% wives in labor force)			
family weekly earnings	190	631.6	410.9
wife weekly earnings	117	264.6	178.1
husband weekly earnings	186	407.3	266.8
wife hourly earnings	117	7.1	3.7
husband hourly earnings	186	9.8	5.7
wife weekly work hours	117	36.3	12.8
husband weekly work hours	186	40.4	8.6
South America (60.9% wives in labor force)			
family weekly earnings	207	676.6	420.2
wife weekly earnings	122	322.0	199.3
husband weekly earnings	203	474.7	258.3
wife hourly earnings	122	8.4	4.0
husband hourly earnings	203	11.3	6.0
wife weekly work hours	122	37.8	14.2
husband weekly work hours	203	41.5	8.5
The Caribbean (68.9% wives in labor force)			
family weekly earnings	181	696.1	375.9
wife weekly earnings	125	340.2	163.4
husband weekly earnings	177	493.2	273.1
wife hourly earnings	125	9.2	6.9
husband hourly earnings	177	11.4	4.9
wife weekly work hours	125	38.3	10.4
husband weekly work hours	177	42.4	12.1
Mexico (48.9% wives in labor force)			
family weekly earnings	723	558.2	373.8
wife weekly earnings	355	263.0	164.3
husband weekly earnings	709	387.7	284.1
wife hourly earnings	355	6.8	3.5
husband hourly earnings	709	9.1	6.3
wife weekly work hours	355	38.0	14.6
husband weekly work hours	709	41.7	11.1

Sources: June 1986, 1988, 1991, and November 1989 Current Population Survey Supplement; Bureau of Labor Statistics, Consumer Price Index.

Table 5.4.9 Weighted Means of Labor Force Participation Regressors by Region-of-Origin, Asians, Pooled Sample

Variable	Total Asians	East Asia	Southeast Asia	South Asia
Region of Residence				
northeast	21.7	22.8	12.9	34.5
midwest	13.7	11.0	12.8	24.6
south	18.1	14.8	17.9	26.3
west	46.5	51.5	56.4	14.6
MSA Status				
in central city	39.6	42.4	46.1	23.8
not in central city	45.2	44.9	37.7	58.9
not in msa	4.2	3.1	5.8	3.8
suppressed	11.0	9.5	10.4	13.5
Husband's Level of Education				
less than 7th grade	5.2	2.8	9.1	0.1
7-12th grade	27.3	27.9	30.5	14.3
college education	67.5	69.3	60.4	85.7
Origin Country				
China	19.3	50.8	na	na
India	14.9	na	na	94.5
Japan	6.0	15.9	na	na
Korea	12.7	33.3	na	na
Laos		na	8.5	na
Philippines	22.0	na	52.3	na
Vietnam	15.9[1]	na	27.5	na
other Asians	9.2	na	11.7	5.5
Immigration Cohort				
prior to 1970	9.4	12.2	8.1	3.6
1970-74	15.8	17.8	14.9	14.2
1975-79	23.6	22.9	24.6	21.8
1980-84	30.8	24.6	37.3	33.8
1985-91	20.4	22.5	15.1	26.7

Table 5.4.9 (continued)

Variable	Total Asians	East Asia	Southeast Asia	South Asia
Wife's Level of Education				
less than 7th grade	6.5	4.6	10.5	0.5
7-12th grade	35.4	40.5	34.0	23.4
college education	58.1	54.9	55.6	76.1
Marital Status at Migration and Migration Patterns				
single	26.8	27.3	28.4	20.2
married, after husband	32.6	31.8	31.5	42.2
married, with husband	35.8	36.7	34.4	33.1
married, before husband	4.8	4.2	5.7	4.4
Wife's Age				
30 or less	32.5	28.2	33.3	37.4
over 30	67.5	71.8	66.7	62.6
Husband's Level of Education				
US-born	20.3	24.3	23.8	2.4
recent immigrant	5.3	6.0	2.2	7.1
established immigrant	74.4	69.7	74.0	90.5
Husband's Usual Weekly Earnings, in 1991 Dollars				
less than $170	6.2	7.0	7.1	3.0
$170-$400	29.4	27.0	33.5	22.5
over $400	64.4	66.0	59.4	74.5
Year of Survey				
1986	34.7	33.2	32.5	36.4
1988	29.1	28.4	32.3	25.0
1991	36.2	38.4	35.2	38.7
Number of Children/Other Adults in Household				
children 6-17	1.0	0.9	1.1	0.7
children less than 6	0.6	0.5	0.6	0.7
adults	0.5	0.4	0.5	0.5

Sources: June 1986, 1988, and 1991 Current Population survey supplements; Bureau of Labor Statistics, Consumer Price Index.

1. Includes Vietnam, Laos, and Cambodia.

Table 5.4.10 Weighted Means of Hourly Earnings and Hours of Work regressors by Region-of-Origin, Asians, Pooled Sample

Variable	Total Asians	East Asia	Southeast Asia	South Asia
Region of Residence				
northeast	20.5	24.0	11.1	34.8
midwest	14.3	10.4	14.8	24.1
south	16.6	13.5	16.9	23.9
west	48.6	52.1	57.3	17.2
MSA Status				
in central city	40.1	46.9	47.0	25.7
not in central city	45.7[1]	40.7	39.8	56.6
not in msa	4.1	3.6	4.7	4.1
suppressed	10.2	8.8	8.5	13.6
Husband's Level of Education				
less than 7th grade	5.5	3.7	8.6	0.0
7-12th grade	26.4	28.6	26.9	16.4
college education	68.1	67.7	64.6	83.6
Origin Country				
China	19.7	57.8	na	na
India	14.2	na	na	95.3
Japan	3.7	10.7	na	na
Korea	10.7	31.5	na	na
Laos		na	7.6	na
Philippines	26.7	na	55.9	na
Vietnam	16.8[1]	na	25.6	na
other Asians	8.2	na	10.9	4.7
Immigration Cohort				
prior to 1970	12.3	18.1	9.1	4.1
1970-74	16.1	18.8	15.2	13.6
1975-79	25.3	23.0	27.2	25.8
1980-84	30.9	24.8	36.4	34.3
1985-91	15.4	15.4	12.2	22.2

Table 5.4.10 (continued)

Variable	Total Asians	East Asia	Southeast Asia	South Asia
Wife's Level of Education				
less than 7th grade	5.4	4.7	7.3	0.6
7-12th grade	33.7	38.9	32.9	21.3
college education	60.9	56.3	59.8	78.1
Marital Status at Migration and Migration Patterns				
single at migration	30.1	30.9	30.1	21.7
married, after husband	30.9	31.9	27.8	43.5
married, with husband	32.9	32.0	35.1	28.7
married, before husband	6.1	5.2	7.0	6.1
Wife's Age				
30 or less	31.1	25.8	33.6	30.0
over 30	68.9	74.2	66.4	70.0
Husband's Immigration Status				
US-born	20.4	26.2	21.3	3.0
recent immigrant	3.4	2.6	1.7	5.5
established immigrant	76.2	71.2	77.0	91.5
Husband's Usual Weekly Earnings, in 1991 Dollars				
less than $170	7.6	10.2	6.7	4.9
$170-$400	31.3	29.3	34.0	27.6
over $400	61.0	60.6	59.3	67.5
Year of Survey				
1986	33.7	31.9	31.3	36.4
1988	30.4	29.1	33.2	23.4
1991	36.0	39.1	35.5	40.2
Number of Children/Other Adults in Household				
children 6-17	1.0	1.0	1.1	0.8
children less than 6	0.5	0.4	0.5	0.6
adults	0.6	0.6	0.6	0.6

Sources: June 1986, 1988, and 1991 Current Population Survey Supplements; Bureau of Labor Statistics, Consumer Price Index.

1. Includes Vietnam, Laos, and Cambodia.

Table 5.4.11 Weighted Means of Labor Force Participation Regressors by Region-of-Origin, Hispanics, Pooled Sample

Variable	Total Hispanics	Central America	South America	Caribbean	Mexico
Region of Residence					
northeast	14.7	21.1	48.4	38.2	1.7
midwest	6.5	4.4	3.1	3.6	7.9
south	28.9	27.7	29.6	53.1	23.7
west	49.9	46.8	19.0	5.0	66.6
MSA Status					
in central city	50.1	56.3	52.3	56.7	49.5
not in central city	35.1	36.5	38.0	36.4	34.2
not in msa	6.8	1.8	2.5	1.6	7.2
suppressed	8.0	5.5	7.2	5.5	9.1
Husband's Level of Education					
less than 7th grade	29.9	25.7	5.2	6.4	41.4
7-12th grade	47.1	45.1	48.3	60.3	44.7
college education	23.0	29.2	46.4	33.4	13.9
Origin Country					
Colombia	4.2	na	32.5	na	na
Cuba	7.8	na	na	63.3	na
Dominican Republic	4.1	na	na	34.8	na
El Salvador	7.2	54.7	na	na	na
Mexico	59.2	na	na	na	100.0
other Hispanics	17.5	45.3	67.5	1.9	na
Immigration Cohort					
prior to 1970	17.8	8.4	17.1	42.1	15.1
1970-74	16.5	12.4	18.6	15.8	17.9
1975-79	21.5	18.3	18.2	10.7	24.9
1980-84	25.7	37.3	28.9	22.1	23.5
1985-91	18.5	23.6	17.1	9.3	18.6
Wife's Age					
30 or less	45.7	48.2	31.9	37.1	50.2
over 30	54.3	51.8	68.1	62.9	49.8

Table 5.4.11 (continued)

Variable	Total Hispanics	Central America	South America	Caribbean	Mexico
Wife's Level of Education					
less than 7th grade	31.7	21.3	3.3	6.6	45.2
7-12th grade	50.2	57.6	59.8	57.4	45.0
college education	18.1	21.1	36.8	36.0	9.7
Marital Status at Migration and Migration Patterns					
single	35.7	34.4	36.4	48.9	33.6
after husband	28.4	27.1	26.0	15.4	31.7
with husband	30.7	34.5	31.5	26.6	30.3
before husband	5.1	4.1	6.1	9.1	4.4
Husband's Immigration Status					
US-born	17.8	16.7	22.8	18.5	16.4
recent immigrant	1.9	1.4	4.0	1.5	2.0
established immigrant	80.3	81.9	73.2	80.0	81.6
Husband's Usual Weekly Earnings, in 1991 Dollars					
less than $170	8.4	9.0	8.4	6.4	8.4
$170-$400	54.3	55.6	42.2	42.7	59.4
over $400	37.3	35.4	49.4	50.9	32.2
Year of Survey					
aping	32.7	31.2	34.3	39.1	33.2
1988	25.5	30.4	21.8	30.3	24.8
1991	41.8	38.4	43.9	30.6	42.0
Number of Children/Other Adults in Household					
children 6-17	1.3	1.0	0.9	1.0	1.5
children less than 6	0.8	0.8	0.6	0.6	0.9
adults	0.6	0.7	0.4	0.3	0.6

Sources: June 1986, 1988 and 1991 Current Population Survey Supplements; Bureau of Labor Statistics, Consumer Price Index.

Table 5.4.12 Weighted Means of Hourly Earnings and Hours of Work Regressors by Region-of-Origin, Hispanics, Pooled Sample

Variable	Total Hispanics	Central America	South America	Caribbean	Mexico
Region of Residence					
northeast	16.7	19.2	46.7	36.4	2.2
midwest	5.2	7.1	1.4	2.1	6.2
south	29.7	23.8	28.3	56.4	24.3
west	48.4	49.9	23.6	5.1	67.3
MSA Status					
in central city	48.3	59.3	49.1	54.2	44.5
not in central city	35.5	32.1	40.9	39.3	36.5
not in msa	6.7	1.5	3.1	2.0	7.1
suppressed	9.5	7.1	6.9	4.4	11.8
Husband's Level of Education					
less than 7th grade	28.2	26.5	4.6	6.8	41.6
7-12th grade	47.3	44.6	47.3	60.5	43.8
college education	24.6	29.0	48.1	32.7	14.6
Origin Country					
Colombia	4.8	na	33.4	na	na
Cuba	10.3	na	na	66.8	na
Dominican Republic	4.7	na	na	31.4	na
El Salvador	7.7	53.5	na	na	na
Mexico	52.6	na	na	na	100.0
other Hispanics	19.9	46.5	66.6	1.8	na
Immigration Cohort					
prior to 1970	22.2	10.3	22.8	45.0	19.4
1970-74	18.4	12.2	22.5	15.6	20.3
1975-79	22.2	16.9	17.4	11.4	27.3
1980-84	22.8	34.6	23.3	19.4	20.8
1985-91	14.5	25.9	14.0	8.7	12.3
Wife's Age					
30 or less	42.0	44.9	33.2	36.9	46.3
over 30	58.0	55.1	66.8	63.1	53.7

Table 5.4.12 (continued)

Variable	Total Hispanics	Central America	South America	Caribbean	Mexico
Wife's Level of Education					
less than 7th grade	27.0	22.9	2.8	6.3	40.6
7-12th grade	50.9	53.3	53.1	56.2	47.6
college education	22.1	23.8	44.1	37.5	11.8
Marital Status at Migration and Migration Patterns					
single	38.9	33.3	38.5	48.9	38.9
after husband	24.5	26.1	25.1	13.8	26.1
with husband	29.6	36.3	28.8	28.3	27.8
before husband	7.0	4.3	7.6	9.0	7.2
Husband's Immigration Status					
US-born	20.4	18.1	28.1	20.8	19.0
recent immigrant	1.6	1.7	4.5	1.4	1.4
established immigrant	78.0	80.2	67.4	77.8	79.6
Husband's Usual Weekly Earnings, in 1991 Dollars					
less than $170	11.1	12.3	12.7	7.2	10.8
$170-$400	51.4	55.8	35.0	43.7	57.1
over $400	37.5	31.9	52.3	49.1	32.1
Year of Survey					
1986	33.8	37.9	40.7	40.9	30.6
1988	26.0	25.0	18.1	30.7	28.4
1991	40.2	37.1	41.3	28.4	41.0
Number of Children/Other Adults in Household					
children 6-17	1.2	1.0	0.9	1.0	1.5
children less than 6	0.6	0.6	0.5	0.4	0.7
adults	0.6	0.8	0.5	0.4	0.6

Sources: June 1986, 1988 and 1991 Current Population Survey Supplements; Bureau of Labor Statistics, Consumer Price Index.

Table 5.4.13 Weighted Mean Earnings and Hours of Work by Cohort and Age at Migration, Pooled Sample, in 1991 Dollars

Variable	N	Mean	Standard Deviation
Before 1970 Cohort (72.9% wives in labor force)			
family weekly earnings	348	853.7	470.1
wife weekly earnings	255	380.8	248.0
husband weekly earnings	337	593.0	319.0
wife hourly earnings	255	10.1	7.1
husband hourly earnings	337	13.7	6.8
wife weekly work hours	255	38.1	11.8
husband weekly work hours	337	42.5	11.2
1970s Cohort (62.7% wives in labor force)			
family weekly earnings	917	775.1	482.0
wife weekly earnings	595	359.5	231.2
husband weekly earnings	894	554.1	356.3
wife hourly earnings	595	9.4	5.7
husband hourly earnings	894	12.8	7.6
wife weekly work hours	595	38.1	11.5
husband weekly work hours	894	42.8	10.7
1980s Cohort (51.7% wives in labor force)			
family weekly earnings	1137	662.9	430.3
wife weekly earnings	602	311.6	200.6
husband weekly earnings	1109	462.4	313.5
wife hourly earnings	602	7.9	4.0
husband hourly earnings	1109	10.9	6.9
wife weekly work hours	602	38.4	13.2
husband weekly work hours	1109	41.7	10.4
Immigrated Before Age 21 (61.5% in labor force)			
family weekly earnings	953	707.6	449.2
wife weekly earnings	600	333.6	222.4
husband weekly earnings	930	496.7	324.6
wife hourly earnings	600	8.8	5.6
husband hourly earnings	930	11.4	6.8
wife weekly work hours	600	37.9	12.5
husband weekly work hours	930	42.8	11.5
Immigrated After Age 21 (57.2% wives in labor force)			
family weekly earnings	1449	750.4	469.7
wife weekly earnings	852	350.3	225.9
husband weekly earnings	1410	529.1	341.8
wife hourly earnings	852	8.9	5.3
husband hourly earnings	1410	12.4	7.5
wife weekly work hours	852	38.4	12.2
husband weekly work hours	1410	41.9	10.0

Sources: June 1986, 1988, 1991, and November 1989 Current Population Survey Supplement; Bureau of Labor Statistics, Consumer Price Index.

Table 5.4.14 Weighted Means of Labor Force Participation Regressors by Cohort and Age at Migration, Pooled Sample

Variable	Before 1970	1970s	1980s	Before Age 21	After Age 21
Region of Residence					
northeast	18.5	16.8	17.4	14.5	19.4
midwest	8.1	9.6	9.3	7.6	10.5
south	31.5	23.5	23.7	27.5	22.8
west	41.9	50.1	49.5	50.4	47.4
MSA Status					
in central city	39.4	48.4	50.5	47.0	48.9
not in central city	46.1	36.9	37.4	39.1	38.0
not in msa	4.0	5.7	4.3	4.9	4.8
suppressed	10.5	9.0	7.7	9.1	8.3
Origin Country					
China	6.5	8.3	7.0	4.8	9.3
Colombia	3.7	2.7	2.3	3.2	2.2
Cuba	16.9	2.8	2.7	7.6	2.8
Dominican Republic	4.9	2.2	2.3	3.0	2.4
El Salvador	0.0	3.1	7.0	3.2	5.5
India	1.5	5.4	7.3	2.5	8.0
Japan	3.2	1.8	2.4	1.1	3.2
Korea	2.5	5.3	5.3	2.6	6.5
SEA refugees	1.4	6.1	7.7	5.1	6.9
Mexico	38.1	40.6	32.9	48.8	27.8
the Philippines	6.9	7.6	8.7	5.4	9.9
other Asians	2.0	4.4	3.3	3.1	3.9
other Hispanics	12.4	9.7	11.2	9.7	11.6
Wife's Age					
30 or less	30.4	32.0	50.9	65.6	22.5
over 30	69.6	68.0	49.1	34.4	77.5
Immigration Cohort					
prior to 1960	9.5	na	na		
1960-64	32.5	na	na		
1965-69	58.0	na	na	30.4[1]	3.1[1]
1970-74	na	42.2	na	18.2	14.8
1975-79	na	57.8	na	24.1	20.9
1980-84	na	na	59.0	18.8	34.1
1985-91	na	na	41.0	8.5	27.0

Table 5.4.14 (continued)

Variable	Before 1970	1970s	1980s	Before Age 21	After Age 21
Wife's Level of Education					
less than 7th grade	11.3	23.0	24.5	20.3	23.2
7-12th grade	46.8	44.5	43.9	48.3	41.8
college education	41.9	32.4	31.6	31.3	35.0
Husband's Level of Education					
less than 7th grade	10.0	22.7	21.8	19.6	21.0
7-12th grade	46.0	36.4	40.1	46.2	34.7
college education	44.0	40.9	38.2	34.2	44.3
Marital Status at Migration and Migration Patterns					
single	75.8	30.9	20.0	54.5	16.2
married, after husband	12.0	26.2	38.7	20.4	37.0
married, with husband	10.0	34.3	38.4	18.2	43.2
married, before husband	2.2	8.5	2.9	6.9	3.6
Husband's Immigration Status					
US-born	39.5	19.7	11.5	23.9	15.0
recent immigrant	0.0	0.4	6.5	1.1	4.8
established immigrant	60.5	79.9	82.0	75.0	80.2
Husband's Usual Weekly Earnings, in 1991 Dollars					
less than $170	5.3	5.9	9.6	6.6	8.3
$170-$400	32.7	41.4	51.3	48.3	42.3
over $400	62.0	52.7	39.1	45.2	49.5
Year of Survey					
1986	43.0	42.3	23.3	35.3	32.1
1988	32.7	24.9	26.6	24.5	28.6
1991	24.3	32.8	50.1	40.2	39.3
Number of Children/Other Adults in Household					
children 6-17	1.4	1.5	0.8	0.9	1.4
children less than 6	0.5	0.7	0.8	0.8	0.6
adults	0.5	0.5	0.6	0.5	0.6

Sources: 1986, 1988, and 1991 June Current Population Survey Supplements; Bureau of Labor Statistics, Consumer Price Index.

1. Includes all cohorts prior to 1970.

Table 5.4.15 Weighted Means of Hourly Earnings and Hours Regressors by Cohort and Age at Migration, Pooled Sample

Variable	Before 1970	1970s	1980s	Before Age 21	After Age 21
Region of Residence					
northeast	20.2	17.4	18.4	15.8	20.2
midwest	6.0	10.0	9.6	6.9	10.7
south	33.7	21.3	22.8	28.7	20.6
west	40.1	51.4	49.2	48.5	48.5
MSA Status					
in central city	40.3	45.9	51.8	45.6	48.6
not in central city	46.8	38.0	36.7	40.4	38.0
not in msa	3.1	5.6	4.1	3.6	5.2
suppressed	9.8	10.5	7.4	10.3	8.1
Husband Level of Education					
less than 7th grade	7.0	21.8	20.3	16.2	20.3
7-12th grade	45.0	34.6	39.2	44.7	33.5
college education	48.0	43.6	40.5	39.1	46.2
Origin Country					
China	8.4	8.1	8.6	6.0	10.2
Colombia	5.1	2.4	2.1	4.1	1.8
Cuba	17.1	3.7	3.2	9.4	3.3
Dominican Republic	4.9	2.0	2.7	2.9	2.7
El Salvador	0.1	2.9	8.0	2.7	5.9
India	1.4	5.7	8.4	2.5	8.8
Japan	3.6	1.2	1.1	1.2	1.8
Korea	2.6	5.5	4.5	2.7	6.0
SEA refugees	1.4	7.9	9.2	6.3	8.0
Mexico	32.6	35.2	24.4	41.4	21.7
the Philippines	8.6	10.1	13.0	7.7	13.6
other Asians	2.1	4.6	3.0	3.3	3.6
other Hispanics	12.1	10.6	11.9	9.8	12.7
Wife's Age					
30 or less	32.2	30.6	46.3	62.5	17.8
over 30	67.8	69.4	53.7	37.5	82.2

Table 5.4.15 (continued)

Variable	Before 1970	1970s	1980s	Before Age 21	After Age 21
Immigration Cohort					
prior to 1960	10.1	na	na		
1960-64	32.6	na	na		
1965-69	57.3	na	na	36.4[1]	3.7[1]
1970-74	na	42.6	na	18.0	16.9
1975-79	na	57.4	na	23.8	23.2
1980-84	na	na	63.8	16.6	33.7
1985-91	na	na	36.2	5.1	22.4
Wife's Level of Education					
less than 7th grade	6.9	19.2	21.2	14.0	20.7
7-12th grade	46.0	43.7	42.4	48.0	40.1
college education	47.1	37.1	36.4	38.0	39.2
Marital Status at Migration and Migration Patterns					
single	76.7	30.2	21.9	58.8	16.7
married, after husband	11.7	27.0	34.2	17.2	35.0
married, with husband	9.5	32.5	39.0	15.9	42.8
married, before husband	2.1	10.4	4.9	8.1	5.5
Husband's Immigration Status					
US-born	38.4	20.4	12.5	27.0	15.3
recent immigrant	0.0	0.6	5.2	0.9	3.5
established	51.6	79.0	82.3	72.1	81.2
Husband's Usual Weekly Earnings, in 1991 Dollars					
less than $170	6.7	7.7	12.7	8.2	10.7
$170-$400	33.7	38.2	51.5	46.6	40.0
over $400	59.6	54.1	35.7	45.2	49.3
Year of Survey					
1986	43.6	40.9	22.3	35.1	32.7
1988	33.0	25.5	27.9	25.7	29.5
1991	23.4	33.5	49.8	39.2	37.7
Number of Children/Other Adults in Household					
children 6-17	1.3	1.4	0.8	0.9	1.3
children less than 6	0.4	0.6	0.6	0.7	0.5
adults	0.5	0.5	0.7	0.5	0.6

Sources: 1986, 88 and 91 June Current Population Survey Supplements; Bureau of Labor Statistics, Consumer Price Index.

1. Includes all cohorts prior to 1970.

noted. The November 1989 sample is excluded from the pooled sample since this specific supplement did not collect marital history information and could not be obtained through matching in any way. It, however, provides valuable residential information of the immigrants' immediate relatives, and thus was utilized in the analysis of reunification of kin in the U.S.

5.4.1 Year of Survey

Table 5.4.1 shows substantial differences in young immigrant wives' earnings, hours of work and their family weekly earnings by year of survey. In 1986, the young immigrant wives reported earning $9. 1 an hour, highest than any other year. In 1989, young immigrant wives worked more hours, and as a result, had more weekly earnings than any other year. The reverse is true for 1988. In 1991, the immigrant wives worked approximately 38 hours, earned $8. 6 an hour, and $332 a week. In the same year, their husbands earned $493 a week, the lowest level among all survey years, which results in the lowest level of family earnings as well.

Table 5.4.2 shows similar demographic patterns across all survey years. There were an average of 59 percent of the young Asian and Hispanic immigrant wives participating the U.S. labor force from 1986 to 1991, with a slightly decreasing trend over the years. The young immigrant wives are heavily concentrated in the west region of the country, and the concentration is exacerbated in recent years. Meanwhile, immigrant wives are also moving toward the suburban areas[15]. Overall, about 78 percent of the young immigrant wives, and 79 percent of their husbands have high school education or over. Young wives surveyed in 1986 are in general younger than those in other years. On average, each immigrant wife has 2 children in the household, with 35 percent of the children under age 6. In 1989 and 1991, an immigrant wife has about 40 percent of her immediate relatives and 50 percent of her in-laws residing in the U.S. In 1989, one half of the young Asian and Hispanic immigrant wives reported speaking little or no English at all, while their husbands seem to possess better English-speaking abilities. This may reflect the fact that some of the husbands are U.S.-born, or most husbands immigrated prior to the wives, instead of the other way around. On average, about one half of the young immigrant wives' husbands earn over $400 weekly in real terms and one fifth of the young immigrant wives were married to U.S.-born husbands.

The statistics also show distinct racial/ethnic, cohort composition, and marital status and migration patterns across the four samples. In particular, higher percentages of both Mexicans and other Hispanics were surveyed in recent years. The 1991 sample contains about 60 percent of young immigrant wives immigrating sometime during the 1980s with over than one half of them came after 1984. In both 1986 and 1988 samples, there are about 38 percent of young immigrant wives migrating while single, as compared to 23 percent in 1991. The 1991 sample contains more immigrant wives migrating in different periods from their husbands than those found in previous years. The changing racial/ethnic composition in 1991 sample as compared to the earlier samples may have contributed to the higher percentage of young immigrant wives migrating after husbands and the lower percentage of wives migrating while single than those of the previous years.

5.4.2 Country of Origin and Region of Origin

Tables 5.4.4-5.4.12 demonstrate distinct labor market performances and demographic compositions of immigrants wives from various areas and countries in Asia, central and South America. Substantial differences between young Asian and Hispanic immigrant wives are noted. Overall, young Asian immigrant wives are more likely to be in the labor force than the young Hispanic wives. Young Hispanic immigrant wives earn only 70 percent of what their young Asian counterparts earn weekly, a result of both lower hourly earnings and weekly hours of work. Similarly, the husbands of young Hispanic immigrant wives only make 65 percent of what the husbands of young Asian immigrant wives make weekly. This may be attributed to that fact young Asian immigrant wives have more favorable demographic characteristics than their Hispanic counterparts. Young Asian immigrant wives themselves and their husbands are more highly educated than young Hispanic immigrant wives and their husbands respectively. Young Asian immigrant wives tend to be older, have fewer children and other adults in the household. Asian immigrant wives are more likely to reside in the suburban areas then their Hispanic counterparts. Young Hispanic immigrant wives are more likely to immigrate prior to 1970 and be interviewed in 1991 than young Asian immigrant wives. Young Hispanic immigrant wives are most likely to immigrate while single, while Asian immigrant wives are most likely to immigrate as married and immigrating during the same period as their husbands.

Closer examination by region and country of origin shows diverse patterns and composition by the young immigrant wives' country-of-origin and region-of-origin. Young immigrant wives from east Asia are older than the average group, while wives from Mexico and Central America are younger than average. Young immigrant wives from the Southeast Asian refugee countries, i.e., Vietnam, Cambodia, and Laos are much more likely to immigrate during the same period as their husbands than the other groups, which is consistent with findings from previous research that these refugees tend to move as a family or household (Kelly 1986).

The majority of the Asian refugee wives immigrated in the late 1970s or early 1980s, while over 40 percent of the young Caribbean immigrant wives immigrated prior to 1970. The latter group is also less likely to be interviewed in 1991 than any other groups. In contrast, young immigrant wives from south Asia, mainly Asian Indians, are more likely to immigrate in the post-1980 period, 27 percent immigrated after 1984. Two other regions also sent relatively high percentages of recent young immigrant wives, i.e., after 1984: east Asia and Central America. As compared to the average level of educational attainments among immigrant wives, the young Asian refugee wives are relatively poorly educated, so are their husbands. In addition, the young Mexican and Central American immigrant wives also contain high percentage of immigrant wives with high school or below level of education. Similarly, these groups reported relatively low level of husbands' earnings.

Young immigrant wives from the Caribbean countries and southeast Asia, particularly the Philippines have higher than average labor force participation rates, while young Mexican immigrant wives have a lower than average. Furthermore, an average Filipino immigrant wife earns $11. 7 an hour, slightly less than twice that of what an average Mexican immigrant wife earns. Among young Hispanic immigrant wives, those from the Caribbean are the most highly paid, while the young Central American immigrant wives supply the least number of hours in paid work.

As opposed to the high concentration in the west among Asian immigrants, young south Asian immigrant wives, the majority of which are Asian Indians, have a high concentration in the northeast region of the U.S. As an exception, the young Cuban immigrant wives are highly concentrated in the southern region the this country. Young Asian Indian immigrant wives also have a higher concentration in the suburban areas than the Asian average. This may be attributed to the fact that over 80 percent of their husbands have higher than high school education, and 74 percent of their husbands make over $400 a week in 1991 dollars, as compared to 46 percent for the husbands of Southeast Asian refugee wives.

Both young Asian Indian and Filipino immigrant wives are highly educated and enjoy relatively high level of family earnings. However, the young Filipino immigrant wives are lightly older and tend to have lower percentage of husbands with beyond high school education and lower husbands' earnings than the young Asian Indian immigrant wives. The high family earnings found among young Filipino immigrant wives is mostly a result of their high propensities of participating in paid work, and their high earning capacities. In contrast, the Asian Indian wives enjoy high family earnings due to their husbands' high earnings capacities. Although highly educated, they are relatively less likely to work and work fewer hours than average young immigrant wives, if work at all. Moreover, young Filipino immigrant wives are more likely to immigrate independent of their current husbands than young Asian Indian immigrant wives; 33 percent of the young Filipinos immigrated while single and 9 percent migrating married and before their husbands, as compared to 20 percent and 5 percent respectively for Asian Indians. The young Filipino wives show a relatively low propensity of immigrating with their husbands, a pattern which is close to that of the young wives from the Caribbean. Furthermore, young immigrant wives from the Caribbean countries also have a relatively high tendency of migrating while married and before their husbands. Over half of the young Cuban immigrant wives immigrated while single. This is consistent with the fact that over half of them immigrated prior to 1970.

Immigrant wives tend to have relatively low level of fertility than the U.S. wives as a whole. However, both the young Mexican and refugee immigrant wives reported relatively large number of children in the household, 2. 3 and 2. 0 respectively, the majority of which are under age 6. The young Filipino and Central American immigrant wives reported slightly higher number of other adults living in the household than the rest of the young immigrant wives.

5.4.3 Immigration Cohort and Age at Migration

Tables 5.4.13 to 5.4.15 document the composition of young Asian and Hispanic immigrant wives by their timing of immigration and age at immigration. Young immigrant wives entering the U.S. in different time periods are likely to have distinct characteristics and labor market performances due to adaptation effects and cohort effects. Consistent with the adaptation hypothesis, early young immigrant wives are more likely to be in the labor force and report higher levels of earnings than the recent young immigrant wives. Nonetheless, there does not seem to be any substantial differences in terms of weekly hours of work. Young immigrant wives immigrating before age 21 are somewhat more likely to be in the labor force than the migrating-after-21 group. Given working, both groups have similar earning capacities and similar hours of work.

Early young immigrant wives are more likely to marry U.S.-born, more highly educated and highly paid husbands than recent young immigrant wives. The former group is clearly more likely to receive college education than the latter. This continuous trend is consistent with that reported by (Jasso and Rosenzweig 1990a) based on information from the 1980 census. The majority, or 76 percent of the "before 1970" cohort immigrated while single as compared to 20 percent among the 1980s cohort. In contrast, the 1980s cohort are more likely to immigrate while married and after their husbands than the previous cohorts. The 1970s cohort are more likely to immigrate while married and before their husbands than the other cohorts. As this study focus on the experiences of young Asian and Hispanic immigrant wives, i.e., aged 18-44, this result may be an artifact of this selection rule, instead of actual trend.

The age at migration of young immigrant wives may have differential implications on their labor market performance. From the policy perspective, the family reunification legislation defines minor children as those unmarried and under age 21. Thus, those immigrating prior to age 21 are much more likely to be dependents or sponsored by their parents while migrating. It is unlikely that they demonstrate similar migration selectivity as single adult immigrants, even though both groups report the same marital status at migration. From the adaptation perspective, the younger age one launches immigration, the easier he/she can adapt to the new society. Nonetheless, Table 5.4.15 shows surprising similarities between those young wives who immigrated prior to age 21 and those immigrated after age 21, except that the former is younger, more likely to be Hispanic than Asian, more likely to immigrate in early years, and not surprisingly, more likely to immigrated while single than the latter. Notably, young Mexican immigrant wives consist of about half of the young wives immigrated before age 21.

This study contributes to the literature through exploring the young Asian and Hispanic immigrant wives' labor market performance by their marital status and migration patterns. In particular, it provides information on other dimensions of labor market performance, including hourly earnings and weekly hours of work, which are rarely documented in the literature. This section illustrates the variations in the young Asian and Hispanic immigrant wives' labor market performances and their demographic composition by their marital status at migration and migration patterns, country-of-origin, region-of-origin, timing of immigration, and year of survey. Both considerable similarities and differences emerge from the empirical data along these lines, and the descriptive results are largely consistent with findings from previous research.

Summary of Chapter. This chapter describes the availability of contemporary immigration data in the U.S. It demonstrate the advantages of using the Current Population Survey supplements of over the Censuses and the INS administrative records for the purpose of evaluating the migration selectivity effects on immigrant wives' labor market adaptation. It then illustrates the sample selection procedures and means to clean and impute the data. Finally, it presents the sample statistics from the empirical data.

In light of the inadequacy of available immigration data, this study put together information from four CPS immigration supplements for this study. The CPS sample rotation scheme facilitates the matching of information about immigrants from different months and years. A substantial amount of imputations were conducted to recover crucial missing information due to item non-response or non-matched. The procedures documented in this chapter enhance the usefulness of the available immigration data. It was also pointed out that imputation inevitably requires strong assumptions. Should the assumptions fail to hold, the inferences drawn from the data may be unreliable.

Substantial differences in marital status and migration patterns by their country-of-origin as well as timing of immigration exist. In general, young Hispanic immigrant wives are more likely to immigrate while single than young Asian immigrant wives. Given both migrated while married, young Asian wives are more likely to migrate in the same period as their husbands than their Hispanic counterparts. A majority of young Cuban immigrant wives migrated while single and prior to 1970. Young Filipino immigrant wives and young wives from the Caribbean are least likely to immigrate with their husbands. Young wives who immigrated prior to 1970 are most likely to immigrate while single and as minors, a fact that is consistent with their current age profile.

The young immigrant wives' marital status at migration and migration patterns appear to have significant labor market implications.

Overall, young wives migrating before their husbands are most likely to be in the labor force. Young wives migration before husbands and migrating while single enjoy relatively high weekly earnings through high hourly earnings, while young wives migrating after husbands earn similar weekly earnings through imputing extra hours of work.

The sample statistics demonstrate substantial demographic differences among young immigrant wives. To control for these demographic differences, multivariate analyses are conducted in estimating the young immigrant wives' labor supply and earnings. The next chapter presents the regression results.

NOTES

1. The marital history supplements asked number of times married and the timing of the beginning and ending of each marriage for ever-married women aged 18-65. The fertility and birth expectation supplements collect age at first marriage along with fertility information for ever-married women aged 18-44.

2. Previous experiences show that, in practice there is about 80 percent of the overlapping households may be matched over June, July, Aug., and Sept. Over time, the respondents may not be tracked down due to death, divorce, mobility, or refusal.

3. The 1983 April CPS supplement is not used for this study since the actual match between the April and June supplements is only 43 percent.

4. The super-universe is the union of the four populations, assuming negligible variations in the population over the eight years.

5. A multiple imputation technique can reduce this potential bias by generating more than one acceptable values representing a distribution of possible values (Rubin 1987).

6. in real terms, i.e., the values assigned to 1986 recipients were converted to the 1986 dollars; the values assigned to 1988 recipients were converted to the 1988 dollars.

7. These particular years are selected since the March CPS annual demographic survey asks earnings and work experiences information related to the year before the survey.

8. The total earnings is the sum of wage and salary earnings, the non-farm self-employment earnings, and the farm self-employment earnings. The March income supplement has a consistent topcoding scheme as that of the non-March surveys; all types of annual income are topcoded at $100,000, i.e., 1923 per week.

9. The reason why the number of donor husbands far outnumbers the number of donor wives in each March CPS is that (1) only the Asian and Hispanic wives are included, while the donor husband may be of any racial or ethnic background and may be married to wives of any race, and females are less likely to be self-employed than males (Haber, Lamsa and Lichtenstein 1986).

10. In accordance to the sponsor criteria in the immigration legislation, the CPS collected relative information on parents, brothers, sisters, and children. Hence, this research refers immediate relatives to

these four types of relatives.

11. This was done because the questionnaire did not allow the respondent to give a "no" or "zero" answer to the specific relative questions.

12. This matching rate is much far from the theoretical 100 percent matching rate. This shows that it is much difficult to track people over a one-year period.

13. The dependent variable in the estimation was the log of the wife's age at first marriage in terms of months.

14. The pooled whole sample here refers to the combined 1986, 1988 and 1991 samples, while the pooled employed sample include only immigrant wives who are in the labor force from the combined sample.

15. Without further analyses, it is not clear whether this reflects the internal migration of the old immigrants, or a changed settlement choice among the new immigrants.

6

Results and Discussion

The empirical analysis of this book examines whether marital status at migration and migration patterns are important factors differentiating young Asian and Hispanic immigrant wives' labor supply and earnings in the U.S. Furthermore, it explores the potential interaction effects between these variables and country-of-origin and timing of immigration. The hypothesized selectivity biases in the estimation of the origin country and immigration cohort effects due to the immigrant woman's decision on the mode of entry and her marital status at migration are examined. The reduced-form selection bias-corrected regression procedures are employed to correct for the potential sample selection bias resulted from the endogenous work decision. The labor force participation probit regression, the hourly earnings ordinary least squares (OLS) regression and the hours of work OLS regression are separately estimated with the same set of independent variables.

This chapter describes the results from regression estimation and hypothesis testing. Section 6.1 presents results from the labor force participation estimation. Section 6.2 discusses estimates from the hourly earning regressions. Section 6.3 addresses the results from the hours of work estimation. Each section contains two sub-sections. The first sub-section discusses the significance of migration selectivity variables in the labor supply estimation and how it varies by the young immigrant wives' country-of-origin and timing of migration. In addition, it summarizes the test results on the extent to which migration selectivity impact on the observed country-of-origin and cohort effects. The second sub-section highlights the signs and magnitudes of the estimates of other control variables. Test results pertaining to the significance of the country-of-origin, cohort, and period effects are also presented.

6.1 IMMIGRANT WIVES' LABOR FORCE PARTICIPATION

Constrained by limited time resources like other married women, immigrant wives are making choices between household work and market work. The neoclassical labor supply theory suggests that a married woman' human capital, family resources and her life-cycle events are important determinants of her labor force participation behavior. Specific to an immigrant wife is the fact that she had undergone a self-selection process in the course of immigration, which might reflect in her decision to participate in the U.S. labor force. The regression results show that the young immigrant wives' marital status at migration and migration pattern significantly differentiate the labor force participation decision among young immigrant wives. These differential effects appear to vary across country-of-origin and timing of immigration.

This section reports the estimates from the labor force participation probit regression, as summarized in Tables 6.1.1-6.1.12. Section 6.1.1 focuses on the effect of migration selectivity, i.e., marital status at migration, migration patterns and the presence of immediate relatives in the U.S. It also addresses the potential confounding country-of-origin and cohort effects due to the omitted marital status and migration pattern variables. Section 6.1.2 discusses the coefficient estimates of the other control variables. Marginal probability for the independent variables included in the probit regression are calculated as the change in the probability of being in the labor force due to a unit change in the continuous variable or changing from the base group to the dummy variable category evaluated at the mean (Caudill and Jackson 1989).

6.1.1 Migration Selectivity and Labor Force Participation

This section reports the significance and magnitude of the migration selectivity variables i.e., marital status at migration, migration patterns, and the presence of immediate relatives, in the labor force participation estimation. As the immigrant wives' characteristics and migration selectivity may contribute to their labor force participation behavior differently by country-of-origin, region-of-origin, timing of immigration, age at immigration, and year of survey, the regressions are estimated separately along these dimensions to allow for possible interaction effects.

Tables 6.1.1-6.1.4 present the coefficient estimates and marginal probabilities from the labor force participation probit regressions based on

Table 6.1.1 Labor Force Participation Probit Regression by Year of Survey (Standard Errors in Parentheses)

Variable	1986	1988	1989	1991
intercept	3.7928*	3.4339*	2.0300*	2.1395
	(1.4210)	(1.3561)	(1.0313)	(1.2899)
Region of Residence (dummies, base group is west)				
northeast	-.1934	-.0967	.0061	.0430
	(.1625)	(.1799)	(.1554)	(.1459)
midwest	-.1636	-.0189	-.0003	.1290
	(.1798)	(.2029)	(.1841)	(.1725)
south	-.1170	-.1502	-.0445	-.1630
	(.1352)	(.1477)	(.1302)	(.1257)
MSA Status (dummies, base group is MSA suppressed)				
in central city	-.4789*	-.3349	.0407	.2841
	(.2029)	(.2006)	(.1806)	(.1728)
not in central city	-.4018	-.2083	-.0317	.1740
	(.2102)	(.2079)	(.1846)	(.1750)
not in msa	-.3912	-.3481	-.2186	.3739
	(.2699)	(.3022)	(.2801)	(.2826)
Origin Country (dummies, base group is the Philippines for Asians, Mexico for Hispanics)				
Asian	.4675*	.5919*	.7879*	1.0322*
	(.2227)	(.2521)	(.2746)	(.2298)
China	-.3025	-.2870	-.6407*	-.7643*
	(.2591)	(.2963)	(.3045)	(.0032)
Colombia	.4846	-.0519	-.0356	-.1404
	(.3298)	(.4053)	(.3274)	(.3024)
Cuba	.8953*	.1349	.5135	.2604
	(.2749)	(.3048)	(.3037)	(.2657)
Dominican Republic	-.3361	.2800	-.7104	.0869
	(.3472)	(.3465)	(.3636)	(.3548)
El Salvador	.5891*	-.3727	.3641	.4368*
	(.2852)	(.3024)	(.2553)	(.2065)
India	-.2985	-.2191	-.4210	-.4899
	(.2852)	(.3092)	(.3508)	(.2810)
Japan	-1.0972*	-.7577*	-.9315*	-1.0327*
	(.4079)	(.3721)	(.4092)	(.3963)
Korea	-.6325*	-.6261*	-.6062	-.7776*
	(.3101)	(.3042)	(.3303)	(.2776)
SE Asian refugees	.1787	.3954	-.2298	-.7555*
	(.2808)	(.3160)	(.3436)	(.2883)
other Asians	-.0736	-.0540	-.7931*	-1.5160*
	(.2929)	(.3652)	(.3229)	(.3499)
other Hispanics	.4252*	-.1980	.1256	.3441*
	(.2029)	(.2175)	(.1809)	(.1614)

Table 6.1.1 (continued)

Variable	1986	1988	1989	1991
Immigration Cohort (dummies, base group is pre-1970 cohort)				
1970-74	-.2231	-.1334	.0045	-.0382
	(.1749)	(.2185)	(.2067)	(.2142)
1975-79	-.1506	-.2255	-.2010	-.0047
	(.1850)	(.2138)	(.2090)	(.2027)
1980-84	-.6597*	-.5058*	-.2940	-.1391
	(.2103)	(.2170)	(.2136)	(.2008)
1985-91	-.7501*	-.8370*	-.3760	-.5772*
	(.3202)	(.3323)	(.2551)	(.2122)
Wife's Level of Education (dummies, base group is college education)				
less than 7th grade	-.7315*	-.4153	-.3806	-.3224
	(.2159)	(.2436)	(.2076)	(.1803)
7-12th grade	-.0793	-.3874*	-.2197	-.2677*
	(.1563)	(.1651)	(.1474)	(.1274)
Number of Children, Other Adults, or Immediate Relatives in Household (continuous)				
children 6-17	-.1137*	-.1390*	-.0729	-.1073*
	(.0486)	(.0545)	(.0488)	(.0470)
children less than 6	-.4643*	-.4445*	-.3594*	-.3040*
	(.0667)	(.0810)	(.0670)	(.0616)
adults	.1687*	.1515*		
	(.0582)	(.0691)		
wife's kin			.2230	.1405
			(.1595)	(.1301)
husband's kin			.0022	.2102*
			(.0988)	(.0885)
Marital Status at Migration and Migration Patterns (dummies, base group is married and migrated before husband)				
single at migration	-.6624	-1.0590*		-.2179
	(.3916)	(.4902)		(.2056)
married, after husband	-.9050*	-1.2394*	-.1424[1]	-.1924
	(.3949)	(.4940)	(.2211)	(.2036)
married, with husband	-.8573*	-1.0705*	.0466[1]	-.1792
	(.3854)	(.4851)	(.1999)	(.1944)
Wife's Age (linear splines)				
30 or less	.0477*	.0365	.0695*	.0472*
	(.0237)	(.0280)	(.0216)	(.0204)
over 30	-.0703*	-.0378	-.0916*	-.0531
	(.0331)	(.0379)	(.0294)	(.0277)
Husband's Immigration Status (dummies, base group is established immigrants)				
US-born	-.0992	.1886	.1029	.0206
	(.1533)	(.1702)	(.2559)	(.1461)
recent immigrant	-.0104	-.0008	-.2562	-.0892
	(.1857)	(.3103)	(.2050)	(.1607)

Table 6.1.1 (continued)

Variable	1986	1988	1989	1991
Husband's Usual Weekly Earnings (linear splines)				
less than $170	-.5472*	-.2660	-.4713*	-.5315*
	(.2333)	(.1955)	(.1549)	(.2210)
$170-$400	.8198*	-.7166	.5212	.1930
	(.3640)	(.3807)	(.3082)	(.3347)
over $400	-.6702*	.5735	-.4482	.0939
	(.3343)	(.3887)	(.3275)	(.3065)
Husband's Level of Education (dummies, base group is college education)				
less than 7th grade	.1667	.3725	.0679	.1569
	(.2056)	(.2494)	(.2040)	(.1736)
7-12th grade	-.3154*	.2365	-.0443	.1157
	(.1524)	(.1648)	(.1457)	(.1276)
Wife's English-Speaking Abilities (dummies, base group is English only)				
very well			-.1743	
			(.2730)	
well			-.0997	
			(.2871)	
little or no English			-.7079*	
			(.2997)	
Husband's English-Speaking Abilities (dummies, base group is English only)				
very well			-.2256	
			(.2394)	
well			-.2072	
			(.2659)	
little or no English			.1698	
			(.2810)	
Percentage of Immediate Relatives living in the U.S. (continuous)				
wife's kin			.1197	.2413*
			(.1308)	(.1215)
husband's kin			-.2699*	.0878
			(.1359)	(.1209)
Memo items:				
number of observations	804	645	922	953
dependent variable mean	59.5%	61.2%	58.4%	57.1%
log likelihood	-434.1	-349.7	-504.8	-554.2

* $p<.05$.

Sources: June 1986, 1988, and 1991 Current Population Survey Supplements; Bureau of Labor Statistics, Consumer Price Index.

1. Marital status at migration unknown.

Table 6.1.2 Marginal Probability Calculated from the Labor Force Participation Probit Regression by Year of Survey (Standard Errors in Parentheses)

Variable	1986	1988	1989	1991
Region of Residence (dummies, base group is west)				
northeast	-.0762	-.0375	.0024	.0168
midwest	-.0644	-.0072	-.0001	.0499
south	-.0459	-.0585	-.0174	-.0647
MSA Status (dummies, base group is MSA suppressed)				
in central city	-.1892	-.1320	.0158	.1073
not in central city	-.1591	-.0815	-.0124	.0669
not in msa	-.1549	-.1373	-.0866	.1388
Husband's Level of Education (dummies, base group is college education)				
less than 7th grade	.0630	.1323	.0263	.0605
7-12th grade	-.1249	.0868	-.0173	.0449
Origin Country (dummies, the Philippines is the base group for Asians; Mexico is the base group for Hispanics)				
Asian	.1654	.1975	.2573	.3160
China	.0624	.1101	.0563	.1015
Colombia	.1707	-.0200	-.0139	-.0556
Cuba	.2767	.0505	.1819	.0988
Dominican Republic	-.1331	.1017	-.2748	.0338
El Salvador	.2015	-.1471	.1338	.1600
India	.0639	.1324	.1347	.1936
Japan	-.2465	-.0647	-.0567	-.0002
Korea	-.0649	-.0131	.0691	.0967
SE Asian refugees	.2172	.2861	.1954	.1047
other Asians	.1420	.1825	-.0020	-.1908
other Hispanics	.1521	-.0775	.0482	.1285
Immigration Cohort (dummies, base group is pre-1970 cohort)				
1970-74	-.0881	-.0519	.0017	-.0150
1975-79	-.0592	-.0884	-.0796	-.0019
1980-84	-.2575	-.1995	-.1166	-.0551
1985-91	-.2899	-.3217	-.1491	-.2258
Number of Children/Other Adults in the Household (continuous)				
children 6-17	-.0446	-.0541	-.0286	-.0425
children less than 6	-.1836	-.1755	-.1425	-.1208
adults	.0637	.0565		
wife's kin			.0843	.0543
husband's kin			.0009	.0804

Table 6.1.2 (continued)

Variable	1986	1988	1989	1991
Marital Status at Migration and Migration Patterns (dummies, base group is married and migrated before husband)				
single at migration	-.2585	-.3927		-.0866
married, after husband	-.3419	-.4422	-.0562[1]	-.0764
married, with husband	-.3264	-.3961	.0181[1]	-.0711
Wife's Age (linear splines)				
30 or less	.0184	.0138	.0269	.0184
over 30	-.0088	-.0005	-.0086	-.0023
Wife's Level of Education (dummies, base group is college education)				
less than 7th grade	-.2833	-.1640	-.1509	-.1280
7-12th grade	-.0310	-.1529	-.0870	-.1064
Husband's Immigration Status (dummies, base group is established immigrants)				
US-born	-.0388	.0699	.0396	.0081
recent immigrant	-.0041	-.0002	-.1016	-.0353
Husband's Usual Weekly Earnings (linear splines)				
less than $170	-.2155	-.1046	-.1862	-.2088
$170-$400	.1010	-.3694	.0193	-.1344
over $400	-.1574	-.1615	-.1578	-.0972
Percentage of Immediate Relatives Living in the U.S. (continuous)				
wife's kin			.0460	.0918
husband's kin			-.1070	.0342
Wife's English-Speaking Abilities (dummies, base group is English only)				
very well			-.0689	
well			-.0392	
little or no			-.2740	
Husband's English-Speaking Abilities (dummies, base group is English only)				
very well			-.0894	
well			-.0820	
little or no			.0647	

Sources: June 1986, 1988, and 1991 Current Population Survey Supplements; Bureau of Labor Statistics, Consumer Price Index.

1. Marital status at migration unknown.

Table 6.1.3 Labor Force Participation Probit Regression, Combined Samples (Standard Errors in Parentheses)

Variable	1989 1991	1986 1988 1991[1]	1986 1988 1991[2]
intercept	1.5933*	2.6936*	2.9435*
	(.7126)	(.7240)	(.7255)
Region of Residence (dummies, base group is west)			
northeast	.0303	-.0640	-.0798
	(.1018)	(.0884)	(.0868)
midwest	.0486	-.0749	-.0808
	(.1196)	(.1023)	(.1021)
south	-.1093	-.1178	-.1057
	(.0863)	(.0735)	(.0718)
MSA Status (dummies, base group is MSA suppressed)			
in central city	.1859	.2284	.2184
	(.1190)	(.1632)	(.1635)
not in central city	.1003	.1532	.1455
	(.1207)	(.1647)	(.1649)
not in msa	.1368	.4740	.4684
	(.1886)	(.2686)	(.2685)
Origin Country (dummies, the Philippines is the base group for Asians; Mexico is the base group for Hispanics)			
Asian	1.0102*	.6504*	
	(.1681)	(.1285)	
China	-.7394*	-.4295*	
	(.1894)	(.1496)	
Colombia	-.0783	.1096	
	(.2143)	(.1855)	
Cuba	.3946*	.3771*	
	(.1889)	(.1536)	
Dominican Republic	-.3358	.0386	
	(.2381)	(.1892)	
El Salvador	.4169*	.2693	
	(.1549)	(.1382)	
India	-.4618*	-.3082	
	(.2104)	(.1612)	
Japan	-1.0490*	-.9861*	
	(.2694)	(.2171)	
Korea	-.7123*	-.6258*	
	(.2043)	(.1647)	
SE Asian refugees	-.5551*	-.0701	
	(.2104)	(.1619)	
other Asians	-1.0105*	-.4377*	
	(.2164)	(.1796)	
other Hispanics	.3052*	.1970	
	(.1142)	(.1051)	

Table 6.1.3 (continued)

Variable	1989 1991	1986 1988 1991[1]	1986 1988 1991[2]
Originating Region (dummies, base group is the Spanish-speaking Caribbean)			
Mexico			-.2556*
			(.1082)
east Asia			-.1664
			(.1173)
southeast Asia			.3974*
			(.1199)
south Asia			.0977
			(.1483)
south America			-.1040
			(.1288)
central America			-.0085
			(.1298)
Immigration Cohort (dummies, base group is pre-1970)			
1970-74	-.0548	-.2253*	-.2524*
	(.1391)	(.1093)	(.1083)
1975-79	-.1851	-.2254*	-.2476*
	(.1359)	(.1068)	(.1055)
1980-84	-.3199*	-.4719*	-.4989*
	(.1376)	(.1107)	(.1099)
1985-91	-.6357*	-.7757*	-.8017*
	(.1459)	(.1275)	(.1258)
Husband's Level of Education (dummies, base group is college education)			
less than 7th grade	.1094	.2317*	.2338*
	(.1260)	(.1120)	(.1117)
7-12th grade	.0405	.0069	.0062
	(.0914)	(.0801)	(.0794)
Number of Children/Other Adults in Household (continuous)			
children 6-17	-.0914*	-.1248*	-.1241*
	(.0321)	(.0273)	(.0272)
children less than 6	-.3156*	-.3676*	-.3668*
	(.0429)	(.0374)	(.0373)
adults		.1133*	.1188*
		(.0303)	(.0302)
wife's kin	.1854		
	(.0958)		
husband's kin	.1061		
	(.0613)		
Wife's Level of Education (dummies, base group is college education)			
less than 7th grade	-.3782*	-.5135*	-.5251*
	(.1294)	(.1144)	(.1134)
7-12th grade	-.2593*	-.2506*	-.2629*
	(.0920)	(.0811)	(.0794)

Table 6.1.3 (continued)

Variable	1989 1991	1986 1988 1991[1]	1986 1988 1991[2]
Marital Status at Migration and Migration Patterns (dummies, base group is married and migrated before husband)			
single at migration		-.4401*	-.4447*
		(.1526)	(.1522)
married, after husband	-.1119[3]	-.5381*	-.5438*
	(.0885)	(.1542)	(.1540)
married, with husband	-.0129[3]	-.4894*	-.4934*
	(.0912)	(.1507)	(.1500)
Wife's Age (linear splines)			
30 or less	.0545*	.0390*	.0396*
	(.0140)	(.0128)	(.0127)
over 30	-.0660*	-.0443*	-.0464*
	(.0191)	(.0176)	(.0175)
Husband's Immigration Status (dummies, base group is established immigrants)			
US-born	.1193	.0645	.0293
	(.1037)	(.0836)	(.0823)
recent immigrant	-.2123	-.2251	-.2656
	(.1557)	(.1716)	(.1691)
Husband's Usual Weekly Earnings (linear splines)			
less than $170	-.4448*	-.4400*	-.4317*
	(.1143)	(.1173)	(.1168)
$170-$400	.2542	.1773	.1585
	(.2051)	(.1923)	(.1917)
over $400	-.1122	-.0568	-.0585
	(.2102)	(.1851)	(.1841)
Year of Survey (dummies, base group is 1991)			
1986		-.0903	-.0896
		(.0798)	(.0796)
1988		-.0062	-.0166
		(.0816)	(.0816)
1989	.0511		
	(.0651)		
Percentage of Immediate Relatives Living in the U.S. (continuous)			
wife's kin	.2020*		
	(.0840)		
husband's kin	-.0869		
	(.0848)		
Memo items:			
number of observations	1875	2402	2402
dependent variable mean	57.7%	59.0%	59.0%
log likelihood	-1092.4	-1407.2	-1409.1

* p<.05.

Sources: June 1986, 1988, and 1991 Current Population Survey Supplements; Bureau of Labor Statistics, Consumer Price Index.

1. Includes country-of-origin dummies. 2. Includes region-of-origin dummies. 3. Marital status at migration unknown.

Table 6.1.4 Marginal Probability Calculated from the Labor Force Participation Probit Regression, Combined Samples (Standard Errors in Parentheses)

Variable	1989 1991	1986 1988 1991[1]	1986 1988 1991[2]
Region of Residence (dummies, base group is west)			
northeast	.0118	-.0250	-.0313
midwest	.0189	-.0293	-.0317
south	-.0431	-.0463	-.0415
MSA Status (dummies, base group is MSA suppressed)			
in central city	.0710	.0858	.0822
not in central city	.0388	.0583	.0554
not in msa	.0527	.1685	.1667
Origin Country (dummies, the Philippines is the base group for Asians; Mexico is the base group for Hispanics)			
Asian	.3085	.2199	
China	.1020	.0831	
Colombia	-.0308	.0420	
Cuba	.1449	.1372	
Dominican Republic	-.1333	.0149	
El Salvador	.1523	.1003	
India	.1940	.1255	
Japan	-.0152	-.1331	
Korea	.1116	.0095	
SE Asian refugees	.1648	.2003	
other Asians	-.0001	.0801	
other Hispanics	.1142	-.0744	
Husband's Level of Education (dummies, base group is college education)			
less than 7th grade	.0422	.0870	.0877
7-12th grade	.0158	.0027	.0024
Originating region (dummies, base group is the Spanish-speaking Caribbean)			
Mexico			-.1012
east Asia			-.0656
southeast Asia			.1440
south Asia			.0375
south America			-.0408
central America			-.0033
Immigration Cohort (dummies, base group is pre-1970 cohort)			
1970-74	-.0215	-.0891	-.0999
1975-79	-.0733	-.0892	-.0980
1980-84	-.1270	-.1865	-.1969
1985-91	-.2476	-.2982	-.3071

Table 6.1.4 (continued)

Variable	1989 1991	1986 1988 1991[1]	1986 1988 1991[2]
Number of children/Other Adults in the Household (continuous)			
children 6-17	-.0360	-.0491	-.0488
children less than 6	-.1253	-.1457	-.1454
adults		.0434	.0454
wife's kin	.0708		
husband's kin	.0410		
Wife's Level of Education (dummies, base group is college education)			
less than 7th grade	-.1500	-.2026	-.2070
7-12th grade	-.1029	-.0992	-.1041
Marital Status at Migration and Migration Patterns (dummies, base group is married and migrated before husband)			
single at migration		-.1741	-.1760
married, after husband	-.0442[3]	-.2119	-.2141
married with husband	-.0050[3]	-.1933	-.1948
Husband's Immigration Status (dummies, base group is established immigrants)			
US-born	.0460	.0249	.0113
recent immigrant	-.0842	-.0890	-.1052
Husband's Usual Weekly Earnings (linear splines)			
less than $170	-.1759	-.1741	-.1709
$170-$400	-.0755	-.1040	-.1082
over $400	-.1202	-.1266	-.1315
Year of Survey (dummies, base group is 1991)			
1986		-.0354	-.0351
1988		-.0024	-.0065
1989	.0199		
Wife's Age (linear splines)			
30 or less	.0212	.0151	.0153
over 30	-.0044	-.0021	-.0026
Percentage of Immediate Relatives Living in the U.S. (continuous)			
wife's kin	.0770		
husband's kin	-.0342		

Sources: June 1986, 1988 and 1991 Current Population Survey Supplements; Bureau of Labor Statistics, Consumer Price Index.

1. Includes country-of-origin dummies. 2. Includes region-of-origin dummies. 3. Marital status at migration unknown.

Table 6.1.5 Labor Force Participation Probit Regression by Region of Origin, Asian (Standard Errors in Parentheses)

Variable	Total Asians	East Asia	Southeast Asia	South Asia
intercept	3.9899*	7.1098	2.0919	-.7368
	(1.2955)	(8.9995)	(2.0476)	(3.3526)
Region of Residence (dummies, base group is west)				
northeast	-.0389	.2406	-.3211	-1.3770*
	(.1267)	(.2049)	(.2484)	(.4823)
midwest	.1258	-.0244	.8328*	-1.1500*
	(.1531)	(.2608)	(.3248)	(.5035)
south	-.0400	-.0520	.1332	-1.3038*
	(.1322)	(.2395)	(.2289)	(.4988)
MSA Status (dummies, base group is MSA suppressed, except for South Asia)				
in central city	.5755*	.8837*	1.5689*	-.4148
	(.2576)	(.3863)	(.7606)	(.6377)
not in central city	.3113	.3602	1.5137*	-.7938
	(.2566)	(.3791)	(.7648)	(.5648)
not in msa	1.0582*	1.4795	1.2043	
	(.4880)	(.8277)	(1.0121)	
Origin Country (dummies, the Philippines is the base group for Asians; Countries of a specific region are compared to the omitted countries in that region)				
China	-.4458*	.6266*		
	(.1599)	(.2491)		
India	-.3778*			.0680
	(.1735)			(.5590)
Japan	-.9787*			
	(.2283)			
Korea	-.5909*	.5237*		
	(.1731)	(.2570)		
Laos			-.2104	
			(.3919)	
Philippines			.2856	
			(.2895)	
Vietnam	-.0990		-.2080	
	(.1823)		(.3007)	
other Asians	-.4075*			
	(.1879)			

Table 6.1.5 (continued)

Variable	Total Asians	East Asia	Southeast Asia	South Asia
Husband's Level of Education (dummies, base group is college education)				
less than 7th grade	.5562	.6006	.3954	
	(.3002)	(.6232)	(.4210)	
7-12th grade	-.0203	.0718	-.2955	1.3628*
	(.1358)	(.2319)	(.2232)	(.5690)
Wife's Level of Education (dummies, base group is college education)				
less than 7th grade	-.8581*	-.7940	-.7276	-1.3818
	(.2600)	(.4785)	(.3731)	(2.2701)
7-12th grade	-.2711*	-.4459*	-.0614	-1.2366*
	(.1277)	(.2224)	(.2343)	(.4223)
Wife's Age (linear splines)				
30 or less	.0188	.0290	.0181	.2729*
	(.0272)	(.0533)	(.0451)	(.0900)
over 30	-.0053	-.0106	-.0363	-.2319*
	(.0349)	(.0654)	(.0595)	(.1124)
Number of Children/Other Relatives in Household (continuous)				
children 6-17	-.1022	-.0438	-.1930*	-.1855
	(.0560)	(.1111)	(.0916)	(.2153)
children less than 6	-.3622*	-.5086*	-.4243*	-1.0513*
	(.0665)	(.1326)	(.1047)	(.2742)
adults	.1571*	.2298*	.1420	.3334*
	(.0545)	(.0912)	(.1084)	(.1523)
Husband's Immigration Status (dummies, base group is established immigrants)				
US-born	-.1827	-.0341	-.6104*	1.0389
	(.1446)	(.2301)	(.2402)	(.8663)
recent immigrant	-.2845	-.1422	-.9296	-.1319
	(.2361)	(.3965)	(.5795)	(.6204)
Year of Survey (dummies, base group is 1991)				
1986	-.2664	-.5017*	-.2314	.1389
	(.1471)	(.2493)	(.2569)	(.5534)
1988	-.1416	-.5590*	-.0892	-.0059
	(.1487)	(.2597)	(.2499)	(.5422)

Table 6.1.5 (continued)

Variable	Total Asians	East Asia	Southeast Asia	South Asia
Immigration Cohort (dummies, base group is pre-1970 cohort)				
1970-74	-.6027*	-1.0311*	-.2270	.1027
	(.2175)	(.3504)	(.3715)	(.7205)
1975-79	-.5959*	-1.0070*	-.2851	.6338
	(.2158)	(.3499)	(.3700)	(.7471)
1980-84	-.7305*	-.9716*	-.5126	.3505
	(.2211)	(.3690)	(.3576)	(.7867)
1985-91	-1.1511*	-1.5277*	-1.0045*	.0598
	(.2422)	(.4158)	(.4013)	(.8421)
Marital Status at Migration and Migration Patterns (dummies, base group is married and migrated before husbands)				
single	-.1180	.3059	-.2634	-1.0316
	(.2789)	(.4646)	(.5772)	(.8404)
married, after husband	-.2457	.4003	-.4303	-.9049
	(.2790)	(.4724)	(.5788)	(.8155)
married, with husband	-.3924	-.1450	-.0142	-1.4801
	(.2721)	(.4550)	(.5652)	(.8319)
Husband's Usual Weekly Earnings (linear splines)				
less than $170	-.5215*	-1.4094	-.3940	-.5827[2]
	(.1958)	(1.7433)	(.2530)	(.4518)
$170-$400	.5818	1.2025	.8481	
	(.3595)	(1.9103)	(.5580)	
$400	-.5653	-.1922	-.9774	-.2807
	(.3275)	(.5714)	(.5783)	(.6222)
Memo items:				
number of observations	1073	419	413	178
dependent variable mean	65.5%	58.5%	76.2%	61.9%
log likelihood	-491.3	-182.0	-155.7	-68.7

* p<.05.

Sources: June 1986, 1988, and 1991 Current Population survey supplements; Bureau of Labor Statistics, Consumer Price Index.

1. Included in the high school category.

2. Included husbands earnings of less than $400 a week.

Table 6.1.6 Marginal Probability Calculated from the Labor Force Participation Regression by Region of Origin, Asian (Standard Errors in Parentheses)

Variable	Total Asians	East Asia	Southeast Asia	South Asia
Region of Residence (dummies, base group is west)				
northeast	-.0144	.0905	-.1097	-.4776
midwest	.0451	-.0095	.1770	-.4205
south	-.0148	-.0203	.0392	-.4606
MSA Status (dummies, base group is MSA suppressed)				
in central city	.1802	.2791	.2269	-.1635
not in central city	.1062	.1323	.2252	-.3073
not in msa	.2726	.3701	.2105	
Husband's Level of education (dummies, college education)				
less than 7th grade	.1753	.2076	.1041	
7-12th grade	-.0075	.0277	-.1003	.3330
Origin Country (dummies, the Philippines is the base group for Asians; Countries of a specific region are compared to the omitted countries in that region)				
China	-.1737	.2150		
India	-.1466			.0256
Japan	-.3740			
Korea	-.2312	.1849		
Laos			-.0697	
Philippines			.0790	
Vietnam	-.0371		-.0689	
other Asians	-.1585			
Immigration Cohort (dummies, base group is pre-1970 cohort)				
1970-74	-.2358	-.3777	-.0756	.0384
1975-79	-.2331	-.3707	-.0964	.2065
1980-84	-.2849	-.3603	-.1827	.1242
1985-91	-.4290	-.4901	-.3768	.0225
Marital Status at Migration and Migration Patterns (dummies, base group is married and migrated before husband)				
single	-.0444	.1137	-.0886	-.3859
married, after husband	-.0942	.1457	-.1508	-.3454
married, with husband	-.1525	-.0572	-.0044	-.4995

Table 6.1.6 (continued)

Variable	Total Asians	East Asia	Southeast Asia	South Asia
Wife's Level of Education (dummies, base group is college education)				
less than 7th grade	-.3320	-.3037	-.2680	-.4787
7-12th grade	-.1042	-.1764	-.0194	-.4438
Number of Children/Other Adults in Household (continuous)				
children 6-17	-.0384	-.0171	-.0636	-.0723
children less than 6	-.1404	-.2005	-.1485	-.3919
adults	.0559	.0867	.0416	.1186
Wife's Age (linear splines)				
30 or less	.0069	.0112	.0055	.0986
over 30	.0050	.0071	-.0056	.0155
Husband's Immigration Status (dummies, base group is husband established immigrants)				
US-born	-.0694	-.0133	-.2213	.2911
recent immigrant	-.1095	-.0561	-.3479	-.0511
Husband's Usual Weekly Earnings (linear splines)				
less than $170	-.2038	-.4686	-.1370	-.2292[2]
$170-$400	.0219	-.0818	.1164	
$400	-.1973	-.1581	-.1869	-.3314
Year of Survey (dummies, base group is 1991)				
1986	-.1023	-.1979	-.0772	.0516
1988	-.0535	-.2196	-.0284	-.0022

Sources: June 1986, 1988 and 1991 Current Population Survey Supplements; Bureau of Labor Statistics, Consumer Price Index.

1. Included in the high school category. 2. Included husbands earnings less than $400 a week.

Table 6.1.7 Labor Force Participation Probit Regression by Region of Origin, Hispanics (Standard Errors in Parentheses)

Variable	Total Hispanics	Central America	South America	Caribbean	Mexico
intercept	2.4217*	3.1804	29.5233	9.9747	1.6749
	(.9715)	(3.3085)	(2.9676)	(1.0902)	(1.2106)
Region of Residence (dummies, base group is west)					
northeast	-.0847	-.1159	-.6864*	.1822	.1936
	(.1370)	(.3044)	(.3283)	(.6069)	(.4008)
midwest	-.2191	1.8018	-1.8974*	-.1966	-.2075
	(.1562)	(1.2007)	(.6795)	(.8087)	(.1956)
south	-.1580	-.3713	-.7239*	-.1488	-.0672
	(.0965)	(.3145)	(.3491)	(.5937)	(.1284)
MSA Status (dummies, base group is MSA suppressed, except for Central America and the Spanish-speaking Caribbean)					
in central city	.0142	-.7290	-.6019	1.0352	.0277
	(.2358)	(.7574)	(.8068)	(.8197)	(.3079)
not in city	.0326	-.4927	-.7093	1.4988	.0699
	(.2379)	(.7902)	(.8050)	(.7984)	(.3121)
not in msa	.1915		.7057		.0184
	(.3633)		(1.2719)		(.4519)
Origin Country (dummies, Mexico is the base group for Hispanics; Countries of a specific region are compared to the omitted countries in that region)					
Colombia	.2103	.1167			
	(.2124)	(.2648)			
Cuba	.4603*			.2041	
	(.1720)			(.7739)	
Dominican Republic	.1806			-.2832	
	(.2243)			(.8199)	
El Salvador	.3032*	.0657			
	(.1536)	(.2891)			
other Hispanics	.2344				
	(.1199)				
Year of Survey (dummies, base group is 1991)					
1986	.0277	.4700	.2931	.6354	-.1575
	(.1052)	(.3965)	(.3099)	(.4199)	(.1450)
1988	.0673	-.2915	-.3867	.5861	.2102
	(.1076)	(.3733)	(.3315)	(.4094)	(.1502)
Wife's Age (linear splines)					
30 or less	.0500*	.0343	.0816	.0566	.0686*
	(.0160)	(.0558)	(.0519)	(.0627)	(.0222)
over 30	-.0685*	-.0633	-.1662*	-.1273	-.0813*
	(.0230)	(.0829)	(.0772)	(.0878)	(.0318)
Number of Children/Other Adults in Household (continuous)					
children 6-17	-.1285*	-.1121	-.1395	-.3449*	-.1304*
	(.0343)	(.1212)	(.1219)	(.1529)	(.0450)
children less than 6	-.3685*	-.4018*	-.5476*	-.9817*	-.3428*
	(.0495)	(.1658)	(.1845)	(.2070)	(.0656)
adults	.0918*	.1517	.2972	.3526	.0589
	(.0401)	(.1442)	(.1638)	(.2213)	(.0534)

Table 6.1.7 (continued)

Variable	Total Hispanics	Central America	South America	Caribbean	Mexico
Wife's Level of Education (dummies, base group is college education)					
less than 7th grade	-.4332*	-.3042	-1.8571	.0939	-.4230
	(.1481)	(.4280)	(1.0929)	(.5348)	(.2351)
7-12th grade	-.2232	-.4548	-.3700	.1054	-.1270
	(.1179)	(.3364)	(.2720)	(.2935)	(.2155)
Immigration Cohort (dummies, base group is pre-1970 cohort)					
1970-74	-.1089	-.8558	-.3775	-.3948	-.0200
	(.1413)	(.6583)	(.4307)	(.4265)	(.1978)
1975-79	-.1210	-.5593	-.8188	-.5142	.0203
	(.1372)	(.5941)	(.4252)	(.4973)	(.1915)
1980-84	-.4048*	-.6320	-.9988*	-1.0213*	-.2312
	(.1426)	(.6088)	(.4585)	(.4611)	(.2086)
1985-91	-.6467*	-.3161	-1.4228*	-.0799	-.6538*
	(.1676)	(.6404)	(.5355)	(.6410)	(.2386)
Husband's Level of education (dummies, base group is college education)					
less than 7th grade	.2434	.1779	.4245	-.3649	.2083
	(.1390)	(.4083)	(.7386)	(.6474)	(.2083)
7-12th grade	.0496	.3247	.1751	-.0883	-.0595
	(.1104)	(.3473)	(.2604)	(.3143)	(.1860)
Marital Status at Migration and Migration Patterns (dummies, base group is married and migrated before husbands)					
single	-.5539*	-.2921	-.6747	-.8979	-.7591*
	(.1989)	(.6372)	(.5739)	(.5398)	(.3108)
after husband	-.6499*	-.3201	-.7460	-.7349	-1.0024*
	(.2025)	(.6563)	(.6215)	(.5674)	(.3133)
with husband	-.5096*	-.1644	-.7909	-.1120	-.9210*
	(.1974)	(.6252)	(.6021)	(.5498)	(.3075)
Husband's Immigration Status (dummies, base group is husband established immigrants)					
US-born	.1952	.1032	.5323	-.0225	.0961
	(.1134)	(.3866)	(.2980)	(.3710)	(.1635)
recent immigrant	-.1173	-.0001	.5226	-1.7392	-.1193
	(.2839)	(1.2669)	(.6727)	(1.0762)	(.3992)
Husband's Usual Weekly Earnings (linear splines)					
less than $170	-.4135*	-.3247	-5.4672	-2.1146	-.3191
	(.1594)	(.5462)	(4.0939)	(1.9975)	(.1877)
$170-$400	-.0124	-.1427	5.2841	3.2686	-.1719
	(.2523)	(.8679)	(4.3661)	(2.3651)	(.3173)
over $400	.2949	.3451	.5740	-2.4791*	.3581
	(.2705)	(.9061)	(.9191)	(.9294)	(.3735)
Memo items:					
number of observation	1329	190	207	181	723
dependent variable mean	55.0%	60.3%	60.9%	68.9%	48.9%
log likelihood	-896.2	-109.4	-96.1	-82.5	-533.2

* p<.05.

Sources: June 1986, 1988, and 1991 Current Population Survey Supplements; Bureau of Labor Statistics, Consumer Price Index.

Table 6.1.8 Marginal Probability Calculated from the Labor Force Participation Regression by Region of Origin, Hispanics (Standard Errors in Parentheses)

Variable	Total Hispanics	Central America	South America	Caribbean	Mexico
Region of Residence (dummies, base group is west)					
northeast	-.0336	-.0452	-.2680	.0612	.0769
midwest	-.0872	.3775	-.5561	-.0724	-.0819
south	-.0629	-.1468	-.2816	-.0543	-.0268
MSA Status (dummies, base group is MSA suppressed, except for Central America and the Spanish-speaking Caribbean)					
in central city	.0056	-.2363	-.2835	.2476	.0110
not in central city	.0129	-.2759	-.1945	.2876	.0279
not in msa	.0744		.2282		.0073
Origin Country (dummies, Mexico is the base group for Hispanics; Countries of a specific region are compared to the omitted countries in that region)					
Colombia	.0816		.0440		
Cuba	.1710			.0681	
Dominican Republic	.0703			-.1058	
El Salvador	.1160	.0251			
other Hispanics	.0906				
Immigration Cohort (dummies, base group is pre-1970 cohort)					
1970-74	-.0433	-.3269	-.1492	-.1498	-.0080
1975-79	-.0481	-.2202	-.3151	-.1974	.0081
1980-84	-.1599	-.2476	-.3738	-.3903	-.0911
1985-91	-.2489	-.1249	-.4829	-.0287	-.2411
Number of Children/Other Relatives in Household (continuous)					
children 6-17	-.0511	-.0437	-.0545	-.1301	-.0517
children less than 6	-.1459	-.1589	-.2158	-.3764	-.1334
adults	.0361	.0571	.1080	.1120	.0235
Marital Status at Migration and Migration Patterns (dummies, base group is married and migrated before husband)					
single	-.2158	-.1153	-.2637	-.3462	-.2732
after husband	-.2500	-.1265	-.2895	-.2845	-.3374
with husband	-.1995	-.0645	-.3054	-.0405	-.3175

Table 6.1.8 (continued)

Variable	Total Hispanics	Central America	South America	Caribbean	Mexico
Wife's Level of Education (dummies, base group is college education)					
less than 7th grade	-.1708	-.1202	-.5517	.0323	-.1628
7-12th grade	-.0888	-.1798	-.1462	.0362	-.0504
Husband's Level of Education (dummies, base group is college education)					
less than 7th grade	.0940	.0667	.1495	-.1380	.0827
7-12th grade	.0196	.1180	.0653	-.0318	-.0237
Wife's Age (linear splines)					
30 or less	.0197	.0131	.0309	.0197	.0274
over 30	-.0073	-.0112	-.0329	-.0253	-.0051
Husband's Immigration Status (dummies, base group is established immigrants)					
US-born	.0758	.0392	.1819	-.0080	.0383
recent immigrant	-.0467	-.0001	.1791	-.5827	-.0474
Husband's Usual Weekly Earnings (linear splines)					
less than $170	-.1633	-.1283	-.6085	-.6367	-.1245
$170-$400	-.1680	-.1847	-.0717	.2610	-.1869
over $400	-.0521	-.0478	.1389	-.4863	-.0527
Year of Survey (dummies, base group is 1991)					
1986	.0109	.1646	.1067	.1813	-.0624
1988	.0265	-.1151	-.1528	.1706	.0835

Sources: June 1986, 1988, and 1991 Current Population Survey Supplements; Bureau of Labor Statistics, Consumer Price Index.

Table 6.1.9 Labor Force Participation Probit Regression by Country of Origin (Standard Errors are in Parentheses)

Variable	Cuba	China	Philip-pines	India	Korea	Asian Refugees
intercept	.3584	5.3381	2.6129	-1.1043	33.9001	4.1552
	(2.1216)	(12.9279)	(34.0106)	(3.6411)	(35.9987)	(4.2886)
Region of Origin (dummies, base group is west)						
northeast	1.4981	.1668	-.8461	-1.4307*	-.4167	-.5123
	(.9340)	(.3202)	(4.1187)	(.4955)	(.4616)	(.5150)
midwest	.8405	-.0389	1.4735	-1.0963*	-.4217	1.5143*
	(1.1177)	(.3940)	(6.5301)	(.5076)	(.5787)	(.6242)
south	.8910	.0323	.7749	-1.2297*	-.3664	-.0887
	(.8337)	(.4336)	(4.1259)	(.5090)	(.4666)	(.4005)
MSA Status (dummies, base group is not in msa and MSA suppressed, except for China)						
central city	.7651	2.3698*	.9220	-.2667	-.6332	1.3917
	(1.1196)	(.6386)	(1.5922)	(.6735)	(.7436)	(.8831)
not in city	.3513	.9528	.9126	-.6956	-.6159	.8652
	(1.0440)	(.6112)	(1.6244)	(.5779)	(.7082)	(.9322)
not in msa		1.9746				
		(1.3943)				
Origin Country (dummies, base group is Cambodia)						
Laos						-.3946
						(.6193)
Vietnam						-.2956
						(.5668)

Table 6.1.9 (continued)

Variable	Cuba	China	Philip-pines	India	Korea	Asian Refugees
Number of Children/Other Adults in Household (continuous)						
children 6-17	-1.0384*	-.0482	-.1501	-.1925	.4772	-.1024
	(.3143)	(.1893)	(1.7938)	(.2191)	(.2632)	(.1511)
children less than 6	-1.5538*	-.7979*	-.3982	-1.0365*	-.3586	-.5829*
	(.3875)	(.2323)	(1.9813)	(.2787)	(.2429)	(.1880)
adults	.4818	.2897*	.2806	.3143*	-.0227	.1353
	(.3736)	(.1296)	(1.6456)	(.1514)	(.2188)	(.2066)
Marital Status at Migration and Migration Patterns (dummies, base group is married and migrated before husband)						
single	-.3729	.3169	-.1214	-1.0195	.0432	-.1776
	(.8007)	(.7516)	(7.8607)	(.8477)	(.9495)	(1.3143)
after husband	-.4576	.2244	-.7107	-.8257	1.3326	.0009
	(.9025)	(.7547)	(7.6117)	(.8208)	(1.0868)	(1.3333)
with husband	.9297	-.0593	.7104	-1.3989	-1.2640	.4511
	(.9938)	(.7486)	(8.0583)	(.8372)	(.9013)	(1.3051)
Wife's Level of Education (dummies, base group is college education, the less-than-7th-grade and the high school groups are combined for Cuba and India)						
less than 7th grade		-1.3614	-.3660		-1.9921*	-.4796
		(.8167)	(1.0624)		(.9617)	(.6762)
7-12th grade	-.1286	-.7833	-.8955	-1.1550*	-1.1878*	.0243
	(.4486)	(.4126)	(4.1695)	(.4197)	(.4463)	(.4814)

Table 6.1.9 (continued)

Variable	Cuba	China	Philip-pines	India	Korea	Asian Refugees
Immigration Cohort (dummies, base group is pre-1970 cohort)						
1970-74		-.5225	-1.1605	.0906	-2.3947*	1.4900
		(.5590)	(5.4004)	(.7200)	(.8779)	(1.6591)
1975-79	-.2161[2]	-1.0634	-1.1051	.6045	-.6251	.3480
	(.6128)	(.5679)	(5.8402)	(.7540)	(.8247)	(1.0354)
1980-84		-.5094	-.9837	.3399	-1.5257	.5009
		(.6281)	(5.1454)	(.7932)	(.8815)	(1.0617)
1985-91	-1.3906[3]	-1.1344	-2.5938	.1453	-3.0928*	.0872
	(.7567)	(.6888)	(6.1119)	(.8553)	(1.2286)	(1.1935)
Wife's Age (linear splines)						
30 or less	.1610	-.0429	.0639	.2899*	.0847	-.0612
	(.0960)	(.0889)	(.8743)	(.0945)	(.1016)	(.0879)
over 30	-.3307*	.0744	-.0116	-.2502*	-.0549	-.0253
	(.1385)	(.4868)	(1.1146)	(.1184)	(.1308)	(.1191)
Husband's Usual Weekly Earnings (linear splines)						
less than $170	-.7479	-.6534	.1457	-.6274	-6.4074	-.6956
	(3.8024)	(2.4827)	(3.8485)	(.5160)	(7.1358)	(.6260)
$170-$400	3.1276	-.0787	-2.3682		7.1801	1.9772
	(4.1343)	(2.6578)	(13.8746)		(7.5809)	(1.0404)
over $400	-4.7542*	.4939	1.2030	-.1928	-2.2426	-1.3096
	(1.5365)	(.9189)	(13.1155)	(.6832)	(1.2807)	(1.0846)

Table 6.1.9 (continued)

Variable	Cuba	China	Philip-pines	India	Korea	Asian Refugees
Year of Survey (dummies, base group is 1991)						
1986	1.1723	-.7348	-.7554	.0770	-.5285	-.3237
	(.6243)	(.4037)	(4.8757)	(.5841)	(.5350)	(.4782)
1988	.3133	-1.1441*	-1.6875	-.0306	-.3884	.7950
	(.5909)	(.4384)	(4.5603)	(.5616)	(.5399)	(.4755)
Husband's Immigration Status (dummies, base group is established immigrants, except for Cuba and Southeast Asian refugees)						
US-born	-.8122	-.3632	-.8333	.7708	-1.2683*	1.4749
	(.5831)	(.4295)	(3.3933)	(.9409)	(.5955)	(1.0625)
recent immigrant		-.0148	-2.2617	-.0010	.6597	
		(1.1314)	(9.6992)	(.6446)	(.7966)	
Husband's Education (dummies, base group is college education; the less-than-7th-grade and high school groups are combined for Cuba, Philippines, India, and Korea)						
less than 7th grade		1.3383				.5846
		(1.1253)				(.6780)
7-12th grade	-.3223	-.2702	-.2941	1.3346*	.6666	-.2659
	(.4172)	(.4074)	(3.5064)	(.5718)	(.4669)	(.4385)
Memo items:						
number of observations	111	207	211	166	141	162
mean of dependent variable	72.8%	66.4%	81.4%	62.5%	55.2%	69.8%
log likelihood	-40.7	-79.7	-51.4	-65.1	-49.3	-59.8

* $p<.05$.

Sources: June 1986, 1988, and 1991 Current Population Survey Supplements; Bureau of Labor Statistics, Consumer Price Index.

1. Includes husbands earnings less than $400 a week. 2. Includes all 1970 cohorts. 3. Includes all 1980s cohorts.

Table 6.1.10 Marginal Probability Calculated from the Labor Force Participation Probit Regression by Country of Origin (Standard Errors are in Parentheses)

Variable	Cuba	China	Philip-pines	India	Korea	Asian Refugees
Region of Residence (dummies, base group is west)						
northeast	.2548	.0584	-.2953	-.4917	-.1646	-.1954
midwest	.1984	-.0143	.1769	-.4065	-.1665	.2808
south	.2052	.0117	.1382	-.4437	-.1452	-.0316
MSA Status (dummies, base group is not in msa and MSA suppressed, except for China)						
in city	.1872	.3330	.1511	-.1043	-.2443	.2737
not in city	.1031	.2514	.1504	-.2719	-.2382	.2186
not in msa		.3274				
Husband's Level of Education (dummies, base group is college education, the less than 7th grade and the high school groups are combined for Cuba, Philippines, India, and Korea)						
less than 7th grade		.2966				.1669
7-12th grade	-.1161	-.1031	-.0887	.3262	.2354	-.0982
Origin Country (dummies, base group is Cambodia)						
Laos						-.1486
Vietnam						-.1097
Immigration Cohort (dummies, base group is pre-1970 cohort)						
1970-74	[2]	-.2034	-.4195	.0338	-.5402	.2795
1975-79	-.0761	-.4029	-.3980	.1971	-.2415	.1088
1980-84	[3]	-.1982	-.3502	.1200	-.4705	.1479
1985-91	-.5114	-.4255	-.7696	.0536	-.5505	.0297
Wife's Level of Education (dummies, base group is college education, the less-than-7th-grade and the high school groups are combined for Cuba and India)						
less than 7th grade		-.4900	-.1131	-.4234	-.5207	-.1823
7-12th grade	-.0443	-.3045	-.3150		-.4068	.0084
Number of Children/Other Adults in Household (continuous)						
children 6-17	-.3951	-.0178	-.0428	-.0748	.1764	-.0366
children less than 6	-.5561	-.3100	-.1244	-.3885	-.1421	-.2236
adults	.1340	.0980	.0656	.1116	-.0090	.0454

Table 6.1.10 (continued)

Variable	Cuba	China	Philip-pines	India	Korea	Asian Refugees
Marital Status at Migration and Migration Patterns (dummies, base group is married and migrated before husband)						
single	-.1356	.1064	-.0342	-.3832	.0170	-.0645
after husband	-.1688	.0774	-.2417	-.3189	.3763	.0003
with husband	.2101	-.0219	.1315	-.4848	-.4235	.1358
Husband's Immigration Status (dummies, base group is established immigrants, except for Cuba and Southeast Asian refugees)						
US-born	-.3095	-.1399	-.2902	.2372	-.4244	.2787
recent immigrant		-.0054	-.7286	-.0003	.2333	
Husband's Usual Weekly Earnings (linear splines)						
less than $170	-.2842	-.2549	.0364	-.2462[1]	-.5520	-.2682
$170-$400	.2711	-.2852	-.7223		.2648	.2659
over $400	-.6891	-.0905	-.3644	-.3169	-.4618	-.0098
Wife's Age (linear splines)						
30 or less	.0507	-.0158	.0166	.1036	.0333	-.0216
over 30	-.0591	.0114	.0137	.0149	.0117	-.0308
Year of Survey (dummies, base group is 1991)						
1986	.2347	-.2862	-.2593	.0288	-.2066	-.1207
1988	.0933	-.4285	-.6006	-.0116	-.1537	.2074

Sources: June 1986, 1988 and 1991 Current Population Survey Supplements; Bureau of Labor Statistics, Consumer Price Index.

1. Includes husbands earnings less than $400 a week. 2. Includes all 1970 cohorts. 3. Includes all 1980s cohorts.

Table 6.1.11 Labor Force Participation Probit Regression by Cohort and Age at Migration (Standard Errors in Parentheses)

Variable	1970	Before 1970s	1980s	Before Age 21	After Age 21
intercept	91.532	2.8847*	2.1979*	2.6094	2.0201
	(337.2)	(1.1892)	(1.0415)	(1.4011)	(1.1917)
Region of Residence (dummies, base group is west)					
northeast	.0505	-.1170	-.0128	-.0828	-.0388
	(.2484)	(.1471)	(.1273)	(.1660)	(.1107)
midwest	-.6528*	-.0080	.0159	-.1584	-.0213
	(.3071)	(.1637)	(.1545)	(.1809)	(.1308)
south	.1233	-.2914*	-.0925	-.0096	-.1924
	(.2192)	(.1201)	(.1091)	(.1220)	(.0987)
MSA Status (dummies, base group is MSA suppressed)					
in central city	2.0366*	-.0771	.2459	.2223	.3184
	(.7758)	(.2771)	(.2244)	(.2724)	(.2188)
not in central city	1.7598*	-.0758	.1006	-.0048	.3264
	(.7774)	(.2759)	(.2281)	(.2741)	(.2216)
not in msa	2.1724	.7825	.2496	.1911	.8219*
	(1.1413)	(.5043)	(.3578)	(.4423)	(.3638)
Husband's Level of Education (dummies, base group is college education)					
less than 7th grade	-.8949*	.3867*	.2048	.1896	.2312
	(.3909)	(.1828)	(.1622)	(.1864)	(.1506)
7-12th grade	-.3654	.0448	.0151	-.0865	.0405
	(.2283)	(.1326)	(.1207)	(.1378)	(.1058)
Immigration Cohort (dummies, base group is the pre-1970 cohort. In the cohort regressions, each group of a specific cohort was compared to the most recent group of the same cohort.)					
pre-1960	.1468				
	(.3526)				
1960-64	.1314				
	(.1930)				
1965-69					
1970-74		-.0298		-.2533	.0366
		(.0971)		(.1621)	(.2391)
1975-79				-.3449*	.0979
				(.1725)	(.2397)
1980-84			.3949*	-.3458	-.2348
			(.0949)	(.2032)	(.2431)
1985-91				-.8027*	-.4510
				(.2750)	(.2602)

Table 6.1.11 (continued)

Variable	1970	Before 1970s	1980s	Before Age 21	After Age 21
Origin Country (dummies, base group is the Philippines for Asians, and Mexico for Hispanics)					
Asian	.4953*	.4461*	.7823*	.8723*	.6104*
	(.2322)	(.2105)	(.1916)	(.2591)	(.1598)
China		-.6422*	-.3135	-.5010	-.4182*
		(.2351)	(.2233)	(.3309)	(.1747)
Colombia		-.0818	.0320	.5439	-.2324
		(.2944)	(.2833)	(.3159)	(.2581)
Cuba		.8034*	.4755	.2817	.5255*
		(.3518)	(.2707)	(.2183)	(.2506)
Dominican Republic		-.1906	.1612	-.0635	.1352
		(.3151)	(.3167)	(.2925)	(.2733)
El Salvador		-.0964	.3764*	.1550	.3389
		(.2656)	(.1690)	(.2688)	(.1730)
India		-.3205	-.2528	-.7905*	-.1737
		(.2705)	(.2195)	(.3773)	(.1849)
Japan		-1.0737*	-1.2841*	-.6521	-1.0372*
		(.3685)	(.3425)	(.5135)	(.2502)
Korea		-.5739*	-.6867*	-.9076*	-.5358*
		(.2672)	(.2323)	(.3753)	(.1898)
SEA refugees		.2192	-.1637	-.2357	-.0239
		(.2806)	(.2246)	(.3277)	(.1960)
other Asians		-.3456	-.5292*	-.5610	-.4009
		(.2806)	(.2655)	(.3588)	(.2195)
other Hispanics		.0415	.3490*	.1411	.2818*
		(.1826)	(.1528)	(.1785)	(.1420)
Number of Children/Other Adults in Household (continuous)					
children 6-17	-.1929*	-.1259*	-.1374*	-.0702	-.1568*
	(.0812)	(.0447)	(.0420)	(.0544)	(.0336)
children less than 6	-.3974*	-.4488*	-.2964*	-.3607*	-.3907*
	(.1313)	(.0633)	(.0531)	(.0606)	(.0516)
adults	.2829*	.0380	.1848*	.1061	.1181*
	(.1171)	(.0510)	(.0427)	(.0545)	(.0392)
Marital Status at Migration and Migration Patterns (dummies, base group is married and migrated before husband)					
single	-.1797	-.5199*	-.6741*	-.2062	-.8018*
	(.6771)	(.2008)	(.3133)	(.2137)	(.2596)
after husband	.1062	-.3425	-.9049*	-.2928	-.8102*
	(.7100)	(.2120)	(.3070)	(.2267)	(.2526)
with husband	-.5553	-.5181*	-.7675*	-.3003	-.7649*
	(.7274)	(.1965)	(.3072)	(.2233)	(.2485)

Table 6.1.11 (continued)

Variable	1970	Before 1970s	1980s	Before Age 21	After Age 21
Wife's Level of Education (dummies, base group is college education)					
less than 7th grade	-1.0461*	-.6590*	-.3823*	-.6749*	-.3815*
	(.3626)	(.1936)	(.1682)	(.1929)	(.1530)
7-12th grade	-.3231	-.3474*	-.2321	-.1564	-.3063*
	(.2254)	(.1357)	(.1271)	(.1403)	(.1072)
Husband's Usual Weekly Earnings (linear splines)					
less than $170	-17.824	-.4404*	-.4591*	-.5022*	-.4345*
	(65.626)	(.1787)	(.1763)	(.2407)	(.1432)
$170-$400	16.765	.3392	.2055	.2459	.1920
	(65.759)	(.3144)	(.2782)	(.3565)	(.2465)
over $400	.6129	-.1415	-.1866	-.1472	-.0617
	(.7123)	(.3046)	(.2772)	(.3227)	(.2406)
Year of Survey (dummies, base group is 1991)					
1986	.1630	.0845	-.3069*	-.1153	-.0607
	(.2586)	(.1281)	(.1229)	(.1365)	(.1118)
1988	-.0742	.1287	-.1064	-.0790	.0260
	(.2640)	(.1406)	(.1147)	(.1481)	(.1083)
Husband's Immigration Status (dummies, base group is established immigrants)					
US-born	-.3798	.0271	.1622	.1121	-.0196
	(.1971)	(.1392)	(.1431)	(.1296)	(.1204)
recent immigrant				-.3576	-.2204
				(.4798)	(.1920)
wife's Age (linear splines)					
30 or less	.0289	.0363	.0340*	.0506*	.0548
	(.0537)	(.0247)	(.0168)	(.0213)	(.0296)
over 30	-.0467	-.0464	-.0215	-.0852*	-.0471
	(.0676)	(.0317)	(.0249)	(.0322)	(.0351)
Memo items:					
number of observations	348	917	1137	953	1449
dependent variable mean	72.9%	62.7%	51.7%	61.5%	57.2%
log likelihood	-157.0	-534.3	-665.8	-568.1	-817.1

* p<.05.

Sources: June 1986, 1988 and 1991 Current Population Survey Supplements; Bureau of Labor Statistics, Consumer Price Index.

Table 6.1.12 Marginal Probability Obtained from the Labor Force Participation Probit Regression by Cohort and Age at Migration (Standard Errors in Parentheses)

Variable	1970	Before 1970s	1980s	Before Age 21	After Age 21
Region of Residence (dummies, base group is west)					
northeast	.0164	-.0450	-.0051	-.0320	-.0153
midwest	-.2461	-.0030	.0063	-.0617	-.0084
south	.0392	-.1140	-.0369	-.0037	-.0764
MSA Status (dummies, base group is MSA suppressed)					
in central city	.2666	-.0295	.0965	.0816	.1194
not in central city	.2618	-.0290	.0399	-.0019	.1222
not in msa	.2679	.2388	.0979	.0706	.2700
Husband's Level of Education (dummies, base group is college education)					
less than grade	-.3412	.1344	.0807	.0701	.0880
7-12th grade	-.1324	.0168	.0060	-.0334	.0158
Origin Country (dummies, base group is Mexico for Hispanics; the Philippines for Asians)					
Asian	.1363	.1524	.2783	.2629	.2137
China		-.0761	.1785	.1316	.0737
Colombia		-.0313	.0127	.1835	-.0923
Cuba		.2432	.1808	.1020	.1881
Dominican Republic		-.0740	.0638	-.0245	.0522
El Salvador		-.0370	.1454	.0577	.1266
India		.0465	.1994	.0309	.1597
Japan		-.2463	-.1940	.0809	-.1689
Korea		-.0493	.0380	-.0135	.0291
SEA refugees		.2118	.2287	.2085	.2066
other Asians		.0374	.0993	.1120	.0801
other Hispanics		.0156	.1353	.0527	.1064
Immigration Cohort (dummies, base group is the pre-1970 cohort; In the cohort regressions, each group of a specific cohort was compared to the most recent group of the same cohort)					
pre-1960	.0463				
1960-64	.0417				
1965-69					
1970-74		-.0113		-.0994	.0143
1975-79				-.1359	.0380
1980-84			.1521	-.1363	-.0933
1985-91				-.3101	-.1783

Table 6.1.12 (continued)

Variable	1970	Before 1970s	1980s	Before Age 21	After Age 21
Marital Status at Migration and Migration Patterns (dummies, base group is married and migrated before husband)					
single	-.0625	-.2047	-.2532	-.0806	-.3045
after husband	.0340	-.1344	-.3228	-.1152	-.3073
with husband	-.2072	-.2040	-.2828	-.1182	-.2923
Wife's Level of Education (dummies, base group is college education)					
less than 7th grade	-.3977	-.2582	-.1500	-.2640	-.1513
7-12th grade	-.1161	-.1364	-.0921	-.0609	-.1216
Wife's Age (linear splines)					
30 or less	.0095	.0137	.0135	.0192	.0214
over 30	-.0059	-.0038	.0050	-.0133	.0030
Husband's Immigration Status (dummies, base group is established immigrants)					
US-born	-.1380	.0102	.0641	.0421	-.0077
recent immigrant				-.1410	-.0875
Husband's Usual Weekly Earnings (linear splines)					
less than $170	-.7294	-.1734	-.1785	-.1981	-.1719
$170-$400	-.4024	-.0389	-.1005	-.1006	-.0963
over $400	-.1640	-.0946	-.1715	-.1592	-.1208
Number of Children/Other Adults in Household (continuous)					
children 6-17	-.0673	-.0485	-.0548	-.0271	-.0622
children less than 6	-.1448	-.1767	-.1172	-.1423	-.1549
adults	.0849	.0143	.0730	.0398	.0457
Year of Survey (dummies, base group is 1991)					
1986	.0511	.0315	-.1212	-.0447	-.0239
1988	-.0251	.0476	-.0424	-.0305	.0102

Sources: June 1986, 1988 and 1991 Current Population Survey Supplements; Bureau of Labor Statistics, Consumer Price Index.

each sample (1986, 1988, 1989 and 1991 sample) and the pooled samples (1986, 1988 and 1991 as well as 1989 and 1991). Tables 6.1.5 to 6.1.8 document the regression results and corresponding marginal probabilities from regressions estimated separately by region-of-origin based on the pooled sample (1986, 1988 and 1991).[1] Tables 6.1.9-6.1.10 present the estimation results and corresponding marginal probabilities by selected country-of-origin based on the pooled sample. Tables 6.1.11-6.1.12 report the estimation results and corresponding marginal probabilities by period of immigration and age at immigration based on the pooled sample.

Marital Status at Migration, Migration Patterns and Country-Of-Origin. Overall, the probit results show consistently that Asian and Hispanic women immigrating before their husbands are significantly more likely to be in the labor force than those migrating while single, or married and migrating following or during the same period as their husbands. In particular, the difference is greatest between young wives following husbands and wives migrating before husbands. Tables 6.1.5 and 6.1.7 show that the differences are not significant among Asians, while the differences are significant for Hispanics as a whole and young Mexican immigrant wives in particularly. One exception to the strong work attachment among young wives migrating before husbands is that young East Asian immigrant wives migrating while single or migrating after their husbands are more likely to be in the labor force than young wives migrating before their husbands.

Assuming zero mean base-group effect, the effect of marital status at migration and migration patterns may be calculated as compared to young wives migrating with their husbands. Above all, wives migrating after their husbands are the least likely to be in the labor force. The disadvantaged status is most pronounced among young Southeast Asian immigrant wives and the majority of Hispanic immigrant wives. However, migrating following husband does not constrain young Asian wives' labor market activities, except for young wives from Southeast Asia. Based on Table 6.1.9, young Chinese, Asian Indian, and Korean wives migrating after their husbands seem to have a strong tendency to participate in the U.S. labor force.

Young wives migrating while single are overall slightly more likely to be in the labor force than those migrating with their husbands. Other than the Southeast Asian wives, Young Asian wives migrating while single are more likely to be in the labor force than those migrating with their husbands. On the contrary, young Hispanic wives migrating while single tend to be less likely to participate in the labor force than those migrating with their husbands. Except for wives from the Spanish-speaking Caribbean, these differences in the likelihood are relatively small. Based on Table 6.1.9, young Chinese, Korean, and Asian Indian immigrant wives migrating while single are more likely to participate in the labor force than their ethnic counterparts who were married and migrated with their husbands. Young Cuban wives migrating while single are evidently less likely to be in the labor force than Cuban wives migrating with their husbands. In fact, refugee status seems to be associated with highly work-oriented wives migrating with their husbands. Of all young Cuban, Laotian, Vietnamese and Cambodian wives, those migrating with their husbands are most active in the U.S. labor force.

The estimations by region-of-origin and country-of-origin demonstrate mostly insignificant marital status at migration and migration patterns effects on the young immigrant wives' labor force participation decision. This is partly a result of very high standard errors caused by limited number of young immigrant wives migrating before their husbands.

Marital Status at Migration, Migration Patterns and Timing of Migration. Table 6.1.11 indicates that, among the "prior to 1970" cohort, young immigrant wives migrating after their husbands are more likely to be in the labor force than young wives migrating before their husbands, although the differences are not statistically significant at 5 percent level. Young immigrant wives migrating during the same period with their husbands appear to be least likely to participate in the labor force as compared to the "migrating before husband" group. Among the 1970s cohort, young immigrant wives migrating while single and wives migrating in the same period as the husbands are significantly less likely to be in the labor force than young wives migrating before their husbands. The negative effect for young wives migrating following their husbands relative to young wives migrating before husbands is smaller in the 1970s cohort than the 1980s cohort. Among the 1980s cohort, young wives migrating after their husbands are significantly and least likely to participate the labor force than young wives migrating before husbands.

Since the regression based on the "prior to 1970" cohort was unable to control for individual origin countries due to insufficient number of observations in most origin countries, the comparison of the coefficients between this cohort and the other two cohorts requires caution. Furthermore, as only those aged 18 to 44 are included in this study, wives who migrated prior to 1970 are very likely to have immigrated as minor children to get into the sample. Thus, the "single" effect estimated based on the pre-1970 cohort contains both the effect of migrating while single as well as migrating before age 21.

Young wives migrating before age 21 do not seem to vary in their labor force participation propensities by marital status at migration and migration patterns. Wives migrating as adults and before their husbands are significantly more likely to be in the labor force than any other adult migrant women. Other than those migrating before their husbands, wives migrating as adults do not seem to differ from one another by their marital status at migration and migration patterns.

Separate regressions by year of survey indicate significant differences between migrating before husbands and all other young immigrant wives for the 1986 and 1988 samples. However, these differences are not significant for the 1991 sample. Furthermore, the coefficient estimates of the marital status and migration patterns variables by year of survey also differ in both sign and magnitude. First, both the 1986 and 1988 regressions consistently estimated substantial differences between young wives migrating before their husbands and all other young wives, while the 1991 regression estimated relative small differences. Second, those migrating while single are more likely to be in the labor force in 1986 and 1988 than wives migrating with their husbands, while the reverse is true for the 1991 estimates.

The fact that the 1991 estimates differ considerably from those of the 1986 and 1988 even after controlling for everything else requires caution in interpretation. First, as documented in the sample statistics, the 1991 sample contains relatively fewer wives migrating while single and more wives migrating after their husbands than either the 1986 or 1988 sample. This differential composition may reflect the imputation effects on age at first marriage for the 1991 sample, and thus contribute to the different marital status at migration and migration pattern effects observed in different years. Second, factors specific to the year of survey or survey design may depress the labor force participation of wives utilizing a particular migration pattern while encouraging wives utilizing other patterns.

Since the young immigrant wives who migrated before husbands are the base group in the regression estimation, the significance and magnitude of the marital status at migration and migration patterns variables are interpreted relative to this group. Hypothesis testings are conducted to determine whether young immigrant wives demonstrated distinct labor force participation behaviors by their marital status at migration and migration patterns. This hypothesis is formulated as hypothesis 10, and the derived F statistic is presented in Table 6.1.13. It is concluded that the young Asian and Hispanic immigrant wives show significant differences in the probabilities of entering the labor force by their marital status and migration patterns regardless which base group was chosen.

Selectivity Bias in the Estimation of Country-Of-Origin and Cohort Effects. The current study hypothesizes that young immigrant wives self-select themselves to immigrate in various life-cycle stage and migration patterns. This self-selection tends to bias the country-of-origin and cohort effects in the young immigrant wives' labor supply and earnings estimations. Two measures were developed to test this hypotheses. First, the labor force participation, hourly earnings, and hours of work regressions were estimated separately before and after including the marital status at migration and migration patterns. F statistics testing the existence of the country-of-origin or cohort effects are calculated for the regressions before and after including marital status and migration patterns variables. Qualitative conclusions may be drawn regarding the potential bias in the country-of-origin or cohort effects caused by omitted the marital status and migration patterns variables.

The "before" F statistics are presented in Table 6.1.14, and the "after" F statistics in Table 6.1.13. The country-of-origin, region-of-origin and racial/ethnic differences in young immigrant wives' labor force participation do not seem to be substantially influenced by including the marital status and migration patterns variables in the regressions. In contrast, the cohort effects in the young immigrant wives' labor force participation estimation are substantially affected by including the marital status and migration patterns variables. This is reflected in the relatively large likelihood ratios obtained by excluding the marital status and migration patterns variables. This implies that substantial variations in the probabilities of participating in the labor force by immigrant wives' timing of immigration may be explained by their differences in their marital status at migration and migration patterns. Nonetheless, the likelihood ratios calculated from both the "before" and "after" estimations lead to the same conclusions about the country-of-origin, region-of-origin, racial/ethnic, cohort and period effects on the young immigrant wives' labor force participation. The F statistics provide a clear and straightforward tool summarizing the interaction between the marital status at migration and migration patterns and country-of-origin and cohort effects in the young immigrant wives' labor supply and earnings estimations. The results basically image the findings from the regression analyses.

Table 6.1.13 Test Statistics, Labor Force Participation, Controlling for Marital Status and Migration Patterns

Hypothesis	J	$\ln L^*$	$\ln L$	Likelihood ratio	reject*
(1) no country of origin effect	12	-1435.0	-1407.2	55.6	yes
(2) no region-of-origin effect	7	-1435.0	-1409.1	51.8	yes
(3) no difference between Asians and Hispanics	1	-1435.0	-1429.9	10.2	yes
(4) no country-of-origin effect among Asians	6	-505.2	-491.3	27.8	yes
(5) no country-of-origin effect among Hispanics	5	-902.3	-896.3	12.0	yes
(6) no immigrant cohort effect	4	-1430.2	-1407.2	46.0	yes
(7) no immigration cohort effect among Asians	4	-503.8	-491.3	25.0	yes
(8) no immigration cohort effect among Hispanics	4	-908.5	-896.3	24.2	yes
(9) no period effect	2	-1408.1	-1407.2	1.8	no
(10) no difference by marital status and migration patterns	3	-1413.8	-1407.2	13.2	yes

* rejects the null hypothesis at 5 percent level.

Source: June 1986, 1988, and 1991 Current Population Survey supplements.

Note: $\ln L^*$ is the log likelihood evaluated at the restricted estimates; $\ln L$ is the log likelihood evaluated at the unrestricted estimates; J is the number of restrictions.

Table 6.1.14 Test Statistics, Labor Force Participation, Not Controlling for Marital Status and Migration Patterns

Hypothesis	J	lnL^*	lnL	Likelihood ratio	reject*
(1) no country of origin effect	12	-1442.3	-1413.8	57.0	yes
(2) no region-of-origin effect	7	-1442.3	-1415.9	52.8	yes
(3) no difference between Asians and Hispanics	1	-1442.3	-1437.5	9.6	yes
(4) no country-of-origin effect among Asians	6	-508.6	-493.7	29.0	yes
(5) no country-of-origin effect among Hispanics	5	-909.5	-902.5	14.0	yes
(6) no immigrant cohort effect	4	-1449.4	-1413.8	71.2	yes
(7) no immigration cohort effect among Asians	4	-512.0	-493.7	36.6	yes
(8) no immigration cohort effect among Hispanics	4	-921.6	-902.5	38.2	yes
(9) no period effect	2	-1415.5	-1413.8	3.4	no

* rejects the null hypothesis at 5 percent level.

Source: June 1986, 1988, and 1991 Current Population Survey Supplements.

Note: lnL^* is the log likelihood evaluated at the restricted estimates; lnL is the log likelihood evaluated at the unrestricted estimates; J is the number of restrictions.

Table 6.1.15 Weighted Standard Deviations of Country-of-Origin, Cohort and Period Effects in the Labor Force Participation Regression with and Without Including Marital Status and Migration Patterns

Variable	Without (1)	With (2)	Difference (1)-(2)
Hypothesis 11:			
not reducing country-of-origin effect, N=13			
labor force participation	.2608	.2579	.0029
Hypothesis 12:			
not reducing region-of-origin effect, N=8			
labor force participation	.1816	.1800	.0016
Hypothesis 14:			
not reducing Asian country-of-origin effect, N=7			
labor force participation	.1977	.1941	.0036
Hypothesis 15:			
not reducing Hispanic country-of-origin effect, N=6			
labor force participation	.1338	.1239	.0099
Hypothesis 16:			
not reducing cohort effect, N=5			
labor force participation	.3353	.2993	.0360
Hypothesis 17:			
not reducing Asian cohort effect, N=5			
labor force participation	.2725	.2448	.0277
Hypothesis 18:			
not reducing Hispanic cohort effect, N=5			
labor force participation	.2231	.1975	.0256
Hypothesis 19:			
not reducing period effect, N=3			
labor force participation	.0718	.0523	.0195

tendency of participating in the U.S. labor force, even after controlling for everything else. Further investigation shows considerable variations in the migration selectivity effects by country-of-origin groups. Comparing with their ethnic counterparts, Hispanic and Southeast Asian wives migrating after their husbands are less likely to be in the labor force, while other Asian wives migrating after their husbands are more likely to be in the labor force. Cuban and Southeast Asian refugee wives who migrated with their husbands are more likely to be in the labor force than any other refugee wives.

Once the migration selectivity is controlled, there are fewer variations across immigration cohort groups in the immigrant wives' labor force participation as those found across countries-of-origin. No matter whether migrating in the 1970s or the 1980s, those migrating before their husbands are the most likely to participate in the labor force, while those migrating with or after their husbands are the least likely to do so. Hypothesis testing confirms that considerable cohort differences in the Hispanic immigrant wives' labor force participation may be reduced by controlling for migration selectivity.

The presence of both sides of the immigrant wife's kin living in the U.S. seems to have opposite effects on her propensity of participating in the labor force. In particular, the more of her side of relatives are in the U.S., the more likely she will be in the labor force. On the contrary, the more of her in-laws are in the U.S., the less likely she will be in the labor force.

6.1.2 Other Control Variables and Labor Force Participation

In addition to the migration selectivity variables, the labor force participation regression includes an array of independent variables that represent the immigrant wives' market wage offers and the reservation wages. These variables are region of residence, whether living in Metropolitan Statistical Area (MSA), country-of-origin, timing of immigration, husband's education, wife's education, the number of children in the household, the number of other adults in the household, husband's immigration status, and husband's usual weekly earnings. This section discusses the sign and magnitude of the coefficient estimates of these control variables in the labor force participation probit regression presented in Tables 6.1.1-6.1.12.

Number of Young Children at Home. As expected, the number of children under 6 in the household significantly hinders the young immigrant wives' labor force participation in almost all probit regressions estimated. The number of children aged 6-17 also has a similar negative effect on labor force participation, although not as pronounced as the effects for the number of children under 6. The derived marginal probabilities show that the dampening effect is slightly larger for young Hispanic immigrant wives than Asian immigrant wives. Among individual origin countries, the young Cuban, Chinese, and Asian Indian immigrant wives' labor force participation decisions are greatly constrained by the presence of young children at home. The magnitude of the effect does not seem to vary substantially by year of survey or timing of immigration.

Other Adults in the Household. The number of other adults in the household is found to significantly facilitate the young immigrant wives' labor force participation with the combined sample and by year of survey. Among regions of origin, the contributions from other adults in the household is most significant and substantial for young immigrant wives from South Asia and the Spanish-speaking Caribbean. By individual country-of-origin, both the estimations for young Cuban and Asian Indian immigrant wives show largest effect from the number of adults in the household, however, the effects could not be measured precisely due to the relative limited sample size. The facilitating effect from other adults in the household is significant for young Chinese immigrant wives, although the magnitude is not as large as those for Cubans and Asian Indians. The help from other adults is significant for the estimations for the "prior to 1970" and the "1980s" cohort, but not the 1970 cohort. It is also significant for the "migrating after age 21" group, but not the "before 21" group.

The 1989 and 1991 samples provide the information needed to decompose the "other adult" effect into contribution from the young immigrant wives' immediate relatives and from husbands' immediate relatives. The results show both types of relatives encourage the young immigrant wives' labor force participation. Nonetheless, the estimated effects for either type of relatives are mostly not significant at the 5 percent level.

Immigrant Wives' Human Capital. The immigrant wife's age, educational attainments and English-speaking ability are included in the model to control for the immigrant wives' human capital, and thus proxies for her market potential wage offers. It is hypothesized that the more human capital she has, the more likely she will go to work. Overall, the likelihood of participating in the labor force increases significantly with age for all immigrant wives aged 30 or less, and decreases slightly but significantly with age for all young immigrant wives over 30. This pattern holds for most young Hispanic immigrant wives by their region-of-origin. In contrast, the age-profile for young Asian immigrant wives is positive for both age groups, and the effects are only significant for young Asian Indian immigrant wives. The estimations by immigration cohort reveal a mixed picture and most of the effects are not significant at the 5 percent level.

The labor supply theory predicts that higher education increases the opportunity costs of not working, and therefore, is positively related to labor force participation, holding everything else constant. The estimation results basically confirm this prediction. Young immigrant wives with less than a college education are less likely to be in the labor force than the young college-educated wives. The estimation for the combined sample shows that the negative effect from education is about twice as large as that for the less-than-7th-grade group. This differential effect is larger for Asian as a whole than Hispanics as a whole. The differential effect is also pronounced for those who immigrated before age 21, but not for the "after 21" group.

The English-speaking ability information is only available in the 1989 sample. The probit estimation shows that young immigrant wives who speak very little or no English at all are significantly less likely to be in the labor force than young wives who speak English only. This set of dummy variables may be highly correlated with the country-of-origin and immigration cohort dummies, and therefore shows mostly insignificant effects.

Region of Residence. Young immigrant wives living in the west region of the country are more likely to be in the labor force participation than those living in any other regions. Nonetheless, the region-of-residence effects are mostly insignificant. Separate estimations by region-of-origin show significant region-of-origin effects only for the South Asian and South America groups. The effects of living in metropolitan, suburban and non-metropolitan areas have mixed effects on the labor force participation of young Asian and Hispanic immigrant wives and these effects are mostly insignificant.

Husband's Earning Capacities and Nonlabor Income. The immigrant wife's husband's educational attainments, his nativity status, whether he immigrated in the last two years, his English-speaking abilities, and his weekly earnings are included in the model as proxies for husband's earnings capacities and indications of the family economic need. It is predicted that the higher her husband's earning capacities, the less likely she will be in the labor force. The results show that the husbands' educational attainment has little effect on young immigrant wives' labor force participation with mixed signs across all the regressions. Young immigrant wives married to U.S.-born husbands are more likely to be in the labor force, while those married to recent immigrants are less likely to be in the labor force than young wives married to established immigrants. However, these effects are mostly not significant. Two exceptions are found. Young Southeast Asian and Korean immigrant wives married to U.S.-born husbands are significantly less likely to be in the labor force than those married to established immigrant husbands. Young South Asian immigrant wives married to husbands who have lower than college education are significantly more likely to be in the labor force than those married to college-educated husbands.

Overall, the probability of participating the labor force decreases significantly for young immigrant wives with husbands earning less than $170 per week (or $4.25 an hour). Although insignificant, similar negative effects are observed for young immigrant wives with husbands having weekly earnings between $170 and $400 and over $400. The negative effect basically confirms the hypothesis that the higher the family nonlabor income, the less likely the young immigrant wives will be in the labor force. Although the husband's weekly earnings is different from his earnings potential in that he chooses how many hours to work per week to adjust his weekly earnings, this measure is still likely to be correlated with the husband's earning potential in the lack of a better measure of family nonlabor income.

Ethnic or Country-Of-Origin Effects. Controlling for everything else, young Asian immigrant wives are significantly more likely to be in the labor force than young Hispanic immigrant wives. All other Asian immigrant wives are significantly less likely than the Filipinos to be in the labor force. By allowing for differential effects from all other demographic characteristics, the difference in the likelihood of participating in the labor force between the Southeast Asian refugees and the Filipinos disappears. Controlling for all other differences, only young Cuban immigrant wives are significantly more likely to be in the labor force than young Mexican immigrant wives (Table 6.1.3). After allowing for separate effects for all independent variables from Asians, the differences between Salvadoreans and Mexicans emerge (Table 6.1.7).

The estimation with the combined sample including region of origin shows that only young immigrant wives from Southeast Asia are significantly more likely to be in the labor force than those from the Spanish-speaking Caribbean (Table 6.1.3). Among young Hispanic immigrant wives, Cubans, Salvadoreans and other Hispanics are more significantly more likely to be in the labor force than Mexican immigrant wives. According to Table 6.1.11, the separate estimations by immigration cohorts have mixed results in the country-of-origin differences in labor force participation. The young Chinese immigrant wives are significantly less likely to be in the labor force than the young Filipino immigrant wives for the 1970 cohort, but this negative effect is not significant for the 1980 cohort. Similarly, young Cuban immigrant wives are significantly more likely to be in the labor force than the young Mexican immigrant wives for the 1970s cohort, but the effect becomes insignificant for the 1980s cohort. The separate estimations by age at immigration show more significant country-of-origin differences between Asians and Filipinos, and between Mexicans and Hispanics for the "migrating after age 21" than the "migrating before age 21" group.

The results consistently show that young Filipino, Cuban immigrant wives have relatively high level of labor force participation, even after controlling for everything else. Young immigrant wives from Southeast refugee countries also show a high tendency of participating in the labor force, given their unfavorable labor market characteristics. In contrast, young Mexican immigrant wives have low levels of labor force participation, although a substantial portion of the negative effect is due to their relatively unfavorable socioeconomic characteristics. Young Japanese immigrant wives also have relatively low levels of labor force participation, which is still true after controlling for socioeconomic characteristics.

Five hypothesis testings were carried out to test whether there are significant country-of-origin, region-of-origin or racial/ethnic effects, free of the base groups chosen in the regression estimations. The tests are formally laid out in Chapter 4 as hypotheses 1-5. They are conducted on the merged 1986, 1988, and 1991 sample only, and the results are summarized in Table 6.1.13. The testing demonstrates strong evidence of the existence of country-of-origin, region-of-origin and racial/ethnic effects in the young immigrant wives' labor force participation decision.

Cohort Effect. Consistent with the assimilation hypothesis, recent young immigrant wives are significantly least likely to participate in the U.S. labor force, and the negative effect expedites as the number of years of U.S. stay decreases. Table 6.1.4 shows that the likelihood of labor force participation of the 1980-84 cohort is only about two third of that estimated for the post-1984. Separate analyses for Asians and Hispanics shows that all post-1970 cohorts are significantly less likely to be in the labor force than the pre-1970 cohort. In contrast, the two 1970s cohorts do not seem to be very different from the pre-1970 cohort for young Hispanic immigrant wives. Furthermore, Table 6.1.6 and 6.1.8 show that the unfavorable labor force statuses of the 1980s cohorts relative to the pre-1970 cohort for Asians is about twice as large as those for Hispanics. In other words, controlling for everything else, young Hispanic immigrant wives' labor force participation behaviors are more invariant to their timing of immigration, or their length of U.S. stay, than young Asian immigrant wives.

Three hypothesis testings were carried out to test if there are significant cohort effects, regardless of the base group chosen in the regression estimation. The hypotheses are formulated in Chapter 4 as hypothesis 6-8, and the results are summarized in Table 6.1.13. The derived F statistics show overall significant cohort differences and show significant differences separately for young Asian and Hispanic immigrant wives. Table 6.1.13 also concludes the absence of significant period effects in the young immigrant wives' labor force participation.

To sum up, the young immigrant wives' labor force participation decision appear to be affected by market opportunities and family responsibilities at varying degrees by race/ethnicity. Based on the results, a general observation is that young Asian immigrant wives appear to be more responsive to their market opportunities, while young Hispanic immigrant wives are more constrained by their family responsibilities. The results are largely consistent with previous research findings (Stier 1991; Stier and Tienda 1992).

6.2 IMMIGRANT WIVES' HOURLY EARNINGS

Immigrant wives' potential market earnings are largely determined by their stock of human capital. Several factors contribute to their human capital accumulation: migration selectivity, formal education, labor market experience, and training (Mincer 1974; Mincer and Polachek 1974; Borjas 1987). The measurement of the labor market experience for married women becomes difficult in the lack of either longitudinal or retrospective data detailing their past work experience and life-cycle events. Empirically, the presence and age composition of young children in the household are included in the earnings equation to capture the effects of the potential disrupted work experience caused by child-bearing and rearing activities (Long 1980; Stier 1991).

To assess the labor market qualities of the young Asian and Hispanic immigrant wives, this study estimates an OLS regression on their log usual hourly earnings. The mills ratio derived from the labor force participation regression is included in the regression to correct for the potential sample selection bias due to the endogenous work decision. Table 6.2.1-6.2.6 report the results. This section first discusses the effects of migration selectivity variables and secondly, the sign and magnitude of all other variables in the regression.

6.2.1 Migration Selectivity and Hourly Earnings

This book argues that the immigrant wives' marital status at migration, migration patterns and kin connection in the U.S. may carry information on their unobserved labor market qualities. This section reports the significance and magnitude of the migration selectivity variables in the hourly earnings estimation. As the immigrant wives' characteristics and migration selectivity may affect their human capital accumulation differently by country-of-origin, region-of-origin, timing of immigration, age at immigration, and year of survey, the regressions are estimated separately along these dimensions to allow for possible interaction effects.

Tables 6.2.1-6.2.2 present the coefficient estimates from the hourly earnings regression based on each sample (1986, 1988, 1989 and 1991 sample) and the pooled samples (1986, 1988 and 1991 as well as 1989 and 1991). Tables 6.2.3 to 6.2.4 document the results from the hourly earning regressions estimated separately by region-of-origin based on the pooled sample (1986, 1988 and 1991). Table 6.2.5 presents the results from the regressions estimated separately by selected country-of-origin based on the pooled sample. Table 6.2.6 reports the results of regressions estimated separately by period of immigration and age at immigration based on the pooled sample.

Marital Status at Migration, Migration Patterns and Country-Of-Origin. Overall, young immigrant wives do not obtain significantly different levels of earnings by their marital status at migration and migration patterns. Despite of a greater labor force participation propensity, young immigrant wives migrating before their husbands earn slightly less than all other wives. The same statement holds in the estimation for young Hispanic immigrant wives. In contrast, young Asian immigrant wives who were single at migration, and wives who follow their husbands earn less than young wives migrating before their husbands.

Table 6.2.1 Hourly Earnings OLS Regression by Year of Survey (Standard Errors in Parentheses)

Variable	1986	1988	1989	1991
intercept	1.4276*	2.5118*	1.9713*	1.8968*
	(.2965)	(.3481)	(.3070)	(.3270)
Region of Origin (dummies, base group is west)				
northeast	.0919	.0499	.1123*	-.0378
	(.0546)	(.0661)	(.0538)	(.0561)
midwest	-.0950	-.1083	.0294	-.0097
	(.0680)	(.0727)	(.0651)	(.0671)
south	-.1259*	-.0517	-.0983	-.0571
	(.0499)	(.0554)	(.0504)	(.0549)
MSA Status (dummies, base group is MSA suppressed)				
in central city	.1426	.2235*	.0875	-.0745
	(.0765)	(.0788)	(.0647)	(.0859)
not in central city	.2430*	.2423*	.0472	-.0636
	(.0729)	(.0748)	(.0665)	(.0819)
not in msa	.2614*	.1059	-.0624	-.2450
	(.1029)	(.1094)	(.1044)	(.1256)
Origin Country (dummies, base group is the Philippines for Asians; Mexico for Hispanics)				
Asian	.0888	.1714	.1312	.1186
	(.0876)	(.0992)	(.0967)	(.1269)
China	-.1149	-.1146	-.0437	.0856
	(.0827)	(.0934)	(.0962)	(.1110)
Colombia	-.1518	-.0264	-.0672	.3007*
	(.1140)	(.1447)	(.1250)	(.1363)
Cuba	.0028	.0139	.0988	.2779*
	(.1138)	(.1073)	(.1043)	(.1071)
Dominican Republic	-.1976	-.1059	.0261	.2926*
	(.1456)	(.1182)	(.1686)	(.1391)
El Salvador	-.2291*	.3091*	.0328	.0864
	(.1100)	(.1293)	(.1025)	(.0992)
India	.0229	-.1574	-.1283	.0006
	(.0947)	(.1078)	(.1038)	(.0982)
Japan	.2089	.0727	.1223	.0043
	(.2133)	(.1710)	(.1639)	(.1803)
Korea	-.0217	-.0879	-.0896	.0362
	(.1212)	(.1218)	(.1057)	(.1194)
SE Asian refugees	-.0519	-.2067*	.0386	.0859
	(.0892)	(.1015)	(.0963)	(.1214)
other Asians	-.2240*	-.1410	.0421	.3744
	(.0900)	(.1179)	(.1167)	(.2687)
other Hispanic	-.1417	.0064	.0364	.0356
	(.0818)	(.0863)	(.0680)	(.0758)
mills ratio	-.2903	-.0401	-.0143	-.3563
	(.2050)	(.2352)	(.1889)	(.2338)

Table 6.2.1 (continued)

Variable	1986	1988	1989	1991
Immigration Cohort (dummies, base group is pre-1970 cohort)				
1970-74	.0108	-.0309	.0729	.1609*
	(.0597)	(.0717)	(.0677)	(.0787)
1975-79	.0016	.0210	.0509	.1460*
	(.0594)	(.0769)	(.0718)	(.0723)
1980-84	-.0012	-.1288	-.0089	.0110
	(.0908)	(.0933)	(.0788)	(.0759)
1985-91	.1821	-.1770	-.0928	.0922
	(.1447)	(.1454)	(.0938)	(.1071)
Wife's Level of Education (dummies, base group is college education)				
less than 7th grade	-.3090	-.2833*	-.3266*	-.1165
	(.1104)	(.1021)	(.0824)	(.0891)
7-12th grade	-.2619*	-.1439*	-.2409*	-.1288*
	(.0477)	(.0723)	(.0512)	(.0594)
Number of Children/Other Adults in the Household (continuous)				
children 6-17	-.0499*	-.0368	-.0050	.0388
	(.0213)	(.0254)	(.0191)	(.0233)
children less than 6	.0477	.0215	.0449	.1383*
	(.0551)	(.0592)	(.0453)	(.0461)
adults	-.0126	.0149		
	(.0236)	(.0303)		
wife's kin			.0312	.0188
			(.0409)	(.0461)
husband's kin			-.0139	-.0544
			(.0400)	(.0338)
Marital Status at Migration and Migration Patterns (dummies, base group is married and migrated before husbands)				
single at migration	.2185	-.0307		.1064
	(.1204)	(.1368)		(.0753)
married, after husband	.2224	-.1029	-.0037[1]	-.0101
	(.1385)	(.1542)	(.0763)	(.0728)
married, with husband	.2433	.0339	-.0627[1]	.0744
	(.1304)	(.1338)	(.0655)	(.0697)
Husband's Immigration Status (dummies, base group is established immigrants)				
husband US-born	.0620	-.0076	.0645	.0978
	(.0504)	(.0593)	(.0850)	(.0566)
recent immigrant	-.0959	-.2124*	-.0185	-.0568
	(.0682)	(.1033)	(.0810)	(.0721)
Husband's Level of Education (dummies, base group is college education)				
less than 7th grade	-.0112	-.0391	-.0506	-.1518
	(.0762)	(.0964)	(.0766)	(.0774)
7-12th grade	-.0491	-.0217	-.0936	-.0794
	(.0542)	(.0638)	(.0503)	(.0530)

Table 6.2.1 (continued)

Variable	1986	1988	1989	1991
Husband's Usual Weekly Earnings (linear splines)				
less than $170	.0536	-.0749*	-.0311	-.0103
	(.0395)	(.0275)	(.0380)	(.0361)
$170-$400	-.0251	.1781	.2828*	.2418*
	(.1135)	(.1480)	(.1117)	(.0973)
over $400	.3496*	.1825	-.2139	.0170
	(.1345)	(.1499)	(.1321)	(.1235)
Percentage of Immediate Relatives living in the U.S. (continuous)				
wife's kin			.0374	.0392
			(.0486)	(.0579)
husband's kin			-.0669	-.0327
			(.0545)	(.0499)
Wife's English-Speaking Abilities (dummies, base group is English only)				
very well			.0665	
			(.0859)	
well			-.0598	
			(.0890)	
little or no English			-.1285	
			(.1167)	
Husband's English-Speaking Abilities (dummies, base group is English only)				
very well			.0179	
			(.0805)	
well			.0503	
			(.0894)	
little or no English			.0314	
			(.0946)	
Wife's Age (linear splines)				
30 or less	.0070	-.0060	.0058	.0033
	(.0092)	(.0111)	(.0112)	(.0107)
over 30	.0100	.0105	-.0019	-.0123
	(.0129)	(.0146)	(.0145)	(.0134)
Memo items:				
number of observations	495	401	554	556
dependent variable mean	2.0709	2.0597	2.0412	2.0232
R square	.4912	.4030	.4117	.3687
adjusted R square	.4464	.3366	.3557	.3157

* $p<.05$.

Sources: 1986, 1988, and 1991 June Current Population survey supplements; Bureau of Labor Statistics, Consumer Price Index.

1. Marital status at migration unknown.

Table 6.2.2 Hourly Earnings OLS Regression, Combined Samples (Standard Errors in Parentheses)

Variable	1989 1991	1986 1988 1991[1]	1986 1988 1991[2]
intercept	1.9917*	2.0651*	2.1726*
	(.2262)	(.1865)	(.1876)
Region of Residence (dummies, base group is west)			
northeast	.0343	.0048	.0029
	(.0381)	(.0334)	(.0331)
midwest	.0127	-.0682	-.0747
	(.0454)	(.0398)	(.0397)
south	-.0734*	-.0828*	-.0744*
	(.0366)	(.0307)	(.0293)
MSA Status, (dummies, base group is MSA suppressed)			
in central city	.0178	-.0482	-.0539
	(.0517)	(.0760)	(.0760)
not in central city	-.0030	-.0634	-.0640
	(.0503)	(.0746)	(.0746)
not in msa	-.1210	-.2199	-.2274*
	(.0772)	(.1147)	(.1152)
Origin Country (dummies, base group is the Philippines for Asians; Mexico for Hispanics)			
Asian	.1388	.1525*	
	(.0954)	(.0701)	
China	-.0072	-.0467	
	(.0790)	(.0588)	
Colombia	.1140	.0930	
	(.0904)	(.0720)	
Cuba	.1747*	.1489*	
	(.0775)	(.0634)	
Dominican Republic	.2138*	.0476	
	(.1040)	(.0718)	
El Salvador	.0650	.0644	
	(.0738)	(.0608)	
India	-.0497	-.0280	
	(.0711)	(.0584)	
Japan	.0746	.0190	
	(.1335)	(.1247)	
Korea	-.0421	-.0611	
	(.0842)	(.0767)	
SE Asian refugees	.0175	-.0755	
	(.0776)	(.0528)	
other Asians	.1475	-.1231	
	(.1160)	(.0742)	
other Hispanics	.0493	.0089	
	(.0534)	(.0449)	
Wife's Level of Education (dummies, base group is college education)			
less than 7th grade	-.2507*	-.2814*	-.2881*
	(.0637)	(.0680)	(.0687)
7-12th grade	-.2040*	-.2047*	-.2110*
	(.0408)	(.0369)	(.0371)

Table 6.2.2 (continued)

Variable	1989 1991	1986 1988 1991[1]	1986 1988 1991[2]
Marital Status at Migration and Migration Patterns (dummies, base group is married and migrated before husband)			
single at migration		.0739	.0780
		(.0590)	(.0595)
married, after husband	-.0311[3]	.0326	.0309
	(.0352)	(.0656)	(.0661)
married, with husband	-.0337[3]	.0935	.0931
	(.0345)	(.0603)	(.0606)
Immigration Cohort (dummies, base group is pre-1970 cohort)			
1970-74	.0862	.0376	.0309
	(.0485)	(.0426)	(.0437)
1975-79	.0803	.0304	.0185
	(.0503)	(.0422)	(.0431)
1980-84	-.0247	-.0722	-.0764
	(.0573)	(.0573)	(.0596)
1985-91	-.0291	-.1196	-.1225
	(.0809)	(.0849)	(.0884)
Originating Region (dummies, base group is the Caribbean)			
Mexico			-.0866
			(.0480)
East Asia			.0200
			(.0457)
Southeast Asia			.0248
			(.0532)
South Asia			.0265
			(.0571)
South America			-.0536
			(.0486)
Central America			-.0640
			(.0489)
Number of Children/Other Adults in the Household (continuous)			
children 6-17	.0165	-.0162	-.0164
	(.0154)	(.0155)	(.0155)
children less than 6	.0895*	.0498	.0523
	(.0365)	(.0386)	(.0391)
adults		-.0056	-.0050
		(.0151)	(.0155)
wife's kin	.0320		
	(.0318)		
husband's kin	-.0233		
	(.0236)		
Percentage of Immediate Relatives in the Household (continuous)			
wife's kin	.0469		
	(.0381)		
husband's kin	-.0325		
	(.0343)		

Table 6.2.2 (continued)

Variable	1989 1991	1986 1988 1991[1]	1986 1988 1991[2]
Husband's Immigration Status (dummies, established immigrants)			
US-born	.0611	.0255	.0223
	(.0405)	(.0311)	(.0303)
recent immigrant	-.0967	.0189	.0213
	(.0733)	(.0793)	(.0800)
Husband's Level of Education (dummies, base group is college education)			
less than 7th grade	-.1002	-.0509	-.0532
	(.0530)	(.0500)	(.0502)
7-12th grade	-.0835*	-.0363	-.0376
	(.0355)	(.0298)	(.0296)
mills ratio	-.1768	-.1258	-.1379
	(.1829)	(.1772)	(.1797)
Wife's Age (linear splines)			
30 or less	.0036	.0055	.0049
	(.0082)	(.0064)	(.0064)
over 30	-.0060	-.0035	-.0024
	(.0104)	(.0082)	(.0084)
Husband's Usual Weekly Earnings (linear splines)			
less than $170	-.0215	-.0323	-.0291
	(.0286)	(.0236)	(.0235)
$170-$400	.2642*	.2070*	.2022*
	(.0688)	(.0578)	(.0581)
over $400	-.1045	.1139	.1162
	(.0845)	(.0720)	(.0720)
Year of Survey (dummies, base group is 1991)			
1986		-.0286	-.0262
		(.0318)	(.0318)
1988		.0077	.0066
		(.0312)	(.0311)
1989	-.0066		
	(.0261)		
Memo items:			
number of observations	1110	1452	1452
dependent variable mean	2.0321	2.0495	2.0495
R square	.3643	.3525	.3485
adjusted R square	.3386	.3332	.3319

* p<.05.

Sources: June 1986, 1988, and 1991 Current Population Survey Supplements; Bureau of Labor Statistics, Consumer Price Index.

1. Includes country-of-origin dummies. 2. Includes region-of-origin dummies. 3. Marital status at migration unknown.

Table 6.2.3 Hourly Earnings OLS Regression by Region of Origin, Asian, (Standard Errors in Parentheses)

Variable	Asians	East Asia	Southeast Asia	South Asia
intercept	2.0219*	2.8730*	2.6152*	-.0407
	(.3251)	(.5875)	(.5466)	(1.2308)
Region of Residence (dummies, base group is west region)				
northeast	.0193	-.0570	.0199	.2524
	(.0456)	(.0777)	(.0856)	(.3110)
midwest	-.1076*	-.0853	.0088	-.1409
	(.0522)	(.0953)	(.1022)	(.2860)
south	-.0084	-.2342*	.0519	.1414
	(.0485)	(.0922)	(.0684)	(.3014)
MSA Status (dummies, base group is MSA suppressed, except for south Asia)				
in central city	.0713	-.0607	-.0188	.2223
	(.1325)	(.1853)	(.3731)	(.2651)
not in central city	.1003	.1582	-.0499	.3300
	(.1223)	(.1716)	(.3700)	(.2557)
not in msa	-.2939	-.5443	-.2582	
	(.1953)	(.3141)	(.4067)	
Husband's Immigration Status (dummies, base group is established immigrants)				
US-born	-.0155	-.0921	.0238	-.1690
	(.0520)	(.0874)	(.0939)	(.3650)
recent immigrant	.0152	.1589	-.2499	.0190
	(.1056)	(.1956)	(.2122)	(.2646)
Origin Country (dummies, base group is the Philippines for Asians; Countries of a specific region are compared to the omitted countries in that region)				
China	-.0117	-.2041		
	(.0637)	(.1227)		
India	-.0138			.2382
	(.0650)			(.2452)
Japan	.1357			
	(.1319)			
Korea	.0017	-.1696		
	(.0806)	(.1265)		
Laos			.0063	
			(.1254)	
Philippines			.0437	
			(.0906)	
Vietnam	-.0612		-.0001	
	(.0594)		(.0951)	
other Asians	-.0856			
	(.0779)			

Table 6.2.3 (continued)

Variable	Asians	East Asia	Southeast Asia	South Asia
Number of Children/Other Adults in Household (continuous)				
children 6-17	-.0249	-.0226	-.0302	-.0063
	(.0223)	(.0390)	(.0320)	(.0924)
children less than 6	.0765	.2069*	-.0032	.1615
	(.0451)	(.0756)	(.0567)	(.2050)
adults	-.0110	-.0686	.0260	-.0009
	(.0231)	(.0396)	(.0288)	(.0846)
Husband's Level of Education (dummies, base group is college education)				
less than 7th grade	.0148	-.3859	.1570	
	(.1155)	(.2002)	(.1318)	
7-12th grade	.0351	.1245	-.0460	-.0844
	(.0468)	(.0854)	(.0738)	(.2721)
Wife's Level of Education (dummies, base group is college education)				
less than 7th grade	-.3773*	-.1043	-.5528*	-1.1578
	(.1365)	(.2081)	(.1591)	(.7203)
7-12th grade	-.2644*	-.2479*	-.3955*	.0097
	(.0534)	(.0916)	(.0666)	(.2364)
Wife's Age (linear splines)				
30 or less	.0112	-.0126	.0022	.0422
	(.0094)	(.0189)	(.0127)	(.0564)
over 30	-.0152	.0000	-.0049	-.0491
	(.0118)	(.0233)	(.0169)	(.0583)
Immigration Cohort (dummies, base group is pre-1970 cohort)				
1970-74	.0765	.2016	-.0391	.3721
	(.0807)	(.1285)	(.1040)	(.2974)
1975-79	.0591	.1324	-.0515	.3825
	(.0793)	(.1279)	(.1014)	(.3173)
1980-84	-.0683	-.0304	-.1488	.0681
	(.0899)	(.1321)	(.1074)	(.2965)
1985-91	-.0869	-.0165	-.1607	.1554
	(.1343)	(.1859)	(.1577)	(.3097)

Table 6.2.3 (continued)

Variable	Asians	East Asia	Southeast Asia	South Asia
Marital Status and Migration Patterns (dummies, base group is married and migrated before husbands)				
single	-.0670	-.1775	-.1521	.1686
	(.0785)	(.1535)	(.1073)	(.2774)
married, after husband	-.0669	-.2020	-.0746	.0932
	(.0807)	(.1490)	(.1149)	(.2516)
married, with husband	.0361	.0171	-.0182	.0537
	(.0832)	(.1485)	(.1110)	(.3181)
Husband's Usual Weekly Earnings (linear splines)				
less than $170	-.0447	-.0125	-.0659	.0106[2]
	(.0358)	(.0491)	(.0484)	(.0886)
$170-$400	.3263*	.3837*	.2718	
	(.1136)	(.1701)	(.1949)	
$400	.0624	.0723	.1036	.3311
	(.1321)	(.1988)	(.2281)	(.1675)
Year of Survey (dummies, base group is 1991)				
1986	.0300	.1407	.0135	.1931
	(.0579)	(.0970)	(.0782)	(.2193)
1988	.0019	.2406*	.0064	.0041
	(.0521)	(.1031)	(.0716)	(.1980)
mills ratio	-.2692	-.5806*	-.0603	-.1782
	(.2173)	(.2287)	(.2869)	(.4539)
Memo items:				
number of observations	709	257	319	103
dependent variable mean	2.2232	2.2135	2.2263	2.2679
R square	.3550	.4833	.3952	.4260
adjusted R square	.3204	.4094	.3251	.2087

* $p < .05$.

Sources: June 1986, 1988, and 1991 Current Population Survey Supplements; Bureau of Labor Statistics, Consumer Price Index.

1. Included in the high school category. 2. Included husbands earnings less than $400 a week.

Table 6.2.4 Hourly Earnings OLS Regression by Region of Origin, Hispanics (Standard Errors in Parentheses)

Variable	Hispanics	Central America	South America	Caribbean	Mexico
intercept	2.1062*	2.6988*	.9129	2.6889*	2.3665*
	(.2400)	(.8094)	(.6283)	(.9030)	(.3783)
Region of Residence (dummies, base group is west)					
northeast	-.0118	.0148	.1081	-.0495	-.0714
	(.0495)	(.1231)	(.1201)	(.1941)	(.1409)
midwest	-.0299	.6144	-.1427	-.5373	-.0039
	(.0720)	(.6084)	(.4061)	(.3288)	(.0950)
south	-.1391*	-.2820	.1292	-.1959	-.2130*
	(.0431)	(.1830)	(.1278)	(.2160)	(.0486)
MSA Status (dummies, base group is MSA suppressed, except for Central America and the Spanish-speaking Caribbean)					
in central city	-.1516	-.6463	.0136	-.6970*	-.1365
	(.0931)	(.3812)	(.2729)	(.3485)	(.1160)
not in city	-.1774	-.8390	-.2108	-.5941	-.0998
	(.0938)	(.4371)	(.2681)	(.3794)	(.1179)
not in msa	-.1826		-.0087		-.3249
	(.1397)		(.4518)		(.1701)
Origin Country (dummies, base group is Mexico Hispanics; Countries of a specific region are compared to the omitted countries in that region)					
Colombia	.1281		.1028		
	(.0809)		(.0947)		
Cuba	.2306*			.0014	
	(.0823)			(.3031)	
Dominican Republic	.0620			-.1828	
	(.0816)			(.3125)	
El Salvador	.0735	.1838			
	(.0708)	(.1197)			
other Hispanics	.0483				
	(.0538)				
Immigration Cohort (dummies, base group is pre-1970 cohort)					
1970-74	.0194	-.82430	-.1353	-.1446	.1638*
	(.0507)	(.4211)	(.1156)	(.1429)	(.0713)
1975-79	-.0028	-.6167	.0075	-.4166*	.1361
	(.0502)	(.3225)	(.1424)	(.1622)	(.0700)
1980-84	-.0727	-.6743	-.0907	-.4199*	.0111
	(.0750)	(.3507)	(.1628)	(.1735)	(.0907)
1985-91	-.1254	-.5213*	-.1734	-.3152	.0039
	(.1066)	(.2430)	(.2024)	(.2194)	(.1697)

Table 6.2.4 (continued)

Variable	Hispanics	Central America	South America	Caribbean	Mexico
Husband's Usual Weekly Earnings (linear splines)					
less than $170	-.0330	-.1225	-.0766	-.1046	-.0549
	(.0315)	(.0925)	(.0520)	(.0794)	(.0441)
$170-$400	.1761*	-.0268	.3851	.4866	.1955
	(.0786)	(.2608)	(.1987)	(.2881)	(.1193)
over $400	.0785	.4439	-.1318	-.5908	.0291
	(.1114)	(.3723)	(.2868)	(.4348)	(.1652)
mills ratio	-.0249	1.0426	-.1861	.7625*	-.0354
	(.2525)	(.8800)	(.2410)	(.3571)	(.3715)
Wife's Level of Education (dummies, base group is college education)					
less than 7th grade	-.2155*	-.2470	-.1126	-.0765	-.3291*
	(.0820)	(.1965)	(.4388)	(.1874)	(.1238)
7-12th grade	-.1294*	-.3034	-.1417	-.1072	-.2010*
	(.0481)	(.2330)	(.0934)	(.0979)	(.0777)
Marital Status at Migration and Migration Patterns (dummies, base group is married and migrated before husband)					
single	.1098	-.1901	-.0139	-.2207	.2029
	(.0940)	(.3204)	(.1920)	(.1951)	(.1608)
after husband	.0397	-.3122	.0017	-.1503	.0994
	(.1072)	(.3397)	(.2030)	(.1982)	(.2119)
with husband	.0877	-.0693	-.0811	.1810	.0806
	(.0881)	(.2653)	(.1913)	(.1636)	(.1883)
Wife's Age (linear splines)					
30 or less	.0049	.0348	.0502*	.0300	-.0062
	(.0097)	(.0257)	(.0209)	(.0220)	(.0178)
over 30	-.0011	-.0547	-.0409	-.0489	.0126
	(.0136)	(.0412)	(.0313)	(.0330)	(.0220)
Husband's Immigration Status (dummies, base group is established immigrants)					
US-born	.0802	.2218	.1531	.0429	.0346
	(.0471)	(.1442)	(.1077)	(.1109)	(.0609)
recent immigrant	.0788	-.0221	.4434	-.5250	-.0833
	(.1178)	(.4046)	(.2245)	(.4628)	(.1786)

Table 6.2.4 (continued)

Variable	Hispanics	Central America	South America	Caribbean	Mexico
Husband's Level of education (dummies, base group is college education)					
less than 7th grade	-.0723	.05100	-.3010	-.1308	-.0141
	(.0620)	(.1612)	(.2898)	(.2172)	(.0930)
7-12th grade	-.0648	.1244	-.0153	-.1096	-.0189
	(.0402)	(.1840)	(.0902)	(.0947)	(.0706)
Number of Children/Other Adults in Household (continuous)					
children 6-17	-.0134	-.1255	-.0397	-.1210	.0109
	(.0215)	(.0782)	(.0460)	(.0654)	(.0324)
children less than 6	.0147	-.2892	.0709	-.2582	.0232
	(.0575)	(.2020)	(.0907)	(.1512)	(.0805)
adults	-.0049	.0991	.0023	.1018	-.0188
	(.0194)	(.0801)	(.0504)	(.0628)	(.0240)
Year of Survey					
from 1986 sample	-.0453	.1886	-.1170	.1471	.0107
	(.0395)	(.2496)	(.1128)	(.1768)	(.0644)
from 1988 sample	.0333	.0048	-.0276	.1639	.0628
	(.0412)	(.1993)	(.1350)	(.1772)	(.0698)
Memo items:					
number of observations	743	117	122	125	355
dependent variable mean	1.9210	1.8994	2.0649	2.1031	1.8367
R square	.2667	.3790	.4551	.3582	.2816
adjusted R square	.2304	.1623	.2675	.1442	.2150

* p<.05.

Sources: June 1986, 1988, and 1991 Current Population Survey Supplements; Bureau of Labor Statistics, Consumer Price Index.

Table 6.2.5 Hourly Earnings OLS regression by Country of Origin (Standard Errors are in Parentheses)

Variable	Cuba	China	Philip-pines	India	Korea	Asian Refugees
intercept	3.1234*	2.0166*	2.2469*	.2057	1.8740	2.5629*
	(1.2534)	(.7399)	(.8429)	(1.2609)	(1.2422)	(.6741)
Region of Residence (dummies, base group is west)						
northeast	-.2996	-.0222	-.0483	.1404	-.0707	.1031
	(.4597)	(.0960)	(.1172)	(.3159)	(.1652)	(.1556)
midwest	-1.0338	-.1025	.1815	-.1571	-.1459	-.0760
	(.5572)	(.1171)	(.1242)	(.2750)	(.1832)	(.1779)
south	-.3931	-.2025	.1714	.1168	-.3084*	.0223
	(.4325)	(.1366)	(.1204)	(.2898)	(.1461)	(.0976)
MSA Status (dummies, base group is not in MSA or MSA suppressed, except for China)						
in central city	-.7987	-.4177	.7783*	.2671	.0593	-.1522
	(.4218)	(.4021)	(.3779)	(.2544)	(.2458)	(.3126)
not in city	-.9299*	-.0192	.7047	.3854	.2001	-.0854
	(.3947)	(.3240)	(.3785)	(.2465)	(.2159)	(.2964)
not in msa		-.9618				
		(.5580)				
Marital Status at Migration and Migration Patterns (dummies, base group is married and migrated before husband)						
single	-.0504	-.1457	-.2083	.1839	-.0069	.1482
	(.2436)	(.2018)	(.1352)	(.2760)	(.2812)	(.2489)
after husband	.0864	-.0153	-.1858	.0782	-.4699	.1805
	(.2764)	(.1959)	(.1505)	(.2442)	(.2669)	(.2522)
with husband	.1280	-.0603	.0166	.1099	.0796	.1886
	(.2610)	(.2005)	(.1464)	(.3011)	(.3015)	(.2623)

Table 6.2.5 (continued)

Variable	Cuba	China	Philip-pines	India	Korea	Asian Refugees
Immigration Cohort (dummies, base group is pre-1970 cohort)						
1970-74	[2]	-.0637	-.1102	.2497	.3359	-.1376
		(.1308)	(.1295)	(.2884)	(.3094)	(.2990)
1975-79	-.1750	.2589	-.0493	.3949	-.1041	-.3867
	(.1543)	(.1611)	(.1359)	(.3084)	(.2448)	(.2481)
1980-84	[3]	-.1669	-.1943	.0093	.0172	-.4796
		(.1475)	(.1232)	(.2895)	(.2980)	(.2590)
1985-91	-.1868	-.0637	-.2425	.1015	.0012	-.3549
	(.1863)	(.1831)	(.1787)	(.3005)	(.4292)	(.3231)
Husband's Education (dummies, base group is college education; the less-than-7th-grade and high school groups are combined for Cuba, Philippines, India, and Korea)						
less than 7th grade		-.4894				.0334
		(.3062)				(.1622)
7-12th grade	-.2411	.3952*	.0502	-.0727	-.0895	-.1623
	(.1268)	(.1322)	(.1009)	(.2624)	(.1623)	(.1134)
Number of Children/Other Adults in Household (continuous)						
children 6-17	-.1656	-.0304	-.0585	-.0895	.0274	.0227
	(.1063)	(.0601)	(.0437)	(.0864)	(.0756)	(.0454)
children less than 6	-.0615	.3033*	-.0127	.1219	.0610	.0295
	(.1383)	(.1173)	(.0553)	(.1968)	(.1032)	(.0810)
adults	.0504	-.0840	.0483	-.0180	.0919	.0207
	(.0669)	(.0500)	(.0390)	(.0810)	(.0807)	(.0433)
Wife's Level of Education (dummies, base group is college education; the less-than-7th-grade and the high school groups are combined for Cuba and India)						
less than 7th grade		-.0960	-.5603*		.5076	-.5525*
		(.2887)	(.2758)		(.4309)	(.1819)
7-12th grade	-.1259	-.2500	-.4352*	-.0229	-.1288	-.4303*
	(.1363)	(.1458)	(.1153)	(.2180)	(.1875)	(.1136)

Table 6.2.5 (continued)

Variable	Cuba	China	Philip-pines	India	Korea	Asian Refugees
Wife's Age (linear splines)						
30 or less	.0250	.0283	-.0019	.0447	.0240	.0019
	(.0279)	(.0226)	(.0234)	(.0574)	(.0422)	(.0169)
over 30	-.0185	-.0451	.0006	-.0371	-.0330	-.0077
	(.0432)	(.0286)	(.0289)	(.0598)	(.0505)	(.0264)
mills ratio	.0588	-.5521	.1136	-.1234	-.0525	-.1886
	(.3028)	(.2795)	(.2253)	(.4380)	(.2446)	(.3077)
Husband's Usual Weekly Earnings (linear splines)						
less than $170	-.0620	-.0957	-.0945	.0077[1]	-.0926	.0344
	(.1393)	(.0489)	(.0555)	(.0865)	(.0941)	(.0779)
$170-$400	.2376	.6009*	.2126		.2768	-.0048
	(.3676)	(.2182)	(.2665)		(.3579)	(.3212)
over $400	-.0897	-.0648	.2553	.3226	.0454	.1718
	(.4932)	(.2566)	(.2857)	(.1638)	(.4219)	(.3494)
Husband's Immigration Status (dummies, base group is established immigrants except for Cuba and Southeast Asian refugees)						
US-born	-.0462	-.0829	-.0379	-.1791	-.0231	-.2068
	(.1853)	(.1389)	(.1023)	(.3860)	(.1884)	(.2112)
recent immigrant		-.0044	-.4951*	.0010	-.3133	
		(.4278)	(.2405)	(.2617)	(.2992)	

Table 6.2.5 (continued)

Variable	Cuba	China	Philip-pines	India	Korea	Asian Refugees
Origin Country (dummies, base group is Cambodia)						
Laos						.0458
						(.1740)
Vietnam						.0298
						(.1546)
Year of Survey (dummies, base group is 1991)						
1986	.0876	.1516	.0055	.1899	.0955	-.0336
	(.2328)	(.1148)	(.1132)	(.2099)	(.1679)	(.1238)
1988	.1027	.3871*	-.0627	-.0451	.1333	-.0973
	(.2249)	(.1466)	(.1218)	(.1890)	(.1782)	(.1323)
Memo items:						
number of observations	81	140	173	98	86	116
mean of dependent variable	2.1486	2.2339	2.3399	2.2668	2.1427	2.0631
R square	.3771	.6091	.3724	.4484	.5611	.5100
adjusted R square	.1101	.5015	.2504	.2464	.3455	.3371

* p<.05.

Sources: June 1986, 1988, and 1991 Current Population Survey Supplements; Bureau of Labor Statistics, Consumer Price Index.

1. Includes husbands earnings less than $400 a week. 2. Includes all 1970 cohorts. 3. Includes all 1980s cohorts.

Table 6.2.6 Hourly Earnings OLS Regression by Cohort and Age at Migration (Standard Errors in Parentheses)

Variable	Before 1970	1970s	1980s	Before Age 21	After Age 21
intercept	3.0497*	2.2827*	1.9691*	2.3277*	2.0398*
	(.8461)	(.3018)	(.2622)	(.2968)	(.4182)
Region of Residence (dummies, base group is west)					
northeast	.0555	.0578	-.0521	.0092	.0124
	(.0843)	(.0542)	(.0477)	(.0582)	(.0406)
midwest	.0560	-.1456*	-.0236	-.0465	-.0625
	(.1621)	(.0581)	(.0577)	(.0722)	(.0478)
south	-.0679	-.1645*	-.0073	-.1298*	-.0760
	(.0814)	(.0609)	(.0442)	(.0455)	(.0440)
MSA Status (dummies, base group is MSA suppressed)					
central city	-.7332	.0079	-.1107	-.2437*	.0761
	(.6632)	(.1094)	(.0971)	(.1169)	(.1031)
not central city	-.6312	-.0422	-.0794	-.1453	.0105
	(.6485)	(.1087)	(.0948)	(.1131)	(.1045)
not in msa	-.3597	-.1477	-.3865*	-.2313	-.1848
	(.7185)	(.1736)	(.1510)	(.1729)	(.1633)
Husband's Level of Education (dummies, base group is college education)					
less than 7th grade	-.0180	-.0269	-.1331	-.0667	-.0401
	(.1981)	(.0861)	(.0686)	(.0739)	(.0650)
7-12th grade	.0281	-.0848	-.0608	-.0013	-.0402
	(.0871)	(.0462)	(.0474)	(.0480)	(.0406)
Immigration Cohort (dummies, base group is pre-1970 cohort; In the cohort regressions, each group of a specific cohort is compared to the most recent group of the same cohort)					
pre-1960	-.0639				
	(.1202)				
1960-64	.0420				
	(.0788)				
1965-69					
1970-74		.0111		.1209	-.1224
		(.7549)		(.0628)	(.0809)
1975-79				.1133	-.1066
				(.0730)	(.0817)
1980-84			-.0262	-.0339	-.2311*
			(.0556)	(.0834)	(.0866)
1985-91				.1779	-.3421*
				(.1501)	(.1024)
Wife's Level of Education (dummies, base group is college education)					
less than 7th grade	-.2212	-.4501*	-.1379	-.0600	-.3812*
	(.2024)	(.1199)	(.0803)	(.1202)	(.0745)
7-12th grade	-.1953*	-.2985*	-.0719	-.1526*	-.2629*
	(.0820)	(.0638)	(.0562)	(.0487)	(.0538)

Table 6.2.6 (continued)

Variable	Before 1970	1970s	1980s	Before Age 21	After Age 21
Origin Country (dummies, base group is the Philippines for Asians; Mexico for Hispanics)					
Asian	.0448	.1323	.0312	.1155	.1326
	(.0950)	(.0892)	(.1014)	(.1183)	(.0838)
China		-.0348	-.0678	.0346	-.0746
		(.1120)	(.0748)	(.1053)	(.0681)
Colombia		-.0423	.0719	.0372	.1008
		(.1156)	(.1185)	(.1150)	(.1140)
Cuba		.0059	.0949	.1317	.2286*
		(.1351)	(.1159)	(.0790)	(.1077)
Dominican Republic		.0376	-.0637	.0834	.0358
		(.1313)	(.1162)	(.1137)	(.0992)
El Salvador		-.1285	.0490	.0769	.0729
		(.1022)	(.0772)	(.1102)	(.0763)
India		.1231	-.0597	-.1613	.0094
		(.0939)	(.0749)	(.1483)	(.0619)
Japan		-.1945	-.0182	.2970	-.1748
		(.2273)	(.2028)	(.1798)	(.1500)
Korea		-.1058	.0620	.0003	-.0719
		(.1089)	(.1059)	(.1481)	(.0840)
SEA refugees		-.0147	-.1406	-.0960	-.0516
		(.0828)	(.0761)	(.0958)	(.0645)
other Asians		-.2250*	.1029	-.2046	-.0509
		(.1017)	(.1127)	(.1266)	(.0900)
other Hispanics		-.1261	-.0721	.0021	.0107
		(.0669)	(.0724)	(.0688)	(.0634)
Number of Children/Other Adults in the Household (continuous)					
children 6-17	-.0549	-.0160	.0140	-.0075	-.0276
	(.0343)	(.0244)	(.0218)	(.0215)	(.0207)
children under 6	.0389	-.0011	.1041*	.0949	.0174
	(.0683)	(.0685)	(.0403)	(.0508)	(.0496)
adults	-.0468	-.0069	-.0423	-.0401	.0098
	(.0486)	(.0193)	(.0244)	(.0238)	(.0186)
Marital Status at Migration and Migration Patterns (dummies, base group is married and migrated before husband)					
single at migration	-.0128	.0579	.1647	.1149	.0397
	(.2209)	(.0905)	(.0966)	(.0763)	(.0931)
after husband	-.1550	-.0110	.2426*	.0130	.0303
	(.2358)	(.0780)	(.1105)	(.0876)	(.0930)
with husband	-.0763	.0039	.2837*	.0522	.0973
	(.2432)	(.0882)	(.0987)	(.0862)	(.0866)
mills ratio	-.2311	.1307	-.5010*	-.4206	.0138
	(.3088)	(.2829)	(.1937)	(.2551)	(.2004)

Table 6.2.6 (continued)

Variable	Before 1970	1970s	1980s	Before Age 21	After Age 21
Husband's Usual Weekly Earnings (linear splines)					
less than $170	-.0460	-.0693	-.0050	-.0135	-.0485
	(.0446)	(.0410)	(.0274)	(.0373)	(.0274)
$170-$400	.2422	.2464*	.2466*	.2292*	.1940*
	(.2143)	(.0969)	(.0798)	(.0934)	(.0753)
over $400	.2073	.0144	.1278	.1275	.1250
	(.2319)	(.1150)	(.1079)	(.1178)	(.0938)
Husband's Immigration Status (dummies, base group is established immigrants)					
US-born	-.0010	-.0313	.1348*	-.0010	.0345
	(.0855)	(.0495)	(.0574)	(.0471)	(.0449)
recent immigrant				.0651	.0159
				(.2003)	(.0868)
Year of Survey (dummies, base group is 1991)					
1986	.1406	-.0895	.0672	-.0146	-.0514
	(.0910)	(.0483)	(.0591)	(.0535)	(.0421)
1988	.1679	-.0534	.0490	.0473	-.0127
	(.0974)	(.0550)	(.0457)	(.0560)	(.0401)
Wife's Age (linear splines)					
30 or less	-.0053	.0083	.0029	-.0037	.0129
	(.0180)	(.0105)	(.0078)	(.0099)	(.0141)
over 30	.0218	-.0028	-.0119	.0154	-.0156
	(.0240)	(.0133)	(.0102)	(.0155)	(.0156)
Memo items:					
number of observations	255	595	602	600	852
dependent variable mean	2.1632	2.1110	1.9385	2.0503	2.0489
R square	.3202	.4109	.3481	.3551	.3913
adjusted R square	.2360	.3706	.3041	.3065	.3597

* p<.05.

Sources: June 1986, 1988, and 1991 Current Population Survey Supplements; Bureau of Labor Statistics, Consumer Price Index.

Separate regressions by region or country-of-origin reveal high degrees of variation in the earning potentials of young immigrant wives based on their marital status at migration and migration patterns. Young South Asian wives who were single at migration earn 16 percent more than young wives migrating before their husbands. The comparable figures are 9 percent and 5 percent for wives migrating after husbands and in the same period as their husbands respectively. Young immigrant wives migrating after husbands from Central America have the greatest earnings disadvantage as compared to young Central American wives migrating before their husbands. On the contrary, the young wives migrating after husbands from South America obtain similar earnings as what the young South American wives migrating before husbands do. Young Caribbean immigrant wives who were single at migration earn 22 percent less than young Caribbean wives migrating before their husbands.

Among young Cuban, Chinese and Filipino wives, those migrating following husbands have the lowest earning offers relative to comparable wives migrating before husbands. Except for South Asian wives, young Asian wives migrating with their husbands seem to gain earning advantages over other similar Asian wives, whereas wives migrating while single or migrating after husbands appear to fair worst in the U.S. labor market. In particular, young Korean immigrant wives migrating after their husbands earn about 55 percent less than young Korean wives migrating with their husbands, 47 percent less than wives migrating before their husbands. In contrast, those young South Asian wives migrating while single enjoy the highest level of hourly earnings, nearly 17 percent more than those migrating before their husbands and 11 percent more than those migrating with their husbands. Of all young Cuban and Southeast Asian refugee wives, those migrating with husbands earn the most, 13 percent and 19 percent more than their respective ethnic counterpart wives migrating before their husbands.

In general, the earning advantages of the young Hispanic wives migrating with their husbands are not as great as those of their Asian counterparts. Nonetheless, a few Hispanic groups do find that wives migrating with their husbands earn a lot more than others. Young Hispanic wives from Central America and the Caribbean who migrated with their husbands earn substantially more than Central American and Caribbean wives who migrated while single or after their husbands. Among young Mexican wives, those migrating while single gain the highest level of earnings, about 12 percent more than those migrating with their husbands and 20 percent more than those migrating before their husbands.

Marital Status at Migration, Migration Patterns and Timing of Immigration. As demonstrated in Table 6.2.6, the results from the separate estimations of the hourly earnings equation by immigration cohorts show evidence of interaction effects between marital status and migration patterns and timing of immigration. Among the pre-1970 cohort, young wives immigrating before their husbands earn more than any other group, although the differences are not statistically significant. In fact, the group migrating while single and young wives migrating during the same period with their husbands appear to have similar earnings capacities as the young wives migrating before their husbands. As discussed previously, the "single" effect estimated based on the pre-1970 cohort contains both the effect of migrating while single as well as migrating before age 21 due to the age criterion in selecting the sample.

Among the 1970s cohort, young wives migrating before their husbands do not earn substantially different from any other group. Among the 1980s cohort, young wives migrating after or during the same period with their husbands earn significantly 24 percent and 28 percent more respectively than young wives migrating before their husbands. Those migrating while single also earn more than young wives migrating before their husband, although the difference is not significant at the 5 percent level.

Separate regressions by year of survey show little consistent pattern. In 1986, young Asian and Hispanic wives migrating before their husbands supply the most number of work hours. In 1988, young Asian and Hispanic wives migrating with their husbands supply the most number of work hours. In 1991, young Asian and Hispanic wives migrating while single supply the most number of hours in market work.

The regressions estimated separately by immigrant wives' ages at migration show similar levels of earnings by their marital status at migration and migration patterns. Those migrating before their husbands appear to earn slightly less than all other wives no matter whether migrating as adults or minors. Young wives migrating with their husbands appear to earn more than all other wives, except for those migrating before age 21 and single.

Selectivity Bias in the Estimation of Country-Of-Origin and Cohort Effects. The above discussion reveals substantial variations in the immigrant wives' earnings by their marital status at migration, migration patterns, country-of-origin and timing of immigration. Hypothesis testing were conducted to evaluate the extent to which the estimated country-of-origin and cohort effects will be changed by controlling for the young immigrant wives' marital status at migration. These hypotheses were formally laid out in Section 4.4.1. as Hypotheses 11 to 19. Two base-group-free measures, the F statistic and the standard deviation, were derived to evaluate the hypotheses.

Table 6.2.7 and Table 6.2.8 summarize the F statistics obtained from the hourly earnings regression before and after including the marital status and migration patterns variables. The "before" and "after" F statistics are reasonably close in general, except for the ones obtained in testing the country-of-origin effect for the combined sample, and the cohort effect for Hispanics. Furthermore, the significance of the cohort effects in the young Hispanic immigrant wives' hourly earnings disappears after including the marital status at migration and migration patterns variables.

Table 6.2.9 presents the standard deviations calculated from the hourly earning regressions before and after including the marital status at migration and migration patterns variables. Consistent with what the F statistics show, the standard deviations of the cohort are reduced considerably by including the migration selectivity variables, and this is particularly true among Hispanics.

Immediate Relatives in the U.S. The presence of the immigrant wife's own immediate relatives seems to increase her hourly earnings, while the presence of her in-laws in the U.S. seems to depress her earnings. The same patterns are observed in either the 1989 or the 1991 sample, or the combined sample. Nonetheless, both effects are not significant at the 5 percent level. The opposite signs may reflect the fact that young immigrant wives with own relatives in the U.S. are more likely to participate in the U.S. labor force, and therefore gain more labor market experiences than those with in-laws in the U.S. Without any further evidence, this may also suggest that young immigrant wives with in-laws in the U.S. tend to be tied-migrants, i.e., migrating to join their families, while those with own relatives tend to self-motivated in the migration process.

Section Summary. The regression results show substantial variations in the effects of migration selectivity by the immigrant wives' countries-of-origin. Wives migrating after their husbands appear to have an earning disadvantage for Central Americans and for most Asians, including Chinese, Filipinos, and Koreans. Those migrating while single earn the most among South Asian (particularly Asian Indian) and Mexican wives. Among Cuban and Southeast Asian refugee wives, those migrating with their husbands tend to earn the most. Hypothesis testing shows that,

Table 6.2.7 Test Statistics, Hourly Earnings, Controlling for Marital Status and Migration Patterns

	Hypothesis	J	N-K	R^2	R^2_*	F statistics	reject*
(1)	no country-of-origin effect	12	1409	.3525	.3244	5.10	yes
(2)	no region-of-origin effect	7	1415	.3485	.3384	3.13	yes
(3)	no difference between Asians and Hispanics	1	1420	.3436	.3384	11.20	yes
(4)	no country-of-origin effect among Asians	6	672	.3550	.3516	.59	no
(5)	no country-of-origin effect among Hispanics	5	707	.2667	.2477	3.66	yes
(6)	no immigration cohort effect	4	1409	.3525	.3376	8.10	yes
(7)	no immigration cohort effect among Asians	4	672	.3550	.3342	5.42	yes
(8)	no immigration cohort effect among Hispanics	4	707	.2667	.2573	2.27	no
(9)	no period effect	2	1409	.3525	.3513	1.31	no
(10)	no difference by marital status and migration patterns	3	1409	.3525	.3506	1.38	no

* Reject the null hypothesis at 5 percent level.

Source: June 1986, 1988, and 1991 Current Population Survey Supplements.

Note: J is the number of restrictions; N is the number of observations; K is the number of regressors; R^2 is the R square from the unrestricted regression; R^2_* is the R square from the restricted regression.

Table 6.2.8 Test Statistics, Hourly Earnings, Not Controlling for Marital Status and Migration Patterns

Hypothesis		J	N-K	R^2	R_*^2	F statistics	reject*
(1)	no country-of-origin effect	12	1412	.3506	.3362	2.61	yes
(2)	no region-of-origin effect	7	1418	.3463	.3362	3.13	yes
(3)	no difference between Asians and Hispanics	1	1423	.3412	.3362	10.8	yes
(4)	no country-of-origin effect among Asians	6	675	.3509	.3477	.55	no
(5)	no country-of-origin effect among Hispanics	5	710	.2622	.2419	3.91	yes
(6)	no immigration cohort effect	4	1412	.3506	.3341	8.97	yes
(7)	no immigration cohort effect among Asians	4	675	.3509	.3276	6.06	yes
(8)	no immigration cohort effect among Hispanics	4	710	.2622	.2488	3.22	yes
(9)	no period effect	2	1412	.3506	.3493	1.41	no

* Reject the null hypothesis at 5 percent level.

Source: June 1986, 1988, and 1991 Current Population Survey Supplements.

Note: J is the number of restrictions; N is the number of observations; K is the number of regressors; R^2 is the R square from the unrestricted regression; R_*^2 is the R square from the restricted regression.

Table 6.2.9 Weighted Standard Deviations of Country-of-Origin, Cohort and Period Effects in the Hourly Earnings Regression, With and Without Including Marital Status and Migration Patterns

Variable	Without (1)	With (2)	Difference (1)-(2)
Hypothesis 11:			
not reducing country-of-origin effect, N=13			
hourly earnings	.0520	.0570	-.0050
Hypothesis 12:			
not reducing region-of-origin effect, N=8			
hourly earnings	.0367	.0418	-.0051
Hypothesis 14:			
not reducing Asian country-of-origin effect, N=7			
hourly earnings	.0400	.0402	-.0002
Hypothesis 15:			
not reducing Hispanic country-of-origin effect, N=6			
hourly earnings	.0453	.0537	-.0084
Hypothesis 16:			
not reducing cohort effect, N=5			
hourly earnings	.0383	.0582	-.0199
Hypothesis 17:			
not reducing Asian cohort effect, N=5			
hourly earnings	.0418	.0444	-.0026
Hypothesis 18:			
not reducing Hispanic cohort effect, N=5			
hourly earnings	.0279	.0419	-.0140
Hypothesis 19:			
not reducing period effect, N=3			
hourly earnings	.0153	.0169	-.0016

Source: June 1986, 1988, and 1991 Current Population Survey Supplements.

by controlling for migration selectivity, very little country-of-origin difference in earnings is eliminated.

Among the 1980s cohort, young wives migrating with their husbands gain the most by working in the labor market, while those migrating before their husbands fare worst. The young wives of the 1970s cohort do not seem to make substantially different levels of earnings by their marital status at migration and migration patterns. Among the pre-1970 cohorts, young wives migrating after their husbands earn the least, while those migrating before their husbands earn the most. By including the migration selectivity variables, considerable cohort differences in earnings are reduced. This is particularly true for Hispanics.

The immigrant wife's hourly earnings appear to be influenced in opposite directions by the presence of her side of relatives and in-laws. The more of her relatives are in the U.S., the higher the immigrant wife earns. On the contrary, the more of her in-laws are in the U.S., the less she earns.

6.2.2 Other Control Variables and Hourly Earnings

In addition to the migration selectivity variables, the same set of independent variables from the labor force participation probit regression were also included in the hourly earning regression. As factors representing the reservation wage enter the married women's labor force participation decision, they are likely to contribute indirectly to the women's human capital accumulation, and therefore are included in the hourly earning regression. These variables are region of residence, whether living in Metropolitan Statistical Area (MSA), country-of-origin, timing of immigration, husband's education, wife's education, the number of children in the household, the number of other adults in the household, husband's immigration status, and husband's usual weekly earnings. The mills ratio derived from the first-stage labor force participation regression was included in the regression to correct for the potential sample selection bias due to the endogenous work decision.

Educational Attainments. Consistent with the prediction by the conventional human capital theory, the results show that an immigrant wife's offered market wage is highly related to her level of education; the higher her educational level, the more she earns. Furthermore, according to Table 6.2.3 and Table 6.2.4, Asian immigrant wife's wage offers appear to be more responsive to her educational level than her Hispanic counterpart judging from both the magnitude and significance of the education effects. Table 6.2.6 indicates significant education effects for the 1970s cohort, but not the 1980s cohort. As the transfer of education training from one country to another takes time (Chiswick 1978), the 1980s cohort may still not able to obtain wage offers that match with their educational attainments due to their relatively short length of U.S. experiences. As a second indicator of the young immigrant wives' human capital, their English-speaking abilities are significant predictors of the young immigrant wives' earnings, although the estimated signs basically confirm that young immigrant wives with very little English-speaking abilities tend to earn less in the U.S. labor market.

Country of Origin. Significant country-of-origin variations between Mexicans and most of the other Hispanic groups are found in the separate regressions by year of survey, as summarized in Table 6.2.1. However, the significance disappear in the estimation based on the combined sample. Table 6.2.2 shows that on average, young Asian immigrant wives earn 15 percent more than their Hispanic counterparts, controlling for everything else. Among young Hispanic immigrant wives, Cuban immigrant wives earn significantly 15 percent more than what Mexican immigrant wives earn. Despite of the significant tendency of labor force participation among young Filipino immigrant wives, they don't seem to have very different earnings capacities from any other group of young Asian immigrant wives. On the contrary, young Cuban immigrant wives not only are more likely to be in the labor force, but also earn more in the labor market than young Mexican immigrant wives. In the same table, the results also indicate that young immigrant wives living in the South earn significantly less than young wives living in the West region of this country. Separate estimations by region-of-origin and country-of-origin show that these significant negative effects come mostly from young immigrant wives from east Asia (or Korea) and the Spanish-speaking Caribbean.

The hypothesis testings on the country-of-origin, region-of-origin and racial ethnic differences in hourly earnings are conducted and the results are presented in Table 6.2.7. The F statistics show overall significant country-of-origin, region-of-origin, and racial/ethnic effects in the young immigrant wives' hourly earnings determination. However, the young Asian immigrant wives do not seem to earn significantly different from one another.

Reservation Wage Rate Factors. Factors influencing the young immigrant wives' reservation wage rate are incorporated in the earnings estimation to control for the immigrant wives' past work experiences.

These include the immigrant wife's age, the number of children in the household, number of adults in the household, her husbands' earnings potentials, his weekly earnings, educational attainments, and his English-speaking abilities. The regression results consistently show no significant age effects on their hourly earnings. This may be due to the relative limited age range selected into the sample, i.e., 18-44. The concentration in the child-bearing ages means little variations in their work experiences. The effects of the number of children in the household and number of adults in the household on the young immigrant wives' hourly earnings seem inconclusive and insignificant. The separate estimation for young Chinese immigrant wives shows that with one more young children at home, an average Chinese immigrant wife will earn significantly 30 percent more an hour. The positive sign contradicts with the prediction that the presence of children in household reduces the immigrant wife's work experiences, and therefore depresses her market wage offers. In general, the young immigrant wives' market wage offers decrease with husbands' earnings for wives with low earnings husbands (earning less than $170 per week), while increase for wives with middle and high earnings husbands, and these effects are, in many cases, significant.

Immigration Cohort. The estimation on the young immigrant wives' hourly earnings provide some evidence supporting the "changing cohort qualities" hypothesis rather than the "assimilation hypothesis. Table 6.2.2 shows that overall, the 1970s tend to fare better off, while the 1980s cohort (except for the young South Asian immigrant wives) tend to fare worse off than pre-1970 cohort. Separate regressions by Asians and Hispanics demonstrate that this pattern is particularly true among young Asian immigrant wives. In contrast, the young Hispanic immigrant wives as a whole shows little differences between the pre-1970 and the 1970s cohorts, although the post-1984 cohort seem to be less worse off than the pre-1970 cohort. Results from separate estimations by region-of-origin among Hispanics show no consistent patterns. In particular, among young immigrant wives from Central America, the 1970s cohort earns an average 70 percent lower, while the 1980s cohort earns about 60 percent lower than the pre-1970 cohort. Among the young immigrant wives from South America, the 1975-79 cohort seem to be not very different, while other three cohorts earn less than the pre-1970 cohort. Among young immigrant wives from the Spanish-speaking Caribbean, all the four post-1970 cohorts fare worse off than the pre-1970 cohort, this may reflect the well-documented "golden exile" of the Cuban refugees in the late 1950s and early 1960s.

Table 6.2.7 show the derived F statistics in testing the existence of a significant cohort effect in the young immigrant wives' hourly earnings. Overall, there are strong evidence of cohort effect based on the estimation for the whole sample. Similarly, young Asian immigrant wives' hourly earnings are significantly different by immigration cohort. However, young Hispanic immigrant wives do not seem to earn significantly different across immigration cohort. The test on the period effect on the young immigrant wives' hourly earnings show no significant differences in hourly earnings by interviewed in different years.

The earning regressions in general have pretty good fit; on average, the adjusted R squares is about 0.33. The coefficients in the earnings regressions are mostly not significant. Both the hourly earnings and the hours of work regressions were estimated on the employed sample only. This may explain why very few variables have significant effects in the separate estimations by country-of-origin due to the limited degrees of freedom in these regressions.

Notably, the mills ratio in the earnings regression are insignificant most of the time, except for the separate estimations for young immigrant wives from east Asia, the Spanish-speaking Caribbean, and the 1980s cohort. Moreover, its coefficient estimates often carry a negative sign, opposite of what is expected from the empirical model. These results cast doubt on the extent to which the sample selection bias has been corrected. One exception is found in the regression for the young Caribbean immigrant wives, where the mills ratio has an significant and positive effect on earnings, and the effect is large in magnitude.

6.3 IMMIGRANT WIVES' HOURS OF WORK

The conventional labor supply theory posits individuals decide on their number of work hours at the point where their marginal rates of substitution between leisure and goods equate their potential market wage offers. Thus, the number of work hours of the immigrant wives is most likely determined by the same set of variables (i.e., migration selectivity as well as variables representing market wage rate and reservation wage rate) as included in the labor force participation regression. A separate OLS regression on hours of work permits the evaluation of the continuous dimension of labor supply for the young Asian and Hispanic immigrant wives.

This section presents and discusses the regression results from the OLS hours of work regression. The mills ratio estimated from the first-stage labor force participation probit regression was included in the hour regression to control for the potential sample selection bias due to endogenous work decision. Tables 6.3.1 through 6.3.6 document the results from the hours of work regression.

6.3.1 Migration Selectivity and Hours of Work

This section reports the sign and magnitude of the migration selectivity variables i.e., marital status at migration, migration patterns, and the presence of immediate relatives, in the hours of work estimation. As the immigrant wives' characteristics and migration selectivity may contribute to their supply of work hours differently by country-of-origin, region-of-origin, timing of immigration, age at immigration, and year of survey, the regressions are estimated separately along these dimensions to allow for possible interaction effects.

Tables 6.3.1-6.3.2 present the coefficient estimates from the hours of work regressions based on each sample (1986, 1988, 1989 and 1991 sample) and the pooled samples (1986, 1988 and 1991 as well as 1989 and 1991). Tables 6.3.3 to 6.3.4 document the results from the hours of work regressions estimated separately by region-of-origin based on the pooled sample (1986, 1988 and 1991). Table 6.3.5 presents the results from the regressions estimated separately by selected country-of-origin based on the pooled sample. Table 6.3.6 reports the results of regressions estimated separately by period of immigration and age at immigration based on the pooled sample.

Marital Status at Migration, Migration Patterns and Country-Of-Origin. As demonstrated in the results using the combined sample (Table 6.3.2), young immigrant wives migrating before their husbands tend to work more hours than any other groups. Overall, young immigrant wives migrating while single work 3.8 significantly fewer hours per week, while young wives migrating after their husbands work only 1.4 few hours than young wives migrating before their husbands. Separate regressions by region or country-of-origin reveal a mixed picture. Young immigrant wives migrating while single in general supply fewer hours in market work than young wives migrating before husbands for most groups. Nonetheless, young wives from South Asia, South America and the Spanish-speaking Caribbean migrating while single work 4.5 (in particular, 7 for Asian Indians), 7, and 1.6 more hours than their respective ethnic counterparts who migrated before their husbands.

Table 6.3.1 Hour of Work OLS Regression by Year of Survey (Standard Errors in Parentheses)

Variable	1986	1988	1989	1991
intercept	21.126*	52.248*	28.688*	35.122*
	(1.1053)	(1.9853)	(11.578)	(9.5468)
Region of Residence (dummies, base group is west)				
northeast	1.7608	.7691	-1.2159	2.1073
	(1.8614)	(2.0860)	(2.0284)	(1.6388)
midwest	5.0553*	4.0208	-2.5980	-2.2704
	(2.3165)	(2.2945)	(2.4538)	(1.9585)
south	.0867	-.8250	-1.3171	-.0608
	(1.6991)	(1.7470)	(1.9011)	(1.6035)
MSA Status (dummies, base group is MSA suppressed)				
in central city	1.1076	-6.7748*	-1.5965	3.6869
	(2.6073)	(2.4874)	(2.4390)	(2.5090)
not in central city	.8598	-5.2584*	-1.6971	2.5051
	(2.4845)	(2.3599)	(2.5083)	(2.3918)
not in msa	-1.9294	-7.1572*	-1.2435	-.7174
	(3.5074)	(3.4520)	(3.9388)	(3.6677)
Origin Country (dummies, base group is the Philippines for Asians; Mexico for Hispanics)				
Asian	1.6126	4.0152	1.8593	2.6569
	(2.9856)	(3.1306)	(3.6474)	(3.7061)
China	-.6213	-2.0870	-4.6276	-2.8836
	(2.8176)	(2.9470)	(3.6281)	(3.2422)
Colombia	-1.2413	-.6338	1.1338*	-13.0579*
	(3.8853)	(4.5672)	(4.7136)	(3.9797)
Cuba	-5.9101	2.1079	2.3546	-2.5481
	(3.8793)	(3.3851)	(3.9333)	(3.1270)
Dominican Republic	1.0621	3.3366	3.5873	2.4673
	(4.9613)	(3.7319)	(6.3593)	(4.0631)
El Salvador	1.6256	-4.7280	-.8349	-2.8864
	(3.7496)	(4.0825)	(3.8646)	(2.8968)
India	-.9848	-7.7842*	-4.1339	-1.2961
	(3.2275)	(3.4024)	(3.9144)	(2.8675)
Japan	-3.7277	-7.5965	-4.5647	-5.5935
	(7.2685)	(5.3977)	(6.1806)	(5.2654)
Korea	-3.6189	-1.5941	-3.1253	-2.4341
	(4.1305)	(3.8433)	(3.9850)	(3.4850)
SE Asian refugees	-1.4217	1.5282	-8.9775*	-.0239
	(3.0388)	(3.2031)	(3.6332)	(3.5441)
other Asians	-1.6278	3.9552	.1850	-.8433
	(3.0666)	(3.7208)	(4.4013)	(7.8462)
other Hispanics	3.2179	-2.3145	-2.9373	-3.9936
	(2.7866)	(2.7235)	(2.5649)	(2.2134)
mills ratio	-2.3239	15.4758*	-5.8418	7.4258
	(6.9881)	(7.4241)	(7.1254)	(6.8256)

Table 6.3.1 (continued)

Variable	1986	1988	1989	1991
Husband's Level of Education (dummies, base group is college education)				
less than 7th grade	.2850	3.3466	.7080	5.0652*
	(2.5955)	(3.0413)	(2.8882)	(2.2604)
7-12th grade	.0521	-.0705	.3734	2.2247
	(1.8484)	(2.0127)	(1.8981)	(1.5468)
Immigration Cohort (dummies, base group is pre-1970 cohort)				
1970-74	-2.5036	-.8178	-.9338	-5.7278*
	(2.0345)	(2.2644)	(2.5536)	(2.2980)
1975-79	-.8426	-3.6807	.8730	-3.2466
	(2.0247)	(2.4258)	(2.7085)	(2.1123)
1980-84	-4.7050	-2.4531	1.0346	-3.2712
	(3.0964)	(2.9462)	(2.9735)	(2.2159)
1985-91	-1.0136	-1.9541*	-3.4828	-1.5707
	(4.9329)	(4.5887)	(3.5366)	(3.1259)
Wife's Level of Education (dummies, base group is college education)				
less than 7th grade	4.0648	-.2046	1.9374	-3.9098
	(3.7644)	(3.2228)	(3.1070)	(2.6013)
7-12th grade	5.0918*	-4.9743*	.7282	-1.2977
	(1.6243)	(2.2818)	(1.9310)	(1.7339)
Number of Children/Other Adults in the Household (continuous)				
children 6-17	-.7411	-2.5891*	-.7394	-.6588
	(.7254)	(.8006)	(.7185)	(.6802)
children less than 6	.3762	-5.5090*	1.3081	-.5066
	(1.8776)	(1.8687)	(1.7094)	(1.3463)
adults	-.8077	3.4445*		
	(.8043)	(.9561)		
wife's kin			-.9256	.9956
			(1.5431)	(1.3462)
husband's kin			.8132	-.0175
			(1.5086)	(.9880)
Marital Status at Migration and Migration Patterns (dummies, base group is married and migrated before husband)				
single at migration	1.7899	-2.6324		-3.9674
	(4.1029)	(4.3174)		(2.1996)
married, after husband	5.6454	-.4101	3.2332[1]	-1.7655
	(4.7219)	(4.8658)	(2.8765)	(2.1268)
married, with husband	2.2891	-1.6917	1.7128[1]	-1.1348
	(4.4429)	(4.2225)	(2.4721)	(2.0342)
Husband's Immigration Status (dummies, base group is established immigrants)				
US-born	-.3771	-.7690	.3801	-.2991
	(1.7175)	(1.8729)	(3.2042)	(1.6521)
recent immigrant	-3.5918	-4.1928	-5.0715	-4.8164*
	(2.3228)	(3.2614)	(3.0532)	(2.1061)

Table 6.3.1 (continued)

Variable	1986	1988	1989	1991
Husband's Usual Weekly Earnings (linear splines)				
less than $170	-.5312	-1.3812	.3694	-1.0229
	(1.3454)	(.8674)	(1.4339)	(1.0546)
$170-$400	5.8061	1.3342	4.6288	5.1240
	(3.8693)	(4.6720)	(4.2137)	(2.8399)
over $400	-6.6450	-6.0253	-4.8566	-6.4492
	(4.5843)	(4.7304)	(4.9825)	(3.6070)
Percentage of Immediate Relatives Living in the U.S. (continuous)				
wife's kin			-2.1675	3.9271*
			(1.8337)	(1.6896)
husband kin			3.1580	.0357
			(2.0558)	(1.4564)
Wife's English-Speaking Abilities (dummies, base group is English only)				
very well			1.0065	
			(3.2409)	
well			.1055	
			(3.3548)	
little or no English			-.0983	
			(4.4029)	
Husband's English-Speaking Abilities (dummies, base group is English only)				
very well			2.2718	
			(3.0346)	
well			5.6075	
			(3.3712)	
little or no English			5.1002	
			(3.5675)	
Wife's Age (linear splines)				
30 or less	.4813	.0050	.1320	.0898
	(.3137)	(.3508)	(.4224)	(.3117)
over 30	-.5957	-.0745	-.0257	.0626
	(.4390)	(.4619)	(.5480)	(.3912)
Memo items:				
number of observations	495	401	554	556
dependent variable mean	38.56	37.37	39.75	38.13
R square	.1244	.1570	.0764	.1131
adjusted R square	.0472	.0634	-.0114	.0387

* p<.05.

Sources: June 1986, 1988, and 1991 Current Population Survey Supplements; Bureau of Labor Statistics, Consumer Price Index.

1. Marital status at migration unknown.

Table 6.3.2 Hour of Work OLS Regression, Combined Samples (Standard Errors in Parentheses)

Variable	1989 1991	1986 1988 1991[1]	1986 1988 1991[2]
intercept	32.1027*	34.3670*	33.1557*
	(7.6420)	(5.7868)	(5.8266)
Region of Origin (dummies, base group is west)			
northeast	.0116	.9047	.7041
	(1.2901)	(1.0350)	(1.0273)
midwest	-2.3951	1.8567	1.6887
	(1.5364)	(1.2349)	(1.2319)
south	-.0194	-.5814	-1.2401
	(1.2375)	(.9536)	(.9099)
MSA Status (dummies, base group is MSA suppressed)			
in central city	.7474	3.2228	3.2235
	(1.7485)	(2.3571)	(2.3603)
not in central city	.2355	2.0020	2.0070
	(1.7016)	(2.3142)	(2.3168)
not in msa	-2.1516	2.7208	2.5657
	(2.6087)	(3.5603)	(3.5772)
Origin Country (dummies, base group is the Philippines for Asians; Mexico for Hispanics)			
Asian	1.9684	3.9735	
	(3.2256)	(2.1760)	
China	-3.0968	-2.7610	
	(2.6695)	(1.8254)	
Colombia	-.0609	-3.5245	
	(3.0548)	(2.2353)	
Cuba	.0080	-1.7769	
	(2.6187)	(1.9675)	
Dominican Republic	3.2251	1.5826	
	(3.5156)	(2.2289)	
El Salvador	-2.5913	.3514	
	(2.4931)	(1.8869)	
India	-2.6514	-3.8444*	
	(2.4041)	(1.8128)	
Japan	-4.7978	-7.3198	
	(4.5109)	(3.8708)	
Korea	-1.8318	-3.3308	
	(2.8442)	(2.3812)	
SE Asian refugees	-3.2755	-1.8301	
	(2.6230)	(1.6371)	
other Asians	.0560	-.0201	
	(3.9211)	(2.3018)	
other Hispanics	-3.2312	-.2919	
	(1.8043)	(1.3932)	
Husband's Immigration Status (dummies, base group is established immigrants)			
US-born	-1.7543	-1.2977	-1.2168
	(1.3693)	(.9658)	(.9415)
recent immigrant	-.0959	-5.5773*	-5.0924*
	(2.4769)	(2.4603)	(2.4849)

Table 6.3.2 (continued)

Variable	1989 1991	1986 1988 1991[1]	1986 1988 1991[2]
Originating Region (dummies, base group is the Spanish-speaking Caribbean)			
Mexico			-.3515
			(1.4897)
East Asia			.1831
			(1.4183)
Southeast Asia			3.0520
			(1.6515)
South Asia			.1394
			(1.7730)
South America			-.0295
			(1.5085)
Central America			-1.1966
			(1.5176)
Immigration Cohort (dummies, base group is pre-1970 cohort)			
1970-74	-3.1266	-4.1222*	-3.8037*
	(1.6407)	(1.3233)	(1.3575)
1975-79	-1.3871	-2.9551*	-2.5977
	(1.6993)	(1.3103)	(1.3400)
1980-84	-1.5675	-4.9314*	-4.5054*
	(1.9370)	(1.7780)	(1.8504)
1985-91	-1.3239	-4.8049	-4.0416
	(2.7332)	(2.6352)	(2.7459)
Wife's Level of Education (dummies, base group is college education)			
less than 7th grade	-1.2142	-2.0334	-1.9554
	(2.1545)	(2.1092)	(2.1329)
7-12th grade	-.0007	-.3096	-.4578
	(1.3792)	(1.1439)	(1.1526)
Number of Children/Other adults in the Household (continuous)			
children 6-17	-.6192	-1.5791*	-1.4784*
	(.5227)	(.4815)	(.4805)
children less than 6	.2127	-2.1559	-1.9740
	(1.2349)	(1.1991)	(1.2130)
adults		.7797	.8129
		(.4698)	(.4817)
wife's kin	.1963		
	(1.0752)		
husband's kin	-.0606		
	(.7988)		
Husband's Usual Weekly Earnings (linear splines)			
less than $170	-.1767	-1.2984	-1.2067
	(.9684)	(.7332)	(.7291)
$170-$400	5.1692*	4.7646*	4.6017*
	(2.3256)	(1.7935)	(1.8058)
over $400	-6.2251*	-7.0686*	-6.8532*
	(2.8569)	(2.2339)	(2.2373)

Table 6.3.2 (continued)

Variable	1989 1991	1986 1988 1991[1]	1986 1988 1991[2]
Wife's Age (linear splines)			
30 or less	.1607	.3120	.3404
	(.2802)	(.1987)	(.1998)
over 30	-.1047	-.3718	-.4073
	(.3523)	(.2559)	(.2597)
Marital Status at Migration and Migration Patterns (dummies, base group is married and migrated before husband)			
single at migration		-3.7822*	-3.8141*
		(1.8318)	(1.8471)
married, after husband	1.4777[3]	-1.3880	-1.2937
	(1.1916)	(2.0342)	(2.0544)
married, with husband	1.4561[3]	-2.2104	-2.4253
	(1.1666)	(1.8724)	(1.8811)
Year of Survey (dummies, base group is 1991)			
1986		.2559	.4261
		(.9864)	(.9872)
1988		-.5640	-.3414
		(.9667)	(.9650)
1989	1.3842		
	(.8825)		
Percentage of Immediate Relatives Living in the U.S. (continuous)			
wife's kin	.5620		
	(1.2887)		
husband's kin	.3530		
	(1.1613)		
Husband's Level of Education (dummies, base group is college education)			
less than 7th grade	3.4512	2.5197	2.5624
	(1.7915)	(1.5522)	(1.5591)
7-12th grade	1.1233	-.4594	-.4544
	(1.1875)	(.9251)	(.9203)
mills ratio	-.3910	9.7973	9.3697
	(6.1813)	(5.4983)	(5.5804)
Memo items:			
number of observations	1110	1452	1452
dependent variable mean	38.90	38.07	38.07
R square	.0421	.0488	.0410
adjusted R square	.0035	.0205	.0166

* p<.05.

Sources: June 1986, 1988, and 1991 Current Population Survey Supplements; Bureau of Labor Statistics, Consumer Price Index.

1. Includes country-of-origin dummies. 2. Includes origin-of-origin dummies. 3. Marital status at migration unknown.

Table 6.3.3 Hours of Work OLS Regression by Region of Origin, Asian (Standard Errors in Parentheses)

Variable	Asians	East Asia	Southeast Asia	South Asia
intercept	33.7975*	26.5685	36.8477*	16.5256
	(8.9637)	(2.2956)	(12.3136)	(28.3783)
Region of Residence (dummies, base group is west)				
northeast	.9336	1.2525	-1.5651	9.2111
	(1.2560)	(2.6858)	(1.9283)	(7.1705)
midwest	1.4116	1.6092	2.0129	5.2453
	(1.4401)	(3.2917)	(2.3036)	(6.5961)
south	-.2225	-.0068	-.6822	6.0659
	(1.3363)	(3.1840)	(1.5410)	(6.9507)
MSA Status (dummies, base group is MSA suppressed, except for south Asia)				
in central city	1.9738	.7874	8.3163	3.8859
	(3.6535)	(6.3999)	(8.4048)	(6.1138)
not in central city	.4078	-4.0535	6.8514	6.9026
	(3.3719)	(5.9269)	(8.3366)	(5.8974)
not in msa	-.6316	-2.6175	4.4358	
	(5.3840)	(1.8501)	(9.1629)	
Origin Country (dummies, base group is the Philippines for Asians; Countries of a specific region are compared to the omitted countries in that region)				
China	-1.1556	-1.4201		
	(1.7564)	(4.2401)		
India	-2.5966			-3.2652
	(1.7909)			(5.6536)
Japan	-2.4578			
	(3.6377)			
Korea	-.8849	-.1525		
	(2.2234)	(4.3693)		
Laos			-1.4931	
			(2.8269)	
Philippines			1.7697	
			(2.0425)	
Vietnam	-1.0529		-.0129	
	(1.6370)		(2.1427)	
other Asians	2.1993			
	(2.1493)			

Table 6.3.3 (Continued)

Variable	Asians	East Asia	Southeast Asia	South Asia
Immigration Cohort (dummies, base group is pre-1970 cohort)				
1970-74	-2.6273	-6.0516	.6706	5.0390
	(2.2241)	(4.4389)	(2.3443)	(6.8579)
1975-79	-2.0484	-4.4641	.1342	1.5023
	(2.1875)	(4.4201)	(2.2857)	(7.3171)
1980-84	-2.5862	-3.5023	-.4511	-2.5106
	(2.4774)	(4.5654)	(2.4205)	(6.8365)
1985-91	-1.6880	-4.5869	-2.8936	-.6026
	(3.7038)	(6.4221)	(3.5531)	(7.1427)
Number of Children/Other Adults in Household (continuous)				
children 6-17	-.7547	.1975	-1.0816	.3706
	(.6156)	(1.3464)	(.7224)	(2.1321)
children less than 6	-.7512	-.1099	-2.5666*	5.0111
	(1.2428)	(2.6118)	(1.2793)	(4.7266)
adults	.5189	1.1764	.9450	-1.2183
	(.6366)	(1.3677)	(.6502)	(1.9511)
Marital Status at Migration and Migration Patterns (dummies, base group is married and migrated before husbands)				
single	-1.8989	-1.3399	-1.5972	4.4799
	(2.1657)	(5.3025)	(2.4188)	(6.3972)
married, after husband	2.5381	6.2844	-.2752	6.6156
	(2.2253)	(5.1477)	(2.5903)	(5.8017)
married, with husband	-.3737	-1.0078	-.4644	4.9750
	(2.2944)	(5.1313)	(2.5004)	(7.3356)
Wife's Age (linear splines)				
30 or less	.1959	.4671	.0354	.3515
	(.2598)	(.6544)	(.2877)	(1.3013)
over 30	-.0535	-.4717	-.0458	-.6065
	(.3257)	(.8060)	(.3825)	(1.3462)
Husband's Level of Education (dummies, base group is college education)				
less than 7th grade	4.5739	11.1478	3.7214	[1]
	(3.1834)	(6.9179)	(2.9706)	
7-12th grade	-1.9032	-3.2082	-2.9387	-5.9291
	(1.2902)	(2.9495)	(1.6628)	(6.2754)

Table 6.3.3 (Continued)

Variable	Asians	East Asia	Southeast Asia	South Asia
Wife's Level of Education (dummies, base group is college education)				
less than 7th grade	-3.0145	-3.1080	-5.6143	-15.6400
	(3.7632)	(7.1893)	(3.5858)	(16.6084)
7-12th grade	.9664	.9848	.2511	2.8178
	(1.4711)	(3.1658)	(1.5006)	(5.4512)
Husband's Usual Weekly Earnings (linear splines)				
less than $170	.1819	.0933	-1.0255	.3118[2]
	(.9883)	(1.6962)	(1.0915)	(2.0447)
$170-$400	1.2713	5.3336	2.1919	
	(3.1313)	(5.8753)	(4.3911)	
over $400	-4.4504	-11.9460	-2.5695	-2.8112
	(3.6433)	(6.8695)	(5.1391)	(3.8620)
mills ratio	.0685	.3443	8.9436	-6.0325
	(5.9907)	(7.9014)	(6.4637)	(1.4662)
Husband's Immigration Status (dummies, base group is established immigrants)				
US-born	-1.8054	-6.4473*	-2.5283	-4.8243
	(1.4335)	(3.0185)	(2.1169)	(8.4157)
recent immigrant	-1.1672	-2.8054	-3.8597	2.7993
	(2.9120)	(6.7588)	(4.7806)	(6.1020)
Year of Survey (dummies, base group is 1991)				
1986	.2485	.8895	-1.3274	1.4525
	(1.5956)	(3.3528)	(1.7635)	(5.0563)
1988	-.9995	1.1205	-2.3528	-2.9233
	(1.4364)	(3.5614)	(1.6147)	(4.5658)
Memo items:				
number of observations	709	257	319	103
dependent variable mean	38.75	38.45	38.95	37.87
R square	.0686	.1465	.0714	.2353
adjusted R square	.0187	.0245	-.0362	-.0541

* p<.05.

Sources: June 1986, 1988, and 1991 Current Population Survey Supplements; Bureau of Labor Statistics, Consumer Price Index.

1. Included in the high school category. 2. Included husbands earnings less than $400 a week.

Table 6.3.4 Hours of Work OLS Regression by Region of Origin, Hispanics *(Standard Errors in Parentheses)*

Variable	Hispanics	Central America	South America	Caribbean	Mexico
intercept	32.3793*	65.2636*	2.5316	56.5241*	24.4384
	(8.3213)	(25.6844)	(23.4774)	(23.7620)	(14.3576)
Region of Residence (dummies, base group is west)					
northeast	.8141	-.0144	-4.2105	-.9248	-3.2634
	(1.7147)	(3.9078)	(4.4890)	(5.1073)	(5.3471)
midwest	2.0239	-1.7068	15.3668	3.6274	2.0620
	(2.4961)	(19.3086)	(15.1746)	(8.6531)	(3.6069)
south	-.4894	.6692	-8.4072	-.3917	1.2388
	(1.4931)	(5.8097)	(4.7769)	(5.6859)	(1.8465)
MSA Status (dummies, base group is MSA suppressed, except for Central America and the Spanish-speaking Caribbean)					
central city	1.0536	-3.9698	-8.7202	8.2010	4.4552
	(3.2268)	(12.0977)	(1.1971)	(9.1703)	(4.4044)
not central city	1.0537	-3.3721	-8.0454	4.5182	4.3812
	(3.2513)	(13.8726)	(1.0179)	(9.9830)	(4.4760)
not in msa	1.5555		-38.8855*		7.1739
	(4.8421)		(16.8827)		(6.4559)
Origin Country (dummies, base group is Mexico for Hispanics; Countries of a specific region are compared to the omitted countries in that region)					
Colombia	-2.6854		-4.2615		
	(2.8035)		(3.5368)		
Cuba	-1.8162			-5.6891	
	(2.8532)			(7.9778)	
Dominican Republic	2.8309			-.6539	
	(2.8293)			(8.2243)	
El Salvador	1.2462	4.2506			
	(2.4531)	(3.7993)			
other Hispanics	-.0033				
	(1.8666)				
Immigration Cohort (dummies, base group is pre-1970 cohort)					
1970-74	-3.6184*	-3.5846	-3.8661	-2.8153	-2.7397
	(1.7581)	(13.3652)	(4.3209)	(3.7613)	(2.7076)
1975-79	-2.1955	-3.4056	-8.1637	-4.9800	-.2051
	(1.7402)	(1.2351)	(5.3240)	(4.2682)	(2.6562)
1980-84	-4.6078	-1.8415	-5.6214	-2.0620	-1.2257
	(2.6018)	(11.1292)	(6.0861)	(4.5676)	(3.4433)
1985-91	-2.8124	2.3406	.8155	-4.4796	3.5558
	(3.6971)	(7.7112)	(7.5627)	(5.7730)	(6.4410)

Table 6.3.4 (continued)

Variable	Hispanics	Central America	South America	Caribbean	Mexico
Husband's Usual Weekly Earnings (linear splines)					
less than $170	-1.2278	-1.9186	-.5425	-2.2462	.6777
	(1.0928)	(2.9359)	(1.9426)	(2.0906)	(1.6759)
$170-$400	4.8641	16.5328*	6.9271	9.8394	6.3448
	(2.7241)	(8.2775)	(7.4242)	(7.5819)	(4.5275)
over $400	-4.1720	-8.2805	1.2668	-5.0781	-11.9029
	(3.8624)	(11.8166)	(1.7163)	(11.4411)	(6.2717)
mills ratio	7.9448	-2.2757	8.6428	-3.1763	-5.0385
	(8.7556)	(27.9248)	(9.0042)	(9.3968)	(14.0987)
Number of Children/Other Adults in Household (continuous)					
children 6-17	-1.5482*	1.0524	-1.8737	-.7093	-1.1086
	(.7449)	(2.4816)	(1.7194)	(1.7228)	(1.2319)
children under 6	-1.4374	2.5881	-.0026	-.3845	1.1277
	(1.9942)	(6.4107)	(3.3901)	(3.9804)	(3.0583)
adults	.4399	-2.0038	-.6245	2.7248	-.4329
	(.6730)	(2.5422)	(1.8836)	(1.6526)	(.9121)
Marital Status at Migration and Migration Patterns (dummies, base group is married and migrated before husband)					
single	-3.4568	-5.5153	7.0461	1.5548	-.4214
	(3.2609)	(1.1686)	(7.1727)	(5.1352)	(6.1029)
after husband	-2.2401	-.1763	5.8930	5.0285	2.8140
	(3.7168)	(1.7816)	(7.5854)	(5.2165)	(8.0437)
with husband	-1.4036	-5.7114	6.8219	3.5219	4.3232
	(3.0541)	(8.4199)	(7.1459)	(4.3054)	(7.1476)
Year of Survey (dummies, base group is 1991)					
1986	1.4036	3.1655	9.4342*	-8.0467	-1.0161
	(1.3683)	(7.9225)	(4.2153)	(4.6525)	(2.4444)
1988	.4106	9.6474	4.6499	-5.0562	-2.2926
	(1.4302)	(6.3241)	(5.0433)	(4.6643)	(2.6495)

Table 6.3.4 (continued)

Variable	Hispanics	Central America	South America	Caribbean	Mexico
Wife's Level of Education (dummies, base group is college education)					
less than 7th grade	-.7947	.6884	7.1526	5.7045	3.4255
	(2.8422)	(6.2380)	(16.3953)	(4.9316)	(4.7004)
7-12th grade	-.4899	.8148	.9847	-.2765	3.0861
	(1.6685)	(7.3935)	(3.4879)	(2.5761)	(2.9485)
Wife's Age (linear splines)					
30 or less	.3848	-.4535	.7036	-.3290	.1205
	(.3379)	(.8180)	(.7815)	(.5814)	(.6785)
over 30	-.7030	-.0471	-1.2390	.0844	-.3845
	(.4701)	(1.3088)	(1.1683)	(.8693)	(.8365)
Husband's Immigration Status (dummies, base group is established immigrants)					
US-born	-.6516	-8.1514	-2.2310	-3.3768	1.9515
	(1.6340)	(4.5781)	(4.0244)	(2.9185)	(2.3140)
recent immigrant	-9.3695*	-9.3684	-9.5046	-3.0648	-8.2388
	(4.0856)	(12.8401)	(8.3900)	(12.1791)	(6.7780)
Husband's Level of Education (dummies, base group is college education)					
less than 7th grade	2.7741	3.4954	6.8164	1.5112	1.2669
	(2.1499)	(5.1167)	(1.8282)	(5.7168)	(3.5301)
7-12th grade	1.1180	-.2529	2.8940	-1.6441	1.5645
	(1.3941)	(5.8388)	(3.3692)	(2.4936)	(2.6814)
Memo items:					
number of observations	743	117	122	125	355
mean of dependent variable	37.56	36.56	37.92	36.95	37.94
R square	.0602	.2822	.3524	.2598	.0795
adjusted R square	.0136	.0318	.1294	.0130	-.0058

* p<.05.

Sources: June 1986, 1988, and 1991 Current Population Survey Supplements; Bureau of Labor Statistics, Consumer Price Index.

Table 6.3.5 Hours of Work OLS regression by Country of Origin (Standard Errors are in Parentheses)

Variable	Cuba	China	Philip-pines	India	Korea	Asian Refugees
intercept	77.1658*	28.6124	5.3202*	17.6945	39.0222	29.6943
	(31.5609)	(31.0672)	(15.7032)	(26.9800)	(35.0909)	(17.9692)
Region of Residence (dummies, base group is west)						
northeast	-13.2068	2.0693	-1.9278	1.8924	3.6492	-5.6006
	(11.5755)	(4.0314)	(2.1844)	(6.7609)	(4.6677)	(4.1486)
midwest	-11.4648	2.9099	2.4096	5.2963	9.1996	4.2091
	(14.0288)	(4.9173)	(2.3143)	(5.8839)	(5.1761)	(4.7437)
south	-11.5221	-6.6035	4.3596	6.7870	9.7695*	-5.0200
	(1.8891)	(5.7356)	(2.2430)	(6.2005)	(4.1265)	(2.6025)
MSA Status (dummies, base group is not in MSA or MSA suppressed, except for China)						
in central city	15.0369	1.2116	-.7059	4.7600	-8.4299	15.9996
	(1.6207)	(16.8844)	(7.0396)	(5.4443)	(6.9432)	(8.3328)
not in city	8.4097	-4.5792	-2.9133	5.4689	-7.7947	15.0851
	(9.9389)	(13.6058)	(7.0523)	(5.2748)	(6.0986)	(7.9013)
not in msa		2.8870				
		(23.4310)				
Origin Country (dummies, base group is Cambodia)						
Laos						-3.7069
						(4.6401)
Vietnam						-1.1501
						(4.1222)

Table 6.3.5 (continued)

Variable	Cuba	China	Philip-pines	India	Korea	Asian Refugees
Immigration Cohort (dummies, base group is pre-1970 cohort)						
1970-74	[2]	-3.8795	1.3380	5.2175	3.7160	-.5903
		(5.4929)	(2.4118)	(6.1709)	(8.7408)	(7.9712)
1975-79	-3.0999	-7.6779	2.1830	-2.3039	4.7160	-3.5713
	(3.8847)	(6.7635)	(2.5318)	(6.5988)	(6.9149)	(6.6134)
1980-84	[3]	-2.8394	1.7136	-4.2891	-3.7975	-2.4265
		(6.1936)	(2.2957)	(6.1951)	(8.4179)	(6.9034)
1985-91	.1255	-7.7142	-2.0230	-5.2346	-.9776	3.3992
	(4.6907)	(7.6885)	(3.3285)	(6.4306)	(12.1252)	(8.6118)
Number of Children/Other Adults in Household (continuous)						
children 6-17	-.5922	2.6862	.7388	.3268	-5.9436*	-.6754
	(2.6776)	(2.5251)	(.8144)	(1.8499)	(2.1343)	(1.2121)
children less than 6	-.2915	-.3045	-.7988	4.5855	-3.0403	-3.2737
	(3.4814)	(4.9268)	(1.0298)	(4.2125)	(2.9161)	(2.1609)
adults	-1.7938	12.4087	-.0387	-5.0636	-8.5233	15.5243
	(7.6243)	(11.7376)	(4.1977)	(9.3734)	(6.9110)	(8.2029)
mills ratio	3.9118*	1.0468	.3714	-.3086	-.8605	.6985
	(1.6838)	(2.0977)	(.7267)	(1.7340)	(2.2786)	(1.1563)
Year of Survey (dummies, base group is 1991)						
1986	-13.1766*	-.6528	-1.5292	.5147	-1.1076	-2.6997
	(5.8606)	(4.8184)	(2.1091)	(4.4924)	(4.7432)	(3.3016)
1988	-5.6485	-2.7383	-2.3563	-5.6659	4.6199	-1.3788
	(5.6620)	(6.1575)	(2.2690)	(4.0453)	(5.0327)	(3.5267)

Table 6.3.5 (continued)

Variable	Cuba	China	Philip-pines	India	Korea	Asian Refugees
Husband's Immigration Status (dummies, base group is established immigrants, except for Cuba and Southeast Asian refugees)						
US-born	-1.1497	-5.1886	-3.7058	5.5049	-4.6703	12.2621*
	(4.6652)	(5.8338)	(1.9062)	(8.2595)	(5.3210)	(5.6304)
recent immigrant		2.9949	-4.3802	1.9885	-3.0147	
		(17.9633)	(4.4805)	(5.6012)	(8.4521)	
Wife's Age (linear splines)						
30 or less	-.7267	.4136	-.2120	.3373	-.7287	-.0129
	(.7025)	(.9485)	(.4359)	(1.2281)	(1.1910)	(.4519)
over 30	.8596	-.5558	.1500	-1.0080	.8253	-.5008
	(1.0872)	(1.2026)	(.5386)	(1.2808)	(1.4276)	(.7060)
Husband's Education (dummies, base group is college education, the less-than-7th-grade and high school groups are combined for Cuba, Philippines, India, and Korea)						
less than 7th grade		12.6242				1.6212
		(12.8560)				(4.3247)
7-12th grade	-1.7563	-8.5227	-2.4952	-5.8920	-4.8872	-5.1458
	(3.1935)	(5.5526)	(1.8806)	(5.6147)	(4.5858)	(3.0237)
Marital Status at Migration and Migration Patterns (dummies, base group is married and migrated before husband)						
single	.5809	-4.4976	-.5184	6.9870	-2.6406	2.1408
	(6.1341)	(8.4736)	(2.5191)	(5.9068)	(7.9431)	(6.6355)
after husband	3.4466	1.5795	.6577	5.1538	6.7388	1.1887
	(6.9584)	(8.2257)	(2.8034)	(5.2249)	(7.5409)	(6.7234)
with husband	-2.8442	-7.6697	-1.0623	5.3524	15.1554	4.7964
	(6.5717)	(8.4188)	(2.7270)	(6.4440)	(8.5183)	(6.9933)

Table 6.3.5 (continued)

Variable	Cuba	China	Philip-pines	India	Korea	Asian Refugees
Wife's Level of Education (dummies, base group is college education, the "less than 7th grade" and "high school" groups are combined for Cuba and India)						
less than 7th grade		-5.5166	.4273		-11.0544	-.0426
		(12.1237)	(5.1382)		(12.1734)	(4.8486)
7-12th grade	.0190	.2689	-.3736	1.0323	5.2880	7.0735*
	(3.4331)	(6.1225)	(2.1476)	(4.6649)	(5.2968)	(3.0300)
Husband's Usual Weekly Earnings (linear splines)						
less than $170	-4.2683	-1.4877	.1786	.4430[1]	6.9604*	-2.7346
	(3.5081)	(2.0532)	(1.0337)	(1.8528)	(2.6583)	(2.0776)
$170-$400	14.1008	1.4948	-4.6469		-17.4846	12.8180
	(9.2553)	(9.1617)	(4.9650)		(1.1110)	(8.5620)
over $400	-6.9556	-21.7043*	5.2584	-4.5619	13.9933	-12.7571
	(12.4174)	(1.7747)	(5.3234)	(3.5052)	(11.9177)	(9.3147)
Memo items:						
number of observations	81	140	173	98	86	116
mean of dependent variable	35.37	38.75	39.39	37.58	38.64	38.21
R square	.3183	.2319	.1383	.2567	.4074	.2513
adjusted R square	.0261	.0205	-.0293	-.0155	.1163	-.0129

* $p<.05$.

Sources: June 1986, 1988, and 1991 Current Population Survey Supplements; Bureau of Labor Statistics, Consumer Price Index.

1. Includes husbands earnings less than $400 a week. 2. Includes all 1970 cohorts. 3. Includes all 1980s cohorts.

Table 6.3.6 Hours of Work OLS Regression by Cohort and Age at Migration (Standard Errors in Parentheses)

Variable	Before 1970	1970s	1980s	Before Age 21	After Age 21
intercept	36.982	25.3476*	36.142*	25.8673*	14.3714
	(22.016)	(8.9550)	(9.3980)	(8.9086)	(13.2452)
Region of Residence (dummies, base group is west)					
northeast	.8540	.9610	1.8476	-.0974	1.4526
	(2.1937)	(1.6069)	(1.7107)	(1.7455)	(1.2871)
midwest	.5692	5.1232*	.5453	-1.5494	3.3147*
	(4.2189)	(1.7247)	(2.0698)	(2.1685)	(1.5130)
south	-3.1383	-.2210	.6115	-.4838	-.2304
	(2.1173)	(1.8059)	(1.5838)	(1.3647)	(1.3931)
MSA Status (dummies, base group is MSA suppressed)					
in central city	-2.3123	2.2768	1.2008	5.4739	1.4463
	(17.2578)	(3.2457)	(3.4805)	(3.5100)	(3.2653)
not in city	-5.4043	3.6292	-1.2356	4.6371	-1.0847
	(16.8756)	(3.2251)	(3.4001)	(3.3956)	(3.3095)
not in msa	-19.2450	8.1815	-5.4934	6.7337	-2.1632
	(18.6952)	(5.1515)	(5.4121)	(5.1898)	(5.1720)
Husband's Level of Education (dummies, base group is college education)					
less than 7th grade	-.1654	2.2172	1.4636	3.6879	1.3946
	(5.1548)	(2.5545)	(2.4610)	(2.2190)	(2.0587)
7-12th grade	.8356	-1.0495	-.7581	-2.4108	.1194
	(2.2662)	(1.3715)	(1.6990)	(1.4415)	(1.2856)
Immigration Cohort (dummies, base group is pre-1970 cohort; In the cohort regressions, each group of a specific cohort was compared to the most recent group of the same cohort)					
pre-1960	-4.0344				
	(3.1279)				
1960-64	-3.2440				
	(2.0505)				
1965-69					
1970-74		-1.2213		-5.2977*	-.5231
		(1.0558)		(1.8852)	(2.5632)
1975-79				-6.7100*	1.3209
				(2.1906)	(2.5880)
1980-84			-1.0029	-8.5757*	.9861
			(1.9917)	(2.5044)	(2.7430)
1985-91				-4.4331	.8397
				(4.5041)	(3.2427)
mills ratio	-7.1265	2.4637	3.5366	19.7687*	4.2675
	(8.0364)	(8.3961)	(6.9439)	(7.6577)	(6.3469)

Table 6.3.6 (continued)

Variable	Before 1970	1970s	1980s	Before Age 21	After Age 21
Origin Country (dummies, base group is the Philippines for Asians and Mexico for Hispanics)					
Asian	-.3218	1.2984	1.0119	5.4878	4.5795
	(2.4707)	(2.6481)	(3.6367)	(3.5517)	(2.6539)
China		-4.5101	-.6257	-2.4310	-2.3460
		(3.3249)	(2.6802)	(3.1620)	(2.1557)
Colombia		-6.1187	-3.9231	-3.8709	3.7518
		(3.4293)	(4.2477)	(3.4521)	(3.6115)
Cuba		-3.6307	-4.2509	-1.0604	-3.6359
		(4.0081)	(4.1550)	(2.3712)	(3.4115)
Dominican Republic		-.7669	.1320	.3001	3.5269
		(3.8957)	(4.1658)	(3.4120)	(3.1436)
El Salvador		-6.3411*	.7193	-.5973	.8683
		(3.0338)	(2.7660)	(3.3068)	(2.4171)
India		-2.5871	-4.5267	-7.3099	-3.5448
		(2.7858)	(2.6863)	(4.4502)	(1.9618)
Japan		-4.8149	-1.7042	-1.2688	-7.6262
		(6.7443)	(7.2711)	(5.3960)	(4.7515)
Korea		-2.2335	.4893	-9.6398*	-.6147
		(3.2329)	(3.7948)	(4.4462)	(2.6605)
SEA refugees		-2.1296	-1.6830	-.1547	-2.4957
		(2.4561)	(2.7286)	(2.8765)	(2.0418)
other Asians		-1.0861	.6712	-2.1661	1.0165
		(3.0188)	(4.0391)	(3.8008)	(2.8491)
other Hispanics		-1.6857	-4.0014	.7409	.6422
		(1.9856)	(2.5946)	(2.0662)	(2.0070)
Number of Children/Other Adults in Household (continuous)					
children 6-17	-.6302	-1.8577*	-.2438	-2.4344*	-.9814
	(.8936)	(.7241)	(.7802)	(.6460)	(.6541)
children under 6	-.2256	-1.9381	.2840	-3.6439*	-1.1849
	(1.7767)	(2.0338)	(1.4462)	(1.5236)	(1.5714)
adults	-.2724	.3023	.5338	.4206	1.0361
	(1.2645)	(.5739)	(.8751)	(.7149)	(.5907)
Marital Status at Migration and Migration Patterns (dummies, base group is married and migrated before husband)					
single	-2.5535	-.3902	-4.3043	-3.3293	-3.4649
	(5.7485)	(2.6860)	(3.4641)	(2.2901)	(2.9493)
after husband	-1.9028	.6425	-.1554	-2.1034	.3242
	(6.1366)	(2.3140)	(3.9628)	(2.6283)	(2.9464)
with husband	.6302	.3225	-2.7658	-1.4385	-1.6459
	(6.3288)	(2.6174)	(3.5370)	(2.5879)	(2.7435)

Table 6.3.6 (continued)

Variable	Before 1970	1970s	1980s	Before Age 21	After Age 21
Wife's Age (linear splines)					
30 or less	.4346	.2724	.2373	.7408*	.7066
	(.4671)	(.3129)	(.2782)	(.2984)	(.4467)
over 30	-.6984	-.2307	-.2469	-1.0273*	-.7264
	(.6252)	(.3943)	(.3662)	(.4661)	(.4949)
Husband's Immigration Status (dummies, base group is established immigrants)					
US-born	1.4529	-1.2313	-1.1264	-1.2817	-1.2841
	(2.2242)	(1.4687)	(2.0586)	(1.4125)	(1.4207)
recent immigrant				-3.9323	-3.7806
				(6.0111)	(2.7495)
Husband's Usual Weekly Earnings (linear splines)					
less than $170	-.2275	.3264	-1.3369	-1.7817	-.7684
	(1.1614)	(1.2155)	(.9841)	(1.1190)	(.8692)
$170-$400	8.2670	4.1052	6.0449*	2.1459	5.7835*
	(5.5761)	(2.8740)	(2.8613)	(2.8019)	(2.3850)
over $400	-12.6100*	-6.9741*	-6.6794	-7.6059*	-7.3079*
	(6.0331)	(3.4127)	(3.8671)	(3.5344)	(2.9700)
Wife's Level of Education (dummies, base group is college education)					
less than 7th grade	2.5515	-.9604	-.3016	-8.6058*	2.3158
	(5.2666)	(3.5579)	(2.8778)	(3.6067)	(2.3583)
7-12th grade	1.3497	1.7465	-.5489	.3569	-.1632
	(2.1330)	(1.8920)	(2.0129)	(1.4621)	(1.7043)
Year of Survey (dummies, base group is 1991)					
1986	-3.9003	1.8645	-.1520	-.0647	.7300
	(2.3667)	(1.4333)	(2.1190)	(1.6071)	(1.3333)
1988	-5.4406*	-.9327	.5730	-.2847	-.8375
	(2.5342)	(1.6326)	(1.6390)	(1.6805)	(1.2700)
Memo items:					
number of observations	255	595	602	600	852
dependent variable					
mean	38.17	37.79	38.30	37.8761	38.2235
R square	.1174	.0889	.0754	.0990	.0792
adjusted R square	.0080	.0266	.0130	.0311	.0314

* p<.05.

Sources: June 1986, 1988, and 1991 Current Population Survey Supplements; Bureau of Labor Statistics, Consumer Price Index.

Young East Asian, South Asian, South American and the Caribbean immigrant wives migrating after their husbands work about 5 to 6 hours more, than their ethnic counterparts who migrated before their husbands. Young South American wives migrating with their husbands work 6.8 hours more than South American wives migrating before their husbands. Young Caribbean wives migrating with their husbands work about 4 hours more than their ethnic counterparts migrating before their husbands. Young Chinese immigrant wives migrating with their husbands work 7.7 hours less, while similar Korean immigrant wives work 15 hours more than their respective ethnic counterparts migrating before their husbands.

Among young Asian wives, those migrating while single supply the least number of hours in market work, whereas those migrating after their husbands supply the most number of works. Among young Hispanic wives, those migrating while single supply the least number of work hours, whereas those migrating before their husbands supply the most number of work hours. Nonetheless, within either racial/ethnic group, the differences by marital status at migration and migration patterns are relatively small. Substantial variations emerge in the separate estimations by region-of-origin and country-of-origin. Young East Asian wives migrating after their husbands work 7.3 hours more than comparable wives migrating with husbands. Among young South Asian wives, those migrating before their husbands work almost 5 hours less than those migrating with their husbands. Young Central American wives migrating with their husbands supply the least number of work hours, about 6 hours less than those migrating before or after their husbands. On the contrary, young Mexican wives migrating with their husbands supply the most number of work hours, 4 hours more than those migrating while single or before their husbands.

Variations in work pattern are also found when comparing the results from separate estimations by country-of-origin. Young Korean wives migrating with their husbands supply the most number of work hours, nearly 18 hours more than those migrating while single, 8 hours more than those migrating after their husbands, and 15 hours more than those migrating before their husbands. Similarly, young Laotian, Cambodian and Vietnamese wives migrating with their husbands supply the most work hours, 2.7 hours more than those migrating while single, 3.6 hours more than those migrating after their husbands, and 4.8 hours more than those migrating before their husbands. Among both young Cuban and Chinese wives, those migrating with their husbands supply the least number of work hours, while those migrating after husbands supply the most number of work hours. The range between those supply the most and the least number of hours is 6.3 hours for Cubans and 9.2 hours for Chinese.

Marital Status at Migration, Migration Patterns and Timing of Immigration. In most parts, the regression estimations on young immigrant wives' hours of work by immigration cohort show no substantial differences between wives migrating before their husbands and any other group, particularly the pre-1980 cohorts. The 1980s cohort who immigrated while single supply 4.3 fewer hours than their cohort counterparts who migrated before their husbands. Those migrating with their husbands work 2.6 hours less than those migrating after their husbands, and 2.8 hours less than those migrating before their husbands.

Surprisingly, the young immigrant wives' age at migration do not seem to interact with their marital status at migration and migration patterns. In other words, young immigrant wives adopting any particular migration patterns supply similar hours of work, regardless of their age at migration. In either "migrated-before-age-21" or "migrated-after-age-21" group, young Asian and Hispanic wives migrating while single supply the least number of work hours, about 3 hours less than those migrating before their husbands.

In both 1988 and 1991, young wives migrating before their husbands supply the most number of work hours, whereas in 1986, they supply the least number of work hours. In both 1988 and 1991, young wives migrating while single supply the least number of work hours. In 1986, those migrating after their husbands work 5.6 hours more than those migrating before their husbands, and 3.4 hours more than those migrating with their husbands.

Selectivity Bias in the Estimation of Country-Of-Origin and Cohort Effects. Table 6.3.7 and 6.3.8 summarize the F statistics testing the country-of-origin, region-of-origin, racial/ethnic, cohort and period effects in the hours of work equation before and after including the marital status and migration patterns variables. Each pair of the "before" and "after" F statistics are pretty close to each other. However, the hours of work estimation before including the marital status and migration patterns variables fails to reject the hypothesis that no overall cohort effect exist, whereas, the regression after including the marital status and migration patterns variables show evidence of significant cohort effects.

The standard deviations of the country-of-origin and cohort effects estimated in the hours of work equation are summarized in Table 6.3.9. The statistics indicate a substantial change in the cohort effect after

Table 6.3.7 Test Statistics, Hours of Work, Controlling for Marital Status and Migration Patterns

	Hypothesis	J	N-K	R^2	R_*^2	F statistics	reject*
(1)	no country-of-origin effect	12	1409	.0488	.0366	1.51	no
(2)	no region-of-origin effect	7	1415	.0410	.0366	.93	no
(3)	no difference between Asians and Hispanics	1	1420	.0386	.0366	2.95	no
(4)	no country-of-origin effect among Asians	6	672	.0686	.0592	1.13	no
(5)	no country-of-origin effect among Hispanics	5	707	.0602	.0514	1.32	no
(6)	no immigration cohort effect	4	1409	.0488	.0417	2.63	yes
(7)	no immigration cohort effect among Asians	4	672	.0686	.0647	.70	no
(8)	no immigration cohort effect among Hispanics	4	707	.0602	.0509	1.75	no
(9)	no period effect	2	1409	.0488	.0473	1.11	no
(10)	no difference by marital status and migration patterns	3	1409	.0488	.0420	3.36	yes

* reject the null hypothesis at 5 percent level.

Source: June 1986, 1988, and 1991 Current Population Survey Supplements.

Note: J is the number of restrictions; N is the number of observations; K is the number of regressors; R^2 is the R square from the unrestricted regression; R_*^2 is the R square from the restricted regression.

Table 6.3.8 Test Statistics, Hours of Work, not Controlling for Marital Status and Migration Patterns

	Hypothesis	J	N-K	R^2	R^2_*	F statistics	reject*
(1)	no country-of-origin effect	12	1412	.0420	.0293	1.56	no
(2)	no region-of-origin effect	7	1418	.0338	.0293	.94	no
(3)	no difference between Asians and Hispanics	1	1423	.0317	.0293	3.53	no
(4)	no country-of-origin effect among Asians	6	675	.0511	.0439	.85	no
(5)	no country-of-origin effect among Hispanics	5	710	.0568	.0485	1.25	no
(6)	no immigration cohort effect	4	1412	.0420	.0364	2.06	no
(7)	no immigration cohort effect among Asians	4	675	.0511	.0487	.43	no
(8)	no immigration cohort effect among Hispanics	4	710	.0568	.0492	1.43	no
(9)	no period effect	2	1412	.0420	.0401	1.40	no

* reject the null hypothesis at 5 percent level.

Source: June 1986, 1988, and 1991 Current Population Survey Supplements.

Note: J is the number of restrictions; N is the number of observations; K is the number of regressors; R^2 is the R square from the unrestricted regression; R^2_* is the R square from the restricted regression.

Table 6.3.9 Weighted Standard Deviations of Country-of-Origin, Cohort and Period Effects in the Hours of Work Regression, With and Without Including Marital Status and Migration Patterns

Variable	Without (1)	With (2)	Difference (1)-(2)
Hypothesis 11:			
not reducing country-of-origin effect, N=13			
hours of work	1.9314	1.8751	.0563
Hypothesis 12:			
not reducing region-of-origin effect, N=8			
hours of work	.9788	.9443	.0345
Hypothesis 14:			
not reducing Asian country-of-origin effect, N=7			
hours of work	1.0151	.9316	.0835
Hypothesis 15:			
not reducing Hispanic country-of-origin effect, N=6			
hours of work	.8676	.8331	.0345
Hypothesis 16:			
not reducing cohort effect, N=5			
hours of work	1.5675	1.9228	-.3553
Hypothesis 17:			
not reducing Asian cohort effect, N=5			
hours of work	.5157	.5287	-.0130
Hypothesis 18:			
not reducing Hispanic cohort effect, N=5			
hours of work	.9110	1.3511	-.4401
Hypothesis 19:			
not reducing period effect, N=3			
hours of work	.6492	.4258	.2234

Source: June 1986, 1988, and 1991 Current Population Survey Supplements.

including the migration selectivity variables. This change of cohort effects, as measured by the standard deviation, is particularly notable among young Hispanic immigrant wives.

Immediate Relatives in the U.S. The percentage of the young immigrant wife's immediate relatives and her in-laws in the U.S. have different effects on the immigrant wives' hours of work, depending on the year surveyed. Specifically, in 1989, the presence of the immigrant wife's own kin in the U.S. decreases her hours of work by 2.2, while in 1991, the presence of her kin increases her hours of work by 3.9. The latter effect is significant at the 5 percent level. The estimation based on the combined sample show a small positive, but insignificant effect from the presence of her own kin in the U.S. The percentage of the immigrant wife's in-laws in the U.S. seems to facilitate her labor supply, however, these effects are not significant at the 5 percent level in any sample estimated.

Section Summary. When examined as a group, the young Asian and Hispanic immigrant wives exhibit few variations in their hours of work by their marital status at migration or migration patterns. However, separate regressions show differential migration selectivity effects by their countries-of-origin. In particular, young wives migrating while single tend to supply relatively few number of work hours, except for those from India and South America. Among most Asian groups, wives migrating after their husbands appear to supply more work hours than other wives of the same countries-of-origin. Among Southeast Asian refugee wives, those migrating with their husbands appear to supply the most work hours. In contrast, Cuban wives migrating with their husbands appear to supply the least hours of work of all Cuban wives. Hypothesis testing shows that little country-of-origin effect was affected by controlling for migration selectivity.

Relatively few variations in the migration selectivity effects were found across immigration cohorts. Young wives migrating while single supply the least number of work hours, regardless when or at what ages they immigrated. Hypothesis testing shows that the uniform effects of migration selectivity variables across cohorts may explain certain cohort differences in the number of work hours, particularly among Hispanics.

The estimated kin effects in the hours of work regression are less conclusive than those obtained from either the labor force participation or the earnings regression. Overall, the more immediate relatives and in-laws the immigrant wife has in the U.S., the more work hours she is likely to supply.

6.3.2 Other Control Variables and Hours of Work

This section summarizes and discusses the effects of variables representing the immigrant wives' market wage offers and reservation wages in the hours of work regression. These variables include region of residence, whether living in Metropolitan Statistical Area (MSA), country-of-origin, timing of immigration, husband's education, wife's education, the number of children in the household, the number of other adults in the household, husband's immigration status, and husband's usual weekly earnings. The mills ratio derived from the first-stage labor force participation regression was included in the regression to correct for the potential sample selection bias due to the endogenous work decision.

Husbands' Characteristics. The husbands' weekly earnings appear to consistently significantly contribute to the variations in the young immigrant wives' hours of work. As demonstrated in Table 6.3.2, an immigrant wife with husband's earning less than $170 weekly, supplies 1 hour less in the market work as her husband's earnings increases one percentage. An immigrant wife with husband's earning between $170 to $400 weekly, supplies 5 hours more in the market work as her husband's earnings increases one percentage. And finally, an immigrant wife with husband's earning over $400 weekly, supplies 7 hours less in the market work as her husband's earnings increases one percentage.

The hypothesis that immigrant wives with recent immigrant husbands may work more to supplement their family income is basically rejected in the combined sample. On the contrary, the results indicate that young immigrant wives with husbands immigrated in the last two years will supply significantly 5.6 fewer hours than those wives married to established immigrant husbands. Separate estimations for Asians and Hispanics show that marrying to a recent immigrant husbands has a much greater dampening effect on hours of work for young Hispanic immigrant wives than their Asian counterparts.

Number of Children in Household. The number of children under 6 in household seem to depress the young immigrant wives' hours of work. This young children effect, although consistently negative, turns out to be insignificant in most estimations except for the ones based on Southeast Asian immigrant wives, and wives immigrated before age 21. Similarly, the number of children aged 6-17 in the household have significantly negative effects in the estimations based on the merged sample as well as the Hispanic sample. Among young Hispanic immigrant wives, one additional child aged 6 to 17 in the household significantly reduces 2 hours of the wives' hours of work. The hours of work for the 1970s cohort and immigrant wives migrating before age 21 also seem to be constrained by the presence of children aged 6-17.

Country of Origin. In the estimation using the combined sample, young Asian immigrant wives work about 4 hours per week more than their Hispanic counterparts, although the difference is not significant at the 5 percent level. Young Asian Indian immigrant wives work significantly fewer hours than the Filipinos, however the differences disappear in the estimation using only the Asian sample. The hypothesis testing results summarized in Table 6.3.7 show no significant sign of any country-of-origin, region-of-origin, or racial/ethnic differences among young immigrant wives' in their supply of work hours.

Immigration Cohort. The estimation based on the combined sample shows that, in general, both the 1970s and 1980s cohorts work significantly fewer hours than the "prior to 1970 cohort" do. However, separate estimates show that the significant differences disappear for Asians, while the early 1970s cohort still work significantly fewer hours than the "prior to 1970" cohort for Hispanics. The hypothesis testing shows an overall significant cohort effect at the 5 percent level. However, tests carried out separately on young Asian and Hispanic immigrant wives reveal no significant cohort effects on their hours of work among either Asians or Hispanics. The hypothesis of no differences in immigrant wives' hours of work by the year they were interviewed can not be rejected at the 5 percent level.

The estimation of the hours of work equation consistently has a poor fit, with an average adjusted R squares around 0.02. This may be due to the fact that the weekly hours of work are difficult to model and that they may be highly correlated with job-specific attributes which are not captured in the current model. Consistent with the prediction based on the empirical model, the coefficient estimates for the mills ratio are mostly positive, although not many of them are significantly different from zero at the 5 percent level.

The Tobit strategy is not used here since the major interests of this study is to obtain separate parameter estimates for labor force participation and hours of work. As mentioned in Chapter 4, the Tobit model restricts the parameters in both hours of work and labor force participation decisions to be the same, and that labor supply is a continuous decision starting from zero hours of work. However, the descriptive statistics discussed in Section 5.4 suggest separate decisions for hours of work and labor force participation.

Chapter Summary and Discussion. This chapter presents and discusses the results from the labor force participation, earnings and hours of work regressions. Overall, most of the regression estimates have expected signs as those predicted by the theory or reported from previous research. The effects of the selectivity factors, i.e., the immigrant wives' marital status at migration and migration patterns exert significant influences on their likelihood of participating in the labor force. As predicted from theory, those migrating before their husbands are most likely to be in the labor force. Strong evidence also suggest that being single at migration is associated with fewer hours of work. Nonetheless, given in the labor force, either those migrating while single or those before their husbands do not have an earnings advantage. In fact, little sign of selectivity effect is found in the earnings regression.

The young immigrant wives' marital status at migration and migration patterns appear to influence the immigrant wives' labor market performance differently, depending on which country or region they immigrated from. Among Asian wives, those migrating with their husbands are the least likely to be in the labor force. Once they work, they supply relatively few hours of work and make the highest level of earnings. Those migrating after their husbands earn the least, and work the most hours. Among Hispanic wives, those migrating before their husbands are the most likely to participate in the labor force, supply the most work hours. Despite of their high work propensity and attachment, they appear to have an earnings disadvantage.

Among refugee wives, those migrating with their husbands demonstrate the greatest propensity of participating in the labor force and have the highest earning potentials. Once in the labor force, they work the most hours among Southeast Asians, while the least work hours among Cubans. Among Asian Indian working wives, those migrating while single gain the highest level of earnings and supply the most work hours. Among Korean wives, those migrating with their husbands are the least likely to be in the labor force, have the highest earning potentials, and work the most hours. Among Mexican wives, those migrating before their husbands are the most likely to be in the labor force, but once they work, they fare the worst in the labor market with the lowest earnings.

Among Chinese wives, those migrating with their husbands are the least likely to be in the labor force and, once employed, they supply the least hours of work. Among Filipino wives, those migrating with their husbands are the most likely to be in the labor force. Once they work, they make the highest earnings and supply the least hours of work. Among

Central American wives, those migrating before their husbands are the most likely to be in the labor force, gain the highest earning potentials and supply the most hours of work. Among South American wives, those migrating with their husbands are the least likely to be in the labor force and once they work, they gain the lowest level of earnings. Among East Asian wives, those migrating with their husbands are the least likely to be in the labor force and have the highest earning potentials, while those migrating after their husbands are the most likely to be in the labor force and have the lowest earning potentials.

The immigrant wives' migration selectivity appear to influence their labor market performance in similar ways across the three major immigration cohorts. Those migrating before their husbands are the most likely to be in the labor force regardless when they immigrated. Across all three major cohorts, migration selectivity fail to substantially differentiate the immigrant wives' earnings or hours of work, except that those migrating in the 1980s and before their husbands fare far worst-off than all other women of the same cohort.

Gurak and colleague (1992) described the function of kin present in the receiving country as selective and adaptive. The results presented in this section show evidence supportive of both functions. The presence of immigrant wives' immediate relatives in the U.S. seems to encourage their labor force participation, while that of their in-laws hinder their labor force participation. Once employed, the immigrant wives' relatives raise their earnings, while in-laws dampen their earnings. Both sides of relatives tend to facilitate many hours of work for the immigrant wives.

Following the selective argument, immigrant wives sponsoring or sponsored by their own immediate relatives are more likely to be in the labor force than wives sponsoring or sponsored by their in-laws, and once they work, they tend to earn more in the market, and work fewer hours. In other words, immigrant wives sponsoring or sponsored by their own immediate relatives are more competitive in the U.S. labor market than those sponsoring or sponsored by their in-laws. This may imply that sponsoring or sponsored by in-laws resembles the situations of tied-migrants, where the motivation for migration is mainly familial.

Based on an adaptive explanation, the presence of the immigrant wives' own relatives facilitates their participation in the paid work, increases their market wage offers through accumulated work experiences and hours of work once they are employed. On the contrary, the presence of their in-laws may deter the immigrant wives' labor force participation and reduce their earnings capacities and hours of work. The disruption function of the in-laws may be due to increased family responsibilities, or preservation of traditional gender roles and family values.

In summary, the overall selectivity effects are in line with those predicted from the theory. Young wives migrating independently, i.e., migrating before their husbands or while single, are more likely to participate in the labor force than wives migrating with or after their husbands. Substantial variations in the selectivity effects in the immigrant wives' labor force participation, earnings, and hours of work emerge when separately examined by country-of-origin. In contrast, separate regressions by immigration cohort show rather constant patterns of selectivity effects. By controlling for migration selectivity, very little country-of-origin effect is changes, while considerable cohort effect is reduced, particularly for Hispanic wives. As one of the measures for migration selectivity, the presence of both sides of the immigrant wives' kin in the U.S. exert differential effects on their labor force participation and earnings.

The next chapter summarizes and concludes the findings presented in this chapter, and draw policy implications. It also addresses the strengths and weakness of this study to provide guidelines for future research.

NOTES

1. As marital history information is not available through the 1989 sample, it was excluded from this pooled sample.

7

Summary and Conclusion

This chapter summarizes the current research findings, provides policy implications and discusses the limitations of the study.

7.1 SUMMARY OF THE RESULTS

Selectivity Effects. This book evaluates the role of the U.S. immigration policy in drawing different types of young Asian and Hispanic immigrant wives to the U.S. In particular, it argues that immigrant wives self-select themselves to immigrate to the U.S. by choosing whether to immigrate while single or married and whether to immigrate independently or to follow their families. It hypothesizes that these self-selection factors represent the immigrant wives' unobserved labor market "qualities", and thus are strongly correlated with their abilities in adapting to the U.S. labor market. As those migrating while single or before their husbands are most likely to be independent immigrants, they are hypothesized to have stronger work involvement and higher earnings in the U.S.

The first research question asks whether there are significant selectivity effects among young immigrant wives, and if so, how do they affect the immigrant wives' labor market adaptation? The empirical data provide evidence on a few general patterns regarding the immigrant wives' labor supply and earnings by their marital status and migration patterns. As expected, immigrant wives migrating before their husbands appear to be the most attached to the labor market. They are most likely to participate in the U.S. labor force compared to immigrant wives adopting other migration patterns, and once they are in the labor force, they supply the most hours of work. However, given their strong involvement in market work, they gain the lowest earnings.

Young immigrant wives migrating while single are also more likely to participate in the labor force than those wives migrating with or after their husbands. While supplying the least hours of work, they do earn more than wives migrating after or before their husbands. Surprisingly, of all the young Asian and Hispanic immigrant wives, those migrating with their husbands appear to have the highest wages. Wives migrating after their husbands are the least likely to participate in the U.S. labor force, and once they are employed, they do not earn as much as the other wives.

To conclude, migration selectivity seems to exert significant effects on the immigrant wives' labor supply, but not on their earnings. Those hypothesized "independent" immigrant women tend to have higher labor force participation propensity than others. Those hypothesized "tied" immigrant women have mixed performance in the labor market, depending on whether they accompany their husbands to the U.S. or not. Those migrating following their husbands do have a low likelihood of participating in the labor force and earn relatively low wages. In contrast, those migrating with their husbands are relatively well-off in the labor market.

Selectivity Effects by Country-Of-Origin. The overall estimation masks substantial heterogeneity of female migration selectivity by immigrants' country-of-origin and immigration cohort. As both the timing and nature of the migration of women are greatly influenced by social and cultural practices of their countries-of-origin, differential selectivity effects along these two dimensions are likely to be significant. Thus, the second research question of this study asks do selectivity effects vary by the immigrant wives' countries-of-origin or timing of immigration?

The regression analyses suggest substantial interaction effects between the immigrant wives' countries-of-origin and their marital status at migration and migration patterns. In other words, immigrant wives from different countries of origin tend to migrate during different stages of the life-cycle and adopt different migration patterns. Moreover, immigrant wives adopting the same migration patterns from different origin countries tend to have different labor market performance. In particular, young wives migrating with their husbands have the highest earning among Koreans, Filipinos, Southeast Asian refugees and Cubans. They are also most likely to participate in the labor force among Filipinos, Southeast Asian refugees and Cubans, but least likely to do so among Koreans, Chinese, and wives from South America. Given in the labor force, they supply the most hours of work among Southeast Asian refugees and

Koreans, while they supply the least hours of work among Cubans, Chinese and Filipinos.

As revealed in the overall picture, those migrating after their husbands appear to earn relatively less compared to other young immigrant wives for most country-of-origin groups. Their earnings disadvantage is most prevalent among Asians, and in particular, among wives from East Asia. Young wives migrating before their husbands tend to have a high labor force participation propensity, particularly among Mexican and Central American wives. They have the lowest earning in the labor market among Mexican wives, while they have the highest earning among Central American wives. Migrating while single exerts a mixed effect in the labor force participation, earnings and hours of work regressions, depending on the immigrant wives' countries of origin. However, most of them do not differ substantially from wives migrating as married, except for Asian Indian wives. In fact, among young working Asian Indian wives, those migrating while single make the highest earnings and supply the most hours of work.

The results imply that single women from one country-of-origin group are likely to be fundamentally different from their counterparts from other groups because they are selected under different processes. To illustrate, of those from countries discouraging mobility of unattached women, only highly selected single women could "afford" to emigrate, and they are very likely to be more active in the labor market than otherwise selected single women immigrants. Single women who had to travel a shorter distance to immigrate to the U.S. are likely to be less selective than single women who immigrated from remote countries. Similarly, wives that migrate following their husbands and came from a nearby country-of-origin are likely to be less selective than the comparable wives from a remote country. Refugee wives migrating with their husbands are likely to be less selective than non-refugee wives migrating with their husbands, since forced migration tends to result in the migration of the whole family. This suggests the importance for further study on the macro-level factors contributing to the differential selectivity in understanding the observed country-of-origin differences in the immigrant wives' labor supply and earnings.

Selectivity Effects by Immigration Cohort. The empirical data suggest that immigrant wives migrating to the U.S. in recent years are more likely to be married and to migrate after their husbands than wives migrating prior to 1970. It also shows that the majority of the early-cohort young wives migrated while single. The later finding coincides with the fact that those young wives mostly migrated as minor children in light of their current ages and their timing of immigration.

Given that different cohorts of young immigrant wives tend to utilize different migration patterns, the regression estimates show relatively few variations in the selectivity effects among immigration cohorts. Those migrating before their husbands are most likely to be in the labor force regardless of when they immigrated. Across all three major cohorts, migration selectivity fail to substantially differentiate either the immigrant wives' earnings or their hours of work, except that those migrating in the 1980s and before their husbands fare far worse than other women of the same cohort.

Since the empirical data is confined to married women, immigrant women of the most recent cohorts who are not married at the time of survey are missed. They are most likely to be never married, and the majority of them will eventually get married in the future. The exclusion of this group of potential immigrant wives may cause certain bias for the recent-cohort immigrant wives who migrated while single since this group may be the most committed to the labor force and make the highest earnings than all other immigrant wives.

Country-Of-Origin and Cohort Effects. Substantial differences in the immigrant wives' labor supply and earnings across their countries of origin are explained by their differential demographic composition. However, after controlling for these compositional differences, Cuban immigrant wives are still more likely to be in the labor force and obtain higher hourly earnings than their Mexican counterparts. Filipino immigrant wives are more likely to be in the labor force than any other Asian immigrant wives. However, after controlling for the compositional differences, the Filipino wives and the Southeast Asian refugees have similar work patterns. Furthermore, after controlling for the compositional differences, the Filipino wives do not seem to earn different amounts or supply different work hours from their other Asian counterparts.

The results also suggest that immigrant wives migrating in different historical times have distinct labor supply behavior and earnings. The 1970s cohort appear to be most better-off in the U.S. labor market, as compared to the pre-1970 and the 1980s cohort. The cohort effect is very apparent for the Asian sample, but not the Hispanic sample.

The substantial differences between the pre-1970, 1970s and 1980s cohorts in their labor market performances has not been extensively examined in the existing literature due to the relative newness of the 1990 census. Previous studies suggest declining immigrant "qualities" based on the analyses of white male immigrants, by comparing 1940, 1960 and the 1970 cohorts. As the family reunification policy was mainly taken advantage of by Asian immigrants, research on Asian immigrants has noted highly selective immigration flows of the 1970s cohort, reflected in their occupational prestige and educational attainments. The findings are also consistent with Lobo's suggestion (1992) that the Hispanic 1970s cohort is not very different from the earlier cohort since the restrictions on western hemisphere immigration were not imposed until the 1970s.

Selectivity Effects and the Estimation of Country-Of-Origin and Cohort Effects. In accordance with previous research, this study finds substantial country-of-origin and cohort effects in the immigrant wives' labor force participation, hourly earnings and hours of work estimations. As migration selectivity is evident from the above discussion, and that migration selectivity varies by immigrants' country-of-origin and timing of immigration, previous estimates of both country-of-origin and cohort effects may be in fact confounded with the omitted migration selectivity effects. This raises the third research question for the current study: are the estimates of country-of-origin and cohort effects biased if not controlling for migration selectivity?

The results based on the F statistics and the weighted standard deviations conclude that the estimate of country-of-origin effect is hardly affected by controlling for the migration selectivity variables. In contrast, considerable cohort differences in the immigrant wives' labor force participation and hours of work are explained by the differences in the marital status and migration patterns between different cohorts. These findings suggest stronger evidence for the "cohort qualities" hypothesis rather than the "adaptation" hypothesis. This may be due to the fact that married women's labor supply and earnings are highly conditioned by their gender role and reproductive activities, so that the number of years in the U.S. fail to accurately reflect their U.S. market experiences.

7.2 POLICY IMPLICATIONS

The empirical results of this study have important implications on immigration policy. Over time, decisions on changes in the U.S. immigration legislation had been made largely uninformed by empirical research (Fuchs 1992). In particular, decisions on how many immigrants should be admitted annually, how should the immigration quota be allocated among sending countries, and how should the available quota be allocated to potential immigrants of a given country-of-origin are mainly compromised by political considerations. The results of the current study show that the U.S. immigration policy can play an active role in selecting well-adapting immigrant wives by giving priority to single women, or wives migrating before or with their husbands to the U.S. Policy encouraging wives to migrate to join their husbands tend to result in less-skilled immigrant wives.

If the goal of the immigration policy is to draw competent immigrant women, the results show that family reunification is likely to attract less-skilled wives migrating to join their husbands. A modification in the policy to facilitate the migration of single women and/or the migration of both husband and wife at the same time while discouraging those migrating following their husbands is likely to bring in higher-earning immigrant women in the U.S. Furthermore, evidence suggests that such a change in policy is likely to raise the labor force participation of the recent cohorts of immigrant wives.

One of the arguments made in favor of family reunification implies that the presence of family members in the U.S. may expand the resources available to immigrant families and hence facilitate the adaptation process. If the goal of the immigration policy is to draw immigrant wives who are able to mobilize their family resources and achieve self-sufficiency in the U.S. as quickly as possible, the results suggest that the economic activities of wives migrating for the purpose of family reunification tend to be restricted by their gender roles. Specifically, wives that migrate to follow their husbands are either constrained by family responsibility or their low wage prospects, that they are less likely to contribute to their family incomes in the U.S. While very competitive in the labor market, those migrating with their husbands are also constrained by family responsibilities and hence exhibit relatively low tendency of labor force participation.

This book examines the selectivity effects from the immigrant wives' perspectives rather than the immigrant families. Nonetheless, the results imply a complex picture of the functions of the immigrant families and potential interactions between the economic role of the immigrant wives and their modes of entry. In order to fully evaluate the policy impacts of family reunification, further study is needed to evaluate the indirect selectivity effects on immigrant men as a result of the direct selectivity on immigrant women.

Since the selectivity effects vary by the immigrant wives' countries-of-origin, a quota system aimed at creating fairness among countries-of-origin may favor different kinds of immigrant wives across origin countries. If the goal of the immigration policy is to reduce the difference among immigrant/minority women in their economic performance in the U.S., the results may imply that special considerations to the country-specific factors should be taken into account to fulfill such a goal, and a more complicated quota system that reflects country-of-origin differences may be desirable. The diversity program recently adopted in 1990 intends to give priority to those who are adversely affected by the 1965 amendments. However, the decision on which country should benefit from the legislation and by how much has been contaminated by political interest groups.

The current study enhances the knowledge on the less-studied gender-specific migration process and the consequence of female migration. It reveals that immigrant wives migrating for the purpose of joining husbands are most constrained by the joint migration decision. This finding has implications on the status of immigrant/minority women per se and relative to that of men. As social and cultural norms of the countries-of-origin apparently affect the migration decision of the immigrant wives, they also cause differential selectivity effects on the immigrant wives.

7.3 LIMITATIONS OF THE STUDY

This book contributes to the immigration literature by identifying gender-specific migration selectivity measures. Furthermore, to overcome the lack of a combination of both immigration and adaptation data, it puts together marital history, timing of migration and labor force participation information from the Current Population Survey to examine the hypothesized selectivity effects.

Nonetheless, it has four major limitations. The first limitation stems from the sample selection criteria. Due to data availability, only those Asian and Hispanic immigrant wives aged 18 to 44 are included in the study. For those immigrated in early years, they had to have immigrated as children (and while single) in order to get into the sample. Thus, the age limitation not only restricts the reference population to those young immigrant wives only, but also confounds the estimate of marital status effect for those that immigrated prior to 1970. In particular, the migrating-while-single coefficient estimate captures both the marital status and the migrating-as-minor effects.

Second, the findings reveal substantial variations in the immigrant wives' selectivity effect across countries of origin. However, as the analysis was constrained by the size of the sample in its ability to control for these two dimensions, the interaction effects were measured with high variability. Future research based on a larger sample would enable more powerful estimates of the interaction effects.

Third, the measure of marital status at migration and migration patterns may give rise to potential bias in the estimation of selectivity effects. The marital history information only contains the immigrant wives' age at first marriage. For immigrant wives married more than once, this measure may not capture her real marital status at migration. Furthermore, the timing of immigration information is reported in five year periods for those who immigrated prior to 1980, and those who immigrated prior to 1960 are censored at 1960. Those married and migrating in the same period are counted as migrating married. This practice may have created differential biases, depending on when the immigrant wives immigrated, and how many year apart their marriage and immigration were.

Fourth, this book evaluates the immigrant wives' labor market adaptation by their labor force participation, hourly earnings and hours of work in the survey reference week. These cross-sectional measures assume away cohort variations in the immigrant wives' abilities to adapt to the U.S. labor market. The estimated cohort effects in this study in fact contain both cohort and adaptation effects. A repeated cross-sectional data set with equal intervals between the year-of-immigration codes, a data set with retrospective labor force information at several points in time after arrival, or a longitudinal data set will allow for separate estimations of both effects.

References

Abadan-Unat, N. 1984. "International labour migration and its effect upon women's occupational and family roles: a Turkish view." in *Women on the Move: Contemporary Changes in Family and Society* UNESCO: Paris.

Arizpe, L. 1984. "Agrarian change and the dynamics of women's rural out-migration in Latin America." in *Women on the Move: Contemporary Changes in Family and Society* UNESCO: Paris.

Arnold, F., B.V. Carino, J.T. Fawcett, & I.H. Park. 1989. "Estimating the immigration multiplier: an analysis of recent Korean and Filipino immigration to the United States." *International Migration Review,* 23(4):813-838.

Bach, R.L. & R. Carroll-Seguin. 1986. "Labor force participation, household composition and sponsorship among southeast Asian refugees." *International Migration Review,* 20(2):381-405.

Bach, R.L. & J.B. Bach. 1980. "Employment patterns of southeast Asian refugees," *Monthly Labor Review,* September:31-38.

Bean, F. & M. Tienda. 1987. *The Hispanic Population of the United States.* New York: Russell Sage.

Bean, F., G.C. Swicegood, & A.G. King, 1985. "Role incompatibility and the relationship between fertility and labor supply among Hispanic women," in G.J. Borjas and M. Tienda, eds. *Hispanics in the US Economy* Institute for Research on Poverty Monograph Series, Academic Press Inc. Orlando, Florida.

Becker, G.S. 1964. *Human Capital* New York: National Nureau of Economic Research; distributed by Columbia University Press.

------. 1965. "A theory of the allocation of time." *Economic Journal,* 75: 493-517.

------. 1981. *A Treatise on the Family* Harvard University Press.

Berg-Eldering, V.L. 1984. Women and migration: trends and priorities. Paper presented at at the Colloquy on Women and Migration, 19-21 November, Council of Europe, Strasboug.

Bilsborrow, R.E. & H. Zlotnik. 1992. "Preliminary report of the United

Nations expert group meeting on the feminization of internal migration." *International Migration Review* 26(1): 138-161

Borjas, G.J. 1980. "The relationship between wages and weekly hours of work: the role of division bias." *Journal of Human Resources,* 15:409-23.

------. 1985a. "The impact of assimilation on the earnings of immigrants: a reexamination of the evidence," Discussion Paper no. 769-84, Institute for Research on Poverty, U of Wisconsin.

------. 1985b. "Assimilation, changes in cohort qualities, and the earnings of immigrants." *Journal of Labor Economics,* 3(4):463-489.

------. 1987. "Self-selection and the earnings of immigrants." *American Economic Review* 77(4):531-553.

------. 1989. "Immigrant and emigrant earnings: a longitudinal study." *Economic Inquiry,* 27:21-37.

------. 1990. *Friends or Strangers: the Impact of Immigrants on the U.S. Economy.* New York: Basic Books.

------. 1991a. "Immigration and self-selection" in J. M. Abowd and R. B. Freeman, eds. *Immigration, Trade, and the Labor Market* Chicago: U of Chicago press.

------. 1991b. Immigrants in the U.S. labor market: 1940-80. AER papers and proceedings.

------. 1991c. Immigration policy, national origin, and immigrant skills: a comparison of Canada and the United States. NEBR working paper no. 3691.

------. & S.G. Bronars, 1990. *Immigration and the Family.* Working Paper No. 3509, National Bureau of Economic Research, INC. Cambridge, Massachusetts.

Boserup, E. 1970. *Women's Role in Economic Development* New York: St. Martin's Press.

Boyd, M. 1982. Sex and generational achivement: Canada. Paper to the International Sociological Association World Conference, Mexico City.

------. 1986. "Immigrant women in Canada." in *International Migration: The Female Experience* (eds.) R. J. Simon and C. B. Brettell, New Jersey: Rowman & Allanheld.

------. 1989. "Family and personal networks in international migration: recent developments and new agendas." *International Migration Review* 23(3): 638-670.

------. 1990. "Migration regulations and sex selective outcomes in settlement and European countries" Paper presented at the United

Nations Expert Group Meeting on International Migration Policies and the Status of Female Migrants, San Miniato, Italy.

Bogue, D.J. & M.J. Hagood. 1953. *Subregional Migration in the United States: 1930-40.* Vol II. Scipps Foundation, Oxford, Ohio.

------. 1961. "Techniques and hypotheses for the study of differential migration: some notes from an experiment with U.S. data." paper presented at the International Population Conference, New York.

Briggs, V.M.Jr. 1992. *Mass Immigration and the National Interest* M.E. Sharpe Inc. New York.

Briody, E.K. 1987. "Patterns of household immigration into south Texas." *International Migration Review* 21(1): 27-47.

Browning, H.L. & N. Rodriguez, 1985. "The migration of Mexican indocumentados as a settlement process: implications for work." in G.J. Borjas, & M. Tienda, eds. *Hispanics in the US Economy* Orlando: Academic Press.

Burawoy, M. 1976. "The function and reproduction of migrant labor: comparative materials from southern Africa and the United States," *American Journal of Sociology* 81: 1050-1087.

Caces, F., F. Arnold, J.T. Fawcett, & R.W. Gardner. 1985. "Shadow households and competing auspices: migration behavior in the Philippines." *Journal of Development Economics* 17: 5-25.

Caudill, S.B. & J.D. Jackson. 1989. "Measuring marginal effects in limited dependent variable models." *The Statistician* 38:203-206.

Chang, T.H.P. 1981. "A review of micro migration research in the third world context," in G.F. De Jong and R.W. Gardner, eds. *Migration Decision Making: Multidisciplinary Approaches to Microlevel Studies in Developed and Developing Countries* New York: Pergamon Press.

Chiswick, B.R. 1978. "The effect of Americanization on the earnings of foreign-born men." *Journal of Political Economy,* 86(5):897-921.

------. 1979. "The economic progress of immigrants: some apparently universal patterns." In W. Fellner ed. *Contemporary Economic Problems.* Washington, D.C.: American Enterprise Institute.

------. 1980a "Immigrant earnings patterns by sex, race, and ethnic groups," *Monthly Labor Review* October:22-25.

------. 1980b. An analysis of the economic progress and impact of immigrants. Final report to the U.S. Department of Labor, Employment and Training Administration. Chicago Circle: Department of Economics, University of Illinois. Mimeographed.

------. 1986. "Human capital and the labor market adjustment if immigrants: testing alternative hypotheses." *Research in Human Capital and Development: Migration, Human Capital and Development* 4:1-26.

Cooney, R.S. & V. Ortiz. 1983. "Nativity, national origin, and Hispanic female participation in the labor force." *Social Science Quarterly* 60:510-523.

Connell, J., B. Dasgupta, B. Laishley, & M. Lipton. 1976. *Migration from Rural Areas: The Eveidence from Village Studies* Delhi: Oxford University Press.

DaVanzo, J. 1981. "Microeconomic approaches to studying migration decisions." in G.F. De Jong & R.W. Gardner, eds. *Migration Decision Making: Multidisciplinary Approaches to Microlevel Studies in Developed and Developing Countries* New York: Pergamon Press.

De Jong, G.F. & R.W. Gardner, 1981. "Introduction and overview." in G.F. De Jong & R.W. Gardner, eds. *Migration Decision Making: Multidisciplinary Approaches to Microlevel Studies in Developed and Developing Countries* New York: Pergamon Press.

De Jong, G.F. & J.T. Fawcett. 1981. "Motivations for migration." in G.F. De Jong & R.W. Gardner, eds. *Migration Decision Making: Multidisciplinary Approaches to Microlevel Studies in Developed and Developing Countries* New York: Pergamon Press.

DeJong G.F., B.D. Root, & R.G. Abad, 1986. "Family reunification and Philippine migration to the United States: The immigrants' perspective." *International Migration Review* 20(3):598-611.

Despradel, L. 1984. "Internal migration of rural women in the Caribbean and its effects on their status." in *Women on the Move: Contemporary Changes in Family and Society* UNESCO: Paris.

Dinerman, I.R. 1978. "Patterns of adaptation among housholds of U.S.-bound migrants from Michoacan, Mexico." *International Migration Review* 12(4):485-501.

Donato, K.M. & A. Tyree. 1986. "Family reunification, health professionals, and the sex composition of immigrants to the United States." *Sociology and Social Research* 70(3): 226-230.

------. 1993. "Current trends and patterns of female migration: evidence from Mexico." *International Migration Review* 27(4):748-771.

Donovan, R.J. & J.L. Norwood. 1982. Technical description of the quarterly data on weekly earnings from the Current Population Survey." Bureau of Labor Statistics bulletin no. 2113.

Ducoff, L.J. 1961. "The migrant population of a metropolitan area in a developing country: a preliminary report on a case study of San Salvador." paper presented at the International Population Conference, New York.

Dumon, W.A. 1989. "Family and migration." *International Migration* 27(2): 251-270.

Eviota, E.U. & P.C. Smith. 1984. "The migration of women in the Philippines." in J.T. Fawcett, S.E. Khoo, & P.C. Smith, eds. *Women in the Cities of Asia: Migration and Urban Adaptation* Colorado, Boulder: Westview.

Fawcett, J.T., S.E. Khoo, & P.C. Smith. 1984. "Urbanization, migration, and the status of women." in J.T. Fawcett, S.E. Khoo, & P.C. Smith, eds. *Women in the Cities of Asia: Migration and Urban Adaptation* Colorado, Boulder: Westview.

Findley, S.E. 1987. "An interactive contextual model of migration in Ilocas Norte, the Philippines." *Demography* 24(2): 163-190.

Fuchs, L.H. 1992. "Migration research and immigration policy." *International Migration Review* 26(4):1069-1076.

Gallaway, L.E. "Age and labor mobility patterns." *Southern Economic Journal* 36(2): 171-180.

Garcia, J.R. 1980. *Operation Wetback: The Mass Deportation of Mexican Undocumented Workers in 1954.* Westport, Conn.: Greenwood Press.

Gardner, R.W. 1981 "Macrolevel Influences on the Migration Decision Process." G.F. De Jong and R.W. Gardner, eds. *Migration Decision Making: Multidisciplinary Approaches to Microlevel Studies in Developed and Developing Countries* New York: Pergamon Press.

Gaude, J. 1976. *Causes and Repercussions of Rural Migration in Developing Countries: A Critical Analysis* Geneva: International Labor Organization, Rural Employment Policy Research Program.

General Accounting Office, 1988. "Immigration: the future flow of legal immigration to the United States." *GAO/PEMD-88-7* Washington, DC: General Printing Office, January.

Goering, J.M. 1987. "Legal immigration to the United States: a demographic analysis of fifth preference visa admissions." *Staff Report* Subcommittee on Immigration and Refugee Affairs, U.S.

Senate, Washington, DC: GAO.

------. 1989. "The 'explosiveness' of chain migration: research and policy issues." *International Migration Review* 23(4):797-812.

Gold, S.J. 1992. *Refugee Communities.* Newbury, California: Sage Publications.

Goodman, J.L. 1981 "Information, uncertainty, and the microeconomic model of migration decision making," in G.F. De Jong & R.W. Gardner, *Migration Decision Making: Multidisciplinary Approaches to Microlevel Studies in Developed and Developing Countries* New York: Pergamon Press.

Gordon, L.W. 1987. The missing children: mortality and fertility of southeast Asian refugees in the U.S. Paper presented at the annual meeting of the Population Association of America, Chicago, May 2.

Gordon, M. 1981. "Caribbean migration: a perspective on women." in D.M. Mortimer & R.S. Bryce-Laporte eds. *Female Immigrants to the United States: Caribbean, Latin American, and African Experiences* , Occational papers No. 2, Research Institute on Immigration and Ethnic Studies, Smithsonian Institution, Washington, D.C.

Grasmuck, S. & P.R. Pessar, 1991. *Between Two Islands: Dominican International Migration* University of California Press, Berkeley and LA, California.

Greenwood, M.J. 1970. "Lagged response in the decision to migrate." *Journal of regional Science* 10(3):375-384.

------. 1972. "Lagged response in the decision to migrate: a reply." *Journal of regional Science* 12(2):311-324.

Gronau, R. 1980. "Home production-a forgotten industry." *Review of Economics and Statistics* 62(3):408-416.

Gujarati, D.N. 1988. *Basic Econometrics* 2nd edition, McGraw-Hill Book Company, New York.

Gurak, D.T. & M.M. Kritz, 1984. "Kinship networks and the settlement process: Dominican and Colombian immigrants in New York city." *Hispanic Research Center Bulletin* (Fordham University) 7(3-4):7-11.

------. 1987. "Family formation and marital selectivity among Colombian and Dominican immigrants in New York city." *International Migration Review* 21(2):275-298.

------., L. Falcon, & M.G. Powers. 1987. Family formation and SES selectivity in the migration of women from Puerto Rico to the mainland. Paper presented at the annual meetings of the American Sociological Association, Chicago, August 20.

------. & G. Gilbertson, 1989. Household transitions in the migrations of Dominicans and Colombians to New York. Working paper series 1.12, October, Cornell University, Population and Development Program, Ithaca.

------. & F. Caces. 1992. "Migration networks and the shaping of migration systems." in M.M. Kritz, L.L. Lim, & H. Zlotnik, eds. *International Migration Systems: A Global Approach* New York: Oxford University Press.

Hanoch, G. 1980. "Hours and weeks in the theory of labor supply." in J.P. Smith. ed. *Female labor supply: theory and estimation.* Princeton University Press, Princeton, New Jersey.

Harbison, S.F. 1981. "Family structure and family strategy in migration decision making." in G.F. De Jong & R.W. Gardner eds. *Migration Decision Making: Multidisciplinary Approaches to Microlevel Studies in Developed and Developing Countries* New York: Pergamon Press.

Heckman, J.J. 1974. "Shadow prices, market wages, and labor supply." *Econometrica,* 42(4):679-694.

------. 1979. "Sample selection bias as a specification error." *Econometrica,* 47(1):153-162.

------., M.R. Killingsworth, & T. MaCurdy. 1981. "Empirical evidence on static labor supply models: a survey of recent developments." in Z. Hornstein, J. Grice, & A Webb, eds. *The economics of the labor market.* Proceedings of a conference on the labor market, London: Her Majesty's Stationary Office, 75-122.

Heinberg, J.D., J.K. Harris, & R.L. York, 1989. "The process of exempt immediate relative immigration to the United States." *International Migration Review* 23(4):839-855.

Hill, K. 1985. "Illegal aliens: an assessment." In D. Levine, K. Hill, & R. Warren. eds. *Immigration Statistics: A Story of Neglect.* Washington, D.C.: National Academy Press.

Hirschman, C. 1982. "Immigrants and minorities: old questions for new directions in research" *International Migration Review* 16(2):474-490.

Hong, S. 1984. "Urban migrant women in the Republic of Korea." in Fawcett, J.T., S.E. Khoo, & P.C. Smith. eds. *Women in the Cities of Asia: Migration and Urban Adaptation* Colorado, Boulder: Westview.

Houstoun, M.F., R.G. Kramer, & J.M. Barrett. 1984. "Female predominance in immigration to the United States since 1930: a first look." *International Migration Review,* 18(4):908-963.

Hugo, G.J. 1981. "Village-community ties, village norms, and ethnic and social networks: a review of evidence from the third world," in G.F. De Jong & R.W. Gardner, eds. *Migration Decision Making: Multidisciplinary Approaches to Microlevel Studies in Developed and Developing Countries* New York: Pergamon Press.

Jasso, G. & M.R. Rosenzweig. 1982. "Estimating the emigration rates of legal immigrants using administrative and survey data: the 1971 cohort of immigrants to the United States" *Demography* 19:279-290.

------. 1986a. "What's in a name? country-of-origin influences on the earnings of immigrants in the United States." *Research in Human Capital and Development: Migration, Human Capital and Development* 4:75-106.

------. 1986b. "Family reunification and the immigration multiplier: U.S. immigration law, origin-country conditions, and the reproduction of immigrants." *Demography* 23(3):291-311.

------. 1987. "Using national recording systems for the measurement and analysis of immigration to the United States." *International Migration Review* 21(4):1212-1244.

------. 1988. "How well do U.S. immigrants do? vintage effects, emigration selectivity, and occupational mobility." *Research in Population Economics* 6:229-253.

------. 1989. "Sponsors, sponsorship rates and the immigration multiplier." *International Migration Review* 23(4):856-888.

------. 1990a. *The New Chosen People: Immigrants in the United States.* Russell Sage Foundation, New York.

------. 1990b. "Self-selection and the earnings of immigrants: comment." *American Economic Review,* 80(1):298-308.

------. 1995. "Do immigrants screened for skills do better than family reunification immigrants?" *Internaitonal Migration Review* 29(1):85-111.

Jelin, E. 1978. "Migration and labour force participation of Latin American women: The domestic servants in the cities." in *Women and National Development: The Complexities of Change* edited by Wellesley Editorial Committee.

Johnson, A.E., S.B. Cohen, & A.C. Monheit. 1989. Imputing hourly wages in the national medical expenditure survey. Paper presented at the Summer Meeting of the American Statistical Association, Washington, D.C.

Kahn, J.R. 1991. Immigrant and native fertility in the U.S. during the 1980s. Paper presented in the annual meeting of the Population Association of America, Washington, D.C., March 21.

Kalton, G. 1983. *Compensation for missing survey data* The University of Michigan, Institute for Social Research.

------. & D. Kasprzyk. 1986. "The treatment of missing survey data." *Survey Methodology* 12(1):1-16.

Keely, C.B. 1971. "Effects of the Immigration Act of 1965 on selected population characteristics of immigrants to the United States." *Demography* 8(2):157-169.

------. 1975. "Effects of U.S. immigration law on manpower characteristics of immigrants." *Demography* 12(2):179-191.

------. 1983. "Current status of U.S. immigration and refugee policy." In M.M. Kritz ed. *U.S. Immigration and Refugee Policy: Global and Domestic Issues.* Lexington, Massachusetts: Lexington Books.

Kelly, G.P. 1977. *From Vietnam to America: A Chronicle of Vietnamese Immigration to the United States.* Boulder, Colorado: Westview.

------. 1986. "Coping with America: Refugees from Vietnam, Cambodia, and Laos in the 1970s and 1980s." *ANNALS, AAPSS,* 487:138-149.

Killingsworth, M.R. 1983. *Labor supply.* Cambridge University Press, Cambridge.

------. & J.J. Heckman, 1986 "Female labor supply: a survey," in O.C. Ashenfelter & R. Layard, eds. *Handbook of Labor Economics* 1: 103-204, North-Holland Publishing Co.

Kritz, M.M. & H. Zlotnik. 1992. "Global interactions: migration systems, processes, and policies." in M.M. Kritz, L.L. Lim, & H. Zlotnik, eds. *International Migration Systems* Clarendon Press, Oxford.

Lee, E. 1961. "Migration differentials by state of birth in the United States." paper presented at the International Population Conference, New York.

------. 1966. "A theory of migration." *Demography* 3(1):47-57.

Lewis, W.A. 1954. "Economic development with unlimited supplies of labor." *The Manchester School* May.

Lim, L.L. 1989. Process shaping international migration flows. Paper presented at the International Population Conference of the

IUSSP, New Delhi.

------. 1990. "The status of women and international migration" Paper presented at the United Nations Expert Group Meeting on International Migration Policies and the Status of Female Migrants, San Miniato, Italy.

Lindstrom, D.P. 1991. "The differential role of family networks in individual migration decisions." Paper presented at the annual meeting of the Population Association of America, Washington, DC.

Liu, J.M., P.M. Ong, & C. Rosenstein, 1991. "Dual chain migration: post-1965 Filipino immigration to the United States." *International Migration Review* 25(3):487-513.

Lobo, P. 1992. "Status of immigrant Asians and Latinos in the 1980s" Paper Presented at the Annual Meeting of the Population Association of America in Denver, Colorado, April, 1992

Long, J.E. 1980. "The effect of Americanization on earnings: some evidence for women." *Journal of Political Economy* 88(3):620-629.

Maddala, G.S. 1983. *Limited Dependent and Qualitative Variables in Econometrics.* New York: Cambridge University Press.

Mark, D.M.L. & G. Chih. 1982. *A Place Called Chinese America.* San Francisco: The Organization of Chinese Americans.

Martin, P.L. 1991. "Labor migration and economic development." In S. Diaz-Briquets & S. Weintraub eds. *Determinants of Emigration from Mexico, Central America, and the Caribbean.* Boulder: Colorado: Westview Press.

Massey, D.S. & J. Reichert. 1979. "Patterns of U.S.-migration from a Mexican sending community: a comparison of legal and illegal migrants," *International Migration Review* 13:599-623.

Massey, D.S. 1981. "Dimensions of the new immigration to the United States and the prospects for assimilation." *Annual Review of Sociology* 7:57-85.

------. 1986. "The settlement process among Mexican migrants to the United States." *American Sociological Review* 51:670-684.

------. & F. Garcia-Espana. 1987. "The social process of international migration." *Science* 237:733-738.

------. R. Alarcon, J. Durand, & H. Gonzalez. 1987. *Return to Aztlan: The Social Process of International Migration from Western Mexico* Berkeley and Los Angeles: University of California Press.

------. 1987. "Understanding Mexican migration to the United States."

American Journal of Sociology 92(6):1372-1403.

------. 1990. "The social and economic origins of immigration." *ANNALS, American Academy of Political and Social Science* 510:60-72.

Medina, B.T.G. & J.N. Natividad, 1985. "Filipino chain migration to the United States." *Philippine Population Journal* 1(4):67-94.

Mincer, J. 1974. *Schooling, experience and earnings* New York: Columbia University Press.

------. & S. Polachek. 1974. "Family investment in human capital: earnings of women." *Journal of Political Economy* 82(2):S76-S108.

Montgomery, M. & J. Trussell. 1986. "Marital status and childbearing." in O. Ashenfelter & R. Layard ed., *Handbook of labor economics.* Amsterdam: Horth-Holland Volume 1.

Morokvasic, M. 1983. "Women in migration: beyond the reductionist outlook." in A. Phizacklea, ed. *One Way Ticket: Migration and Female Labour* London: Routledge & Kegan Paul.

------. 1984a. "Birds of passage are also women" *International Migration Review* 18(4):886-908.

------. 1984b. "Migrant women in Europe: A comparative perspective." in *Women on the Move: Contemporary Changes in Family and Society* UNESCO: Paris.

Mullan, B.P. 1990. "The impact of social networks on the occupational status of migrants." *International Migration* 28(3):69-85.

Nauck, B. 1989. "Assimilation process and group integration of migrant families." *International Migration* 27(1):27-46.

Nee, V. & B.D. Nee. 1973. *Longtime Californ': a Documentary Study of an American Chinatown.* New York, Pantheon Books.

------. & H.Y. Wong. 1985. "Asian American socioeconomic achievement: the strength of the family bond." *Sociological Perspectives* 28(3):281-306.

Nelson, P. 1959. "Migration, real income and information." *Journal of Regional Science* 1(2):43-74.

Neter, J., W. Wasserman, & M.H. Kutner. 1990. *Applied Linear Statistical Models.* Homewood, Illinois: IRWIN Inc.

North, D.S. 1981. "Labor force participation of Indochinese refugees." Mimeo. Washington, D.C.: New Transcentury Foundation, spring.

Ong, P.M. 1987. "Immigrant wives' labor force participation," *Industrial Relations* 26(3):296-303.

Ortiz, V. & R.S. Cooney. 1984. "Sex-role attitudes and labor force participation among young Hispanic females and Non-Hispanic

White females," *Social Science Quarterly* LXV:392-400.

Park, I.H., J.T. Fawcett, F. Arnold, & R.W. Gardner. 1990. Korean immigrants and U.S. immigration policy: a predeparture perspective. Papers of the East-West Population Institute, no. 114. Honolulu, Hawaii.

Parkin, D. ed. 1975. *Town and Country in Central and Eastern Africa* London: Oxford University Press.

Passel, J. & K. Woodrow, 1987. "Comment on family reunification and the immigration multiplier." in J.M. Goering. ed. *Legal Immigration to the United States: A Demographic Analysis of Fifth Preference Visa Admissions* U.S. Senate. Washington, DC General Printing Office.

Perez, L. 1986a. "Immigrant economic adjustment and family organization: the Cuban success story reexamined." *International Migration Review* 20(1):4-20.

------. 1986b. "Cubans in the United States." *ANNALS, AAPSS,* 487:126-137.

Pessar, P.R. 1982. "The role of households in international migration and the case of U.S.-bound migration from the Dominican Republic." *International Migration Review* 16(2):342-364.

Poirier, D.J. 1976. *The Econometrics of Structural Change: with Special Emphasis on Spline Functions* North-Holland Publishing Company.

Portes, A. & R.L. Bach. 1985. *Latin Journey: Cuban and Mexican Immigrants in the United States* Berkeley: University of California Press.

------. 1987. "One field, many views: competing theories of international migration." in J.T. Fawcett & B.V. Carino, eds. *Pacific Bridges: The New Immigration from Asia and the Pacific Islands* New York: Center for Migration Studies.

Prieto, Y. 1986. "Cuban women and work in the United States: a New Jersey case study." in R.J. Simon & C.B. Brettell, eds. *International Migration: The Female Experience* New Jersey: Rowman & Allanheld.

Przeworski, A. & H. Teune. 1970. *The Logic of Comparative Social Inquiry* New York: John Wiley and Sons.

Ravenstein, E.G. 1885. "The laws of migration." *Journal of the Royal Statistical Society* 48:167-235.

------. 1889 "The laws of migration." *Journal of the Royal Statistical Society* 52:242-305.

Reimers, D.M. 1992. *Still the Golden Door: The Third World Comes to America.* Columbia University Press, New York.

Reimers, C.W. 1984a. "Cultural differences in Labor Force Participation among Married Women," Papers and Proceeding for American Economics Association 97th Annual Meeting May:251-255.

------. 1984b "Sources of the family income differentials among Hispanics, Blacks, and White Non-Hispanics" *American Journal of Sociology* 89(4):889-903.

Reubens, E.P. 1981. Interpreting migration: current models and a new integration. Occasional papers, No. 29, December, New York University, Center for Latin America and Caribbean Studies.

Ritchey, P.N. 1976. "Explanations of migration," *Annual Review of Sociology* 2:363-404.

Rubin, D.B. 1987. *Multiple Imputation for Nonresponse in Surveys.* New York: John Wiley & Sons

Rumbaut, R.G. & J.R. Weeks. 1986. "Fertility and adaptation: Indochinese refugees in the United States." *International Migration Review,* 20(2):428-466.

Samuel, T.J. 1988. "Family class immigrants to Canada, 1981-1984: Part I: labour force activity aspects." *International Migration* 26(2): 171-186.

Sassen-Koob, S. 1981. "Exporting capital and importing labor: the role of women." in *Female Immigrants to the United States: Caribbean, Latin American, and African Experiences* in D.M. Mortimer & R.S. Bryce-Laporte eds. Occational papers No. 2, Research Institute on Immigration and Ethnic Studies, Smithsonian Institution, Washington, D.C.

Schultz, T.P. 1975. The determinants of internal migration in Venezuela: an application of the polytomous logistic model. Paper presented at the World Congress of the Econometric Society, Toronto.

Schwartz, A. 1973. "Interpreting the effect of distance on migration." *Journal of Political Economy* 81:1153-1169.

Simon, R.J. & M.C. DeLey. 1986. "Undocumented Mexican women: their work and personal experiences." in R.J. Simon & C.B. Brettell, *International Migration: The Female Experience* New Jersey: Rowman & Allanheld.

Sjaastad, L.A. 1962. "The costs and returns of human migration." *Journal of Political Economy* 70:80-93.

Smith, P.C., S.E. Khoo, & S.P. Go. 1984. "The migration of women to cities: a comparative perspective." in J.T. Fawcett, S.E. Khoo, &

P.C. Smith, eds. *Women in the Cities of Asia: Migration and Urban Adaptation* Colorado, Boulder: Westview.

Sorensen, E., F.D. Bean, L. Ku, & W. Zimmermann, 1992. *Immigrant Categories and the U.S. Job Market: Do They Make a Difference* Urban Institute Report 92-1, The Urban Institute, Washington, D.C.

Stark, O. & D. Levhari. 1982. "On migration and risk in LDCs." *Economic Development and Cultural Change* 31:191-196.

------. 1984a. "Migration decision making: A review article." *Journal of Development Economics* 14:251-259.

------. 1984b. "Rural-to-urban migration in LDCs: A relative deprivation approach." *Economic Development and Cultural Change* 32:475-486.

------. & D.E. Bloom. 1985. The new economics of labor migration. American Economic Association, Papers and Proceedings, May.

------, & J.E. Taylor. 1986. "Testing for relative deprivation: Mexican labour migration." Migration and Development Discussion Paper No. 26, Cambridge, Mass.: Center for Population Studies, Harvard University.

------, & J.E. Taylor. 1989. "Relative deprivation and international migration." *Demography* 26(1):1-14.

------. 1991. "Relative deprivation and migration: theory, evidence, and policy implications." In S. Diaz-Briquets and S. Weintraub, eds. *Determinants of Emigration from Mexico, Central America, and the Caribbean.* Boulder: Colorado: Westview Press.

Stier, H. 1991 "Immigrant women go to work: analysis of immigrant wives' labor supply for six Asian groups," *Social Science Quarterly* 72(1):67-82.

------. & M. Tienda. 1992. "Family, work and women: the labor supply of Hispanic immigrant wives." *International Migration Review* 26(4):1291-1313.

Taylor, R.C. 1969. "Migration and motivation: a study of determinants and types." in J.A. Jackson, ed. *Migration* Cambridge University Press.

Taylor, J.E. 1986. "Differential migration networks, information and risk." *Research in Human Capital and Development: Migration, Human Capital and Development* 4:147-171.

Thadani, V. & M.P. Todaro, 1979. Female Migration in Developing countries: A Framework for Analysis Working Paper No. 47, Center for Policy Studies, Population Council, New York.

Tienda, M. & R. Angel. 1982. "Female headship and extended household composition: comparison of Hispanics, blacks and non-Hispanic whites." *Social Forces* 61(2):508-531.

------. 1983. "Socioeconomic and labor force characteristics of U.S. immigrants: issues and approaches." In M.M. Kritz ed. *U.S. Immigration and Refugee Policy: Global and Domestic Issues.* Lexington, Massachusetts: Lexington Books.

------., L. Jensen, & R. Bach, 1984. "Immigration, gender and the process of occupational change in the United States, 1970-80." *International Migration Review* 18(4):1021-1044.

------. & J. Glass. 1985. "Household structure and labor force participation of black, Hispanic and white mothers." *Demography* 22(3):381-394.

Tilly, C. & C.H. Brown. 1967. "On uprooting, kinship, and the auspices of migration." *International Journal of Comparative Sociology* 8:139-164.

Tucker, R.W., C.B. Keely, & L. Wrigley, eds. 1990. *Immigration and U.S. Foreign Policy.* Boulder, Colorado: Westview Press.

Todaro, M.P. 1969. "A model of labor migration and urban unemployment in less-developed countries." *American Economic Review* 59:138-148.

------. 1976. *Internal Migration in Developing Countries: A Review of Theory, Evidence, Methodology, and Research Priorities* Geneva: International Labor Office.

Tyree, A. & K.M. Donato. 1986. "A demographic overview of the international migration of women." in R.J. Simon & C.B. Brettell, *International Migration: The Female Experience* New Jersey: Rowman & Allanheld.

U.S. Congress, Senate. Subcommittee on Immigration and Refugee Affairs of the Committee on the Judiciary, 1987. *U.S. Immigration Law and Policy: 1952-1986.* Report, 100th Cong., 1st sess. Washington: GPO.

U.S. Department of Commerce, Bureau of the Census. 1978. The Current Population Survey: Design and Methodology. Technical paper 40, Washington, D.C.: Bureau of the Census.

------. 1984. Interviewer's manual: current population survey. Government Printing Office: Washington, DC.

------. 1992. Census of Population and Housing, 1990: Public Use Microdata Sample U.S. Technical Documentation, Washington, D.C.: Bureau of the Census.

------. 1993a. We the American foreign born. Washington, D.C.: Bureau of the Census.

------. 1993b. Current Population Survey, June 1991: Immigration and Emigration survey technical documentation. Washington, D.C.: Bureau of the Census.

U.S. Department of Labor, Bureau of Labor Statistics. 1988. BLS Handbook of Methods. Bureau of Labor Statistics bulletin no. 2285.

U.S. Immigration and Naturalization Service, 1979. *Statistical Yearbook of the Immigraiton and Naturalization Services, 1978.* U.S. Government Printing Office: Washington, DC.

U.S. Immigration and Naturalization Service, 1983. *Statistical Yearbook of the Immigraiton and Naturalization Services, 1982.* U.S. Government Printing Office: Washington, DC.

U.S. Immigration and Naturalization Service, 1987. *Statistical Yearbook of the Immigraiton and Naturalization Services, 1986.* U.S. Government Printing Office: Washington, DC.

U.S. Immigration and Naturalization Service, 1990. *Statistical Yearbook of the Immigraiton and Naturalization Services, 1989.* U.S. Government Printing Office: Washington, DC.

U.S. Immigration and Naturalization Service, 1991. *Statistical Yearbook of the Immigraiton and Naturalization Services, 1990.* U.S. Government Printing Office: Washington, DC.

Wales, T.J. & A.D. Woodland. 1980. "Sample selectivity and the estimation of labor supply function." *International Economic Review* 21(2):437-468.

Warren, R. & J.S. Passel. 1987. "A count of the uncountable: estimates of undocumented aliens counted in the 1980 census." *Demography* 24: 375-393.

------. 1988. Projected immigration to the United States as a result of the legalization program. Paper presented at the Annual Meeting of the Population Association of America, New Orleans.

Weeks, J.R. 1986. *Population: An Introduction to Concepts and Issues* California: Wadsworth Publishing Company.

Whiteford, M.F. 1978. "Women, migration and social change: a Colombian case study." *International Migration Review* 12(2):236-247.

Wong, M.G. & C. Hirschman, 1983 "Labor force participation and socioeconomic attainment of Asian American women." *Sociological Perspectives* 26(4):423-446

Woodrow, K.A., J.S. Passel, & R. Warren. 1987. Preliminary estimates of undocumented immigration to the United States, 1980-1986: analysis of the June 1986 Current Population Survey. Proceedings of the Social Statistics Section of the American Statistical Association. San Francisco, California.

------. 1990. Undocumented immigrants living in the United States. Proceedings of the Social Statistics Section of the American Statistical Association.

------. & A. Peregoy. 1991. Parents, siblings, and children: how many Do immigrants and native-born persons have? Paper presented at the annual meeting of the Population Association of America, Washington, D.C.

Wyon, J.B. & J.E. Gordon. 1971. *The Khanna Study: Population Problems in the Rural Punjab* Cambridge, Mass.: Harvard University Press.

Xenos, P. 1989. Asian Indians in the United States. Papers of the East-West Population Institute. no.111, Honolulu, Hawaii.

Yap, Y.L. 1977. "The attraction of cities: a reivew of the migration literature." *Journal of Devepolment Economics* 4:239-264.

Youssef, N., M. Buvinic, A. Kudat, J. Sebstad, & B. Von Elm. 1979. Women in migration: a third world focus. International Center for Research on Women, Washington D.C.

Zick, C.D. & W.K. Bryant. 1983. "Alternative strategies for pricing home work time." *Home Economics Research Journal,* 12(2):133-144.

Index